THE DESERT WAR

ALAN MOOREHEAD

The North African Campaign 1940/1943

The Des

ert War

HAMISH HAMILTON · LONDON

The text of *The Desert War* is an abridged edition of
African Trilogy which comprised *Mediterranean Front,
A Year of Battle* and *The End in Africa*

First published in Great Britain, 1965
by Hamish Hamilton Ltd
90 Great Russell Street, London, W.C.1

Copyright © 1965 by Alan Moorehead

Printed in England by
Fletcher & Son Ltd., Norwich

By the same Author
ECLIPSE
MONTGOMERY
THE RAGE OF THE VULTURE
THE VILLA DIANA
THE TRAITORS
RUM JUNGLE
A SUMMER NIGHT
GALLIPOLI
THE RUSSIAN REVOLUTION
NO ROOM IN THE ARK
THE WHITE NILE
THE BLUE NILE
COOPER'S CREEK
THE FATAL IMPACT
(*in preparation*)

NORTH AFRICA has always been one of the great battle-grounds of history. Rome and Carthage there decided their long drawn-out contest for the Empire of the Mediterranean—the world of their day. One of the most famous commanders of history, Scipio, won in that struggle his title of Africanus; another, Belisarius, there fought one of his most spectacular campaigns. Two of the world's conquering heroes, Alexander and Napoleon, established themselves in the Egyptian base.

Much blood has been shed in those obliterating sands. It was in accordance with the fitness of history that North Africa should have been the scene of a great struggle in the greatest of all wars, the Second World War.

FIELD MARSHAL VISCOUNT WAVELL, GCB, CMG, MC

I REACHED Egypt by way of Greece. Nothing could disturb that timeless apathy in the eastern Mediterranean. In Athens the diplomats talked leisurely around the point of whether Greece would fight or not; they were rather agreed on the whole that she would not. Neither here nor anywhere in Greece was there a hint that a second Marathon was coming. This was May 1940.

I flew on to Cairo where we bathed in the pool of the green island, Gezira, in the Nile, or watched the cricket. The Turf Club swarmed with officers newly arrived from England, and a dozen open-air cinemas were showing every night in the hot, brightly-lit city. The war was not serious in Egypt at this stage. It was merely a noise on the radio. There were known to be British troops in the Western Desert, of course, but no one doing the round of the parties and the polo in Cairo and Alexandria ever seemed to see them.

The war correspondents were grouped into a unit known as Public Relations, and they began to gather in Cairo with bright green-and-gold tabs on their uniforms, to seek information. Like every other unit, we squabbled and laughed and complained and muddled along. But for that cold news from France it didn't seem to matter very much.

Then the news broke: France fallen; Italy at war; 10th June, 1940. Slowly, painfully, reluctantly, the Middle East dragged itself out of its apathy. For the first time it realized fear over Dunkirk and worse fear too, closer at hand, for Italy's armies loomed menacingly all through Africa and the Mediterranean. How long could Malta hold out? What was to stop Balbo advancing to the Nile? What forces had we in the Sudan and Kenya to withstand Aosta's three hundred thousand in Eritrea and Abyssinia? And above all, how were we to maintain communications with England?

The answer came in the first week. The Italians attacked by land, sea and air. Communications with England were broken. Released from the menace of the French along the Mareth line in Tunis, Balbo hurried his Western Libyan army in thousands of lorries across to the Egyptian border. One after another the lights in the cities round the Mediterranean went out, and in the darkness the fleet in Alexandria was bombed from the Dodecanese Islands.

Then, at last, it was discovered that we had virtually no forces in the Middle East. All the regiments in Cairo and the Western Desert, all the ships at Alexandria, all the garrisons in Sudan and Kenya, all the raw Australians and New Zealanders training in Palestine and Egypt, all the aircraft that swept occasionally over the burnt-out land—all these amounted to not one-tenth of the forces that Mussolini alone was gathering for his great drive on the Suez Canal. In every department of modern warfare, especially in such equipment as tanks and guns, we were pitifully, hopelessly, weak. If you will find greatness in General Wavell, trace it back to the summer months in 1940 when he was beaten on paper before he ever fired a shot. He shut his mouth, confiding in practically no one. He put his trust in the surrounding deserts, he sent appeal after appeal to Churchill for more forces at once, and he held on. It required no great genius, that strategy of simply digging in one's toes and waiting for the enemy to come on. What did require brilliance was the game of bluff on which the General now deliberately embarked.

It was not until some days after the opening of hostilities on the Egyptian border that I got down to the front at Sollum and saw what was happening. Driving out into the desert one early morning from Cairo, I made the first of many journeys to Alexandria, and then turned west along the coast through El Daba, Fuka and Maaten Bagush to Mersa Matruh. This road, some three hundred miles in length, had a relatively good macadam surface, especially on the Cairo–Alexandria section, and running parallel to it beyond Alexandria was the single-track railway. Nothing in the desert justifies either road or railway. El Daba, Fuka and places farther on, like Buq Buq, are merely names on the map. No houses exist there. Bedouin, perhaps, coming on intermittent water-wells, may have given names to these places, but they have nothing to attract either man or beast except this one thing—a spotless white beach that runs steeply into a sea tinted the wonderful shades of a butterfly's wing. To Mersa Matruh went Antony and Cleopatra to enjoy that glorious bathing. On that same beach I found some hundreds of sun-blistered Scots trying to get the desert dust out of their mouths by wallowing naked in the water. Behind them stood Mersa Matruh, and the village at that time was intact. Driving in from the open desert, you suddenly breast a rise and your sun-strained eyes are immediately refreshed by the white township spreading out below and the cool greenish-blue of the bay beyond.

Mersa Matruh had been for years a small watering-place to which the Egyptian pashas and a few of the foreign colony in Egypt used to send their families. Hillier's Hotel, a collection of low, white walls under a flat roof, stood by the water's edge; there was the Governor's cottage, the railway station, the church and the mosque, a few shops down the central village street, and not much else. Artesian water, as at many places along this coast, was drawn from wells, and at Matruh the water was good. Yet only a few weary date-palms and a patch or two of coarse grass and saltbush pushed up through the hot, grey ground.

Yellow rocks, saltbush, grey earth and this perfect beach was the eternal background wherever you looked in the north of the Western Desert. Except at spots along the coast and far inland it never even achieved those picturesque rolling sandhills which Europeans seem always to associate with deserts. It had fresh colours in the morning, and immense sunsets. One clear hot cloudless day followed another in endless progression. A breeze stirred sometimes in the early morning, and again at night when one lay on a camp bed in the open, gazing up into a vaster and more brilliant sky than one could ever have conceived in Europe. I found no subtle fascination there nor any mystery, unless it was the Bedouin who appeared suddenly and unexpectedly out of the empty desert as soon as one stopped one's car. But there was a sense of rest and relaxation in the tremendous silence, especially at night, and now the silence is still the best thing I remember of the desert, the silence, the cool nights, the clear hot days and the eternal flatness of everything.

The morning I drove toward Mersa Matruh, however, looking for Force Head-

The khamseen sandstorm, the most hellish wind on earth; everything stopped, even the war.

quarters, a khamseen was blowing, and that of course changed everything. The khamseen sandstorm, which blows more or less throughout the year, is in my experience the most hellish wind on earth. It picks up the surface dust as fine as baking powder and blows it thickly into the air across hundreds of square miles of desert. All the way through Daba's tent-hospital base and past Fuka it gathered force along the road until at Bagush it blocked visibility down to half a dozen yards. In front of the car little crazy lines of yellow dust snaked across the road. The dust came up through the engine, through the chinks of the car-body and round the corners of the closed windows. Soon everything in the car was powdered with grit and sand. It crept up your nose and down your throat, itching unbearably and making it difficult to breathe. It got in your ears, matted your hair, and from behind sand-goggles your eyes kept weeping and smarting. An unreal yellow light suffused everything. Just for a moment the billows of blown sand would open, allowing you to see a little farther into the hot solid fog ahead, and then it would close in again. Bedouin, their heads muffled in dirty rags, lunged weirdly across the track. You sweated, returned again and again to your water-bottle for a swig of warm sandy water, and lay back gasping. Sometimes a khamseen may blow for days, making you feel that you will never see light and air and feel coolness again.

3

Groping along from point to point, we found headquarters at last, an inexpressibly dreary place. Dugouts nosed up to the surface amid sandbags and rocks. A few low tents flapped pathetically in the wind. Camels plodded about moodily through trucks and armoured vehicles that were dispersed over a couple of miles of desert. Down on the beach in the yellow gloom a group of naked men were trying to wash the dirt away with salt-water soap. One or two grounded aircraft, their engines swathed in canvas, loomed up out of the sandstorm from the airfield across the other side of the camp. Clearly the war was halted by the weather. Inside the dugouts deepening sand covered everything. In the mess-tent we poured lukewarm beer from cans into gritty glasses, and waited for a luncheon of tinned sausages that was frying in a mixture of fat and sand. Only war could have brought men to this place at such a time, and now we were here we could see less sense in war than ever. The storm eased slightly in the evening, but I slept that night on the ground with my sleeping-bag zipped over my head. Another hot sand-swept morning broke—one of those dreary, lifeless mornings which bring no promise of freshness or feeling of having rested.

The road leading on from Mersa Matruh to Sidi Barrani was still good at this time. Camouflaged water-wagons bound for the forward units were moving along, averaging perhaps six or seven miles an hour. At intervals of twenty miles or so little groups of these supply-wagons turned off into the open desert to the south. Moving by compass across that waste, they would eventually meet brigade, battalion and company headquarters that would be resting briefly at some point that was nothing more than a number on the map. Units were seldom directed to places in the desert. They were simply ordered to proceed on a compass bearing to a certain point, and there camp down. Except in action, there was wireless silence, and communications were kept up by a few light aircraft and motor-cyclists.

More and more I began to see that desert warfare resembled war at sea. Men moved by compass. No position was static. There were few if any forts to be held. Each truck or tank was as individual as a destroyer, and each squadron of tanks or guns made great sweeps across the desert as a battle-squadron at sea will vanish over the horizon. One did not occupy the desert any more than one occupied the sea. One simply took up position for a day or a week, and patrolled about it with Bren-gun carriers and light armoured vehicles. When you made contact with the enemy you manoeuvred about him for a place to strike, much as two fleets will steam into position for action. There were no trenches. There was no front line. We might patrol five hundred miles into Libya and call the country ours. The Italians might as easily have patrolled as far into the Egyptian desert without being seen. Always the essential governing principle was that desert forces must be mobile: they were seeking not the conquest of territory or positions but combat with the enemy. We hunted men, not land, as a warship will hunt another warship, and care nothing for the sea on which the action is fought. And as a ship submits to the sea by the nature of its design and the way it sails, so these new mechanized soldiers were submitting to the desert. They found weaknesses in the ruthless hostility of the desert and ways to circumvent its worst moods. They used the desert. They never sought to control it. Always the desert set the pace, made the direction and planned the design. The desert offered colours in browns, yellows and greys. The army accordingly took these colours for its camouflage. There were practically no roads. The army shod its vehicles with huge balloon tyres and did

4

Vehicles on the unmade tracks threw up a smokescreen of fine sand.

without roads. Nothing except an occasional bird moved quickly in the desert. The army for ordinary purposes accepted a pace of five or six miles an hour. The desert gave water reluctantly, and often then it was brackish. The army cut its men—generals and privates—down to a gallon of water a day when they were in forward positions. There was no food in the desert. The soldier learned to exist almost entirely on tinned foods, and contrary to popular belief remained healthy on it. Mirages came that confused the gunner, and the gunner developed precision-firing to a finer art and learned new methods of establishing observation-posts close to targets. The sandstorm blew, and the tanks, profiting by it, went into action under the cover of the storm. We made no new roads. We built no houses. We did not try to make the desert liveable, nor did we seek to subdue it. We found the life of the desert primitive and nomadic, and primitively and nomadically the army lived and went to war.

I make these points at length here because in my belief the Italians failed to accept these principles, and when the big fighting began in the winter it was their undoing. They wanted to be masters of the desert. They made their lives comfortable and static. They built roads and stone houses and the officers strode around in brilliant scented uniforms. They tried to subdue the desert. And in the end the desert beat them.

Already on this midsummer morning when I drove down the road to Sidi Barrani, Marshal Balbo was piling up his great luxurious army along the Egyptian frontier and preparing to roll on across the Western Desert to the Nile. Only a tiny, experienced and toughened little British force stood against him. We came into Sidi Barrani, glaring white in the sun, and the storm was lifting at last. The

5

civilians had long since been evacuated—only a few hundred of them—and the empty houses had been looted by the Bedouin. The first exploratory Italian air raiders had been over the village that morning, and half a dozen dwellings and a general store had been split open. The road was dotted with small, three-foot bomb-craters. There was no sign of the army although half a squadron of British fighter aircraft rested on a remote rise, immobile.

Now we had something almost as bad as the sandstorm to face. The made road ceased in Sidi Barrani. We plunged into knee-deep fine sand that blew up through the floorboards of the car in billowing stifling waves. Every vehicle on the track set up an immense column of dust behind it, creating almost the impression of a destroyer at sea laying a smoke-screen. Drivers of passing vehicles manoeuvred to get to the windward of one another so that they would not be overwhelmed in one another's dust. With each man seeking his own track, a full half-mile width of desert was broken up into drifting sand, and sometimes a car plunging through this uneasy surface would crash upon a hidden rock with a force that knocked the breath out of the passengers. Petrol tins burst. Rations flung madly about in the interior of the trucks. I sat there holding the side of the car, hating the desert.

At a salt-pan beside the sea, which for some reason bears the name Buq Buq, we came on one of the advance headquarters. It was clearer and cooler here, at last, and the soothing whisper of the waves came across the sand-dunes. Guns, tanks and cars were dispersed about rather like an American middle-western caravan at a halt. In the centre of the dried-up lake stood the officers' mess—a plain trestle-table with a camp stove burning beside it. We took tea there, and as we

6

Dressing up dummies to represent an anti-tank gun crew.

drank, a whistle suddenly shrilled from the edge of the camp and we ran for the slit trenches. These were simply narrow graves dug about four feet into the earth. Whenever it stopped for the night, the first job of the crew of every fighting vehicle was to dig one of these trenches. Apart from retaliation, it was the only protection the desert could give against air raids, and it was nearly a hundred per cent. effective. I myself have been in a trench when a bomb has burst three yards away, and come to no harm beyond being partly buried in sand. And so on this day we huddled into the trench and crouched there while a three-engined Savoia bomber, flying low enough for us to see its pilot, swept leisurely over the horizon. We had at that time no effective gun for hitting him. It was just a matter of crouching there and seeing if our camouflage was good or not. He came down to two thousand feet and circled slowly round. The afternoon was now sparkling clear, and it seemed so certain that he must see and dive that it was a curious unlooked-for disappointment when he turned away and nothing happened. We went back to tea.

Now at last we were close to the front and able to see Wavell's game of bluff in action. It was vitally necessary, the general saw, to convince the enemy that we were much stronger than we actually were. This was not easy in so open a place as the desert. Yet it was being done—how successfully we only learned months later. The painfully thin British forces were scattered for hundreds of miles across the desert facing the Libyan frontier. They had one all-important standing order: make one man appear to be a dozen, make one tank look like a squadron, make a raid look like an advance. And so this little Robin Hood force, being unable to withstand any sort of a determined advance by the half-dozen

7

Italian divisions across the border, did the unpredicted, unexpected thing—it attacked. It attacked not as a combined force but in small units, swiftly, irregularly and by night. It pounced on Italian outposts, blew up the captured ammunition, and ran away. It stayed an hour, a day, or a week in a position, and then disappeared. The enemy had no clear idea of when he was going to be attacked next or where. Fort Maddalena fell; Sidi Aziz was invested. British vehicles were suddenly astride the road leading back from Bardia, shooting up convoys. Confused and anxious, the Italians rigged up searchlights and scoured the desert with them while British patrols lay grinning in the shadows. Soon from prisoners we learned that extraordinary stories were going the rounds behind the Italian lines. There were two . . . three . . . five British armoured divisions operating, they said. A large-scale British attack was imminent. Balbo drew in his horns, cut down his own patrols and called for more reinforcements from Rome. The bluff was working.

Back in Cairo, Wavell, consulting with Air Marshall Sir Arthur Longmore and Admiral Cunningham, knew that it had to work. He had to have time. Every day brought the first convoys of reinforcements nearer Egypt, and without them he knew he would not withstand a large-scale Italian attack. Somehow that attack had to be delayed through the summer. Somehow the enemy had to be kept timid, anxious and in doubt. But there were signs that Balbo would not be deluded for ever. Already after the first few weeks he was cautiously trying out his hand, cautiously testing the strength of the British.

It was at one such moment that I had arrived from Buq Buq at Sollum, geographically the most distinctive spot in the Western Desert. The coast here sweeps round in a great curve to the Libyan frontier. Locked in the arc of this shallow bay lies the lower half of the village of Sollum, but easily the most arresting thing, the thing that riveted your eyes from miles away, was the escarpment. This is an immense cliff rising six hundred feet sheer from the Egyptian plain. The cliff, buttressing on its heights the Libyan desert and reaching at its depths the Western Desert, cuts on to the Mediterranean roughly at right angles on a north–south line. South of Sollum, however, it strikes south-east and runs away from the strict north–south line of the Egyptian Libyan border. Two routes wind up the cliff-face from lower Sollum: one which climbs precariously over the very edge of the sea is a wide modern road. The other, Halfaya Pass—Hellfire Pass was the troops' word for it—is no more than a track. It starts from the coast a few miles east of Sollum, and over broken grey rocks and rubble lifts you steeply on to the Libyan desert. Once on the top there you command a broad vision of the Egyptian coast-line sweeping far away to the east. Upper Sollum was then a collection of sun-baked white barracks, the home of an Egyptian frontier force, and a stony airfield. Fifteen or twenty miles away on the coast to the north-west lies Bardia, the first Libyan township, and at this time an important Fascist headquarters. Dividing Sollum and Bardia, and along the whole frontier, Mussolini had constructed a wire fence. This ran southward some hundreds of miles, and was built, it was said, to prevent the Libyan natives escaping into Egypt from the Fascist régime. It consisted of a quadruple line of five-feet metal stakes bedded in concrete and closely woven with barbed wire. It must have been some twenty feet in width. The cost of the fence must have been enormous, its conception absurd, its uses nil. It revealed how strongly a man may be driven by the acquisitive instinct, how ridiculous a lust for property can be. The escaping Libyan threw out his cloak

8

Looking down on Sollum from the 6oo-foot heights of the escarpment.

over the barbed wire, and crawled through. The British tank setting out on patrol into Libya simply nosed the fence aside. Yet that absurd fence, like many another absurd Italian device in the desert, seemed to give the Fascist soldier a sense of security, and he patrolled it with the persistence of a goldfish edging along the confines of his glass jar.

Land mines, like the fence, were another illustration of the Italian passion for defence. The whole distance from Sollum to Benghazi he strewed them across the desert. Later we were to get sufficiently used to them to be able to treat them with contempt. Yet they were good mines. Originally they were designed to explode at the pressure of an ordinary wheeled vehicle, but the detonator wires rusted and they were often sensitive even to the footfall of a man. These mines were laid in lines across the roads and around all fortified positions. They were buried just deep enough to allow a thin layer of sand to rest on top of them, but the depressions could be clearly seen as a rule. A mine going off on the driver's side of a vehicle would have sufficient force to break the legs of the driver or even to destroy him and the vehicle altogether. Tank tracks could be broken by a mine. So special sapper squads were formed to deal with them, and always when an advance was on you would see the sappers going on ahead. The chief danger was that one would stumble on these mines in the darkness.

Next day we climbed the escarpment deep in the desert and on the Libyan plateau there we found units of our armoured forces. It was the first time I had seen these men who were eight months later to make their great march to the Libyan Gulf and overwhelm the last of the broken Italian armies at the battle of Beda Fomm. Already they had been months in the desert. Their faces had blistered red in the sun and after so long an isolation from civilization they were eager to meet any stranger. We were taken to the brigadier and with delight we heard from

9

Fort Capuzzo smashed by heavy shelling.

him that he intended to try to take Fort Capuzzo with his tanks that same night. We went forward to a slight rise some four miles out of Capuzzo, and waited there in the blazing afternoon sun for the attack to begin. Before us the tower and the white walls of the fort rose above the lip of the horizon. On the left flank a half-squadron of our medium tanks had broken through the frontier fence and lay silently waiting for the arrival of a heavily armed enemy squadron which, our intelligence had learned, was making its way from Sidi Aziz toward Capuzzo. On the right flank the main body of British tanks which were to carry the main assault at dusk was creeping in open formation toward the fort. At our feet stood a battery of twenty-five-pounder guns. We had been told that was the battle plan. Now in the hot tense silence of the late afternoon we waited for the drama to unroll. As the sun, growing redder and larger, dipped on Libya, it began to unfold stage by stage. First came the British aircraft to sweep the sky of enemy raiders. They plunged on an Italian flight of three Savoias that was bombing rear headquarters behind us, and put them to flight. Then, a line of black geese in the red sky, the British fighters wheeled over the expectant battlefield, found the sky clear and turned away. The battery before us opened up, not shrilly or loudly for the heavy air seemed to deaden the sound. There was just the steady rhythmical coughing of each gun firing in turn. They were sighting on an Italian battery to the left of the fort, and as each hit registered a great pillar of black sand and smoke flowered upward and spread in the form of a mushroom, making a stain on the clear blue background of the sea beyond. The Italians did not reply. The British tanks, no more than silhouettes now in the waning light, waited motionless. A desert

10

fox ran across the battlefield. Someone laughed. I went over to our car and got out a pot of raspberry jam and some biscuits and handed them around. My shirt had gone dirty black with soaking perspiration. Then the tanks attacked. They had half a mile to go, and each tank, shooting as it went, attacked one of the Italian guns spaced around Capuzzo's walls. The enemy guns waited perhaps two minutes. Then they spouted out a deafening salvo that enveloped the whole fort in smoke. Smoke rose everywhere. A full expanding cloud of blown dust split by gun-flashes rolled out across the desert toward us, and one after another the British tanks dived into it and disappeared. In a moment the battle lost all shape. There was only noise and light growing louder and brighter under the pall of smoke. We waited, straining our eyes until it was full night, and then, while the firing began gradually to die away, we turned back to brigade headquarters to find out what had happened.

Nothing good had happened. The Italians had driven our tanks off. The British colonel in command was wounded. One or two of our tanks were wrecked, others for the moment missing. As we ate bully stew in the mess, ambulances lumbered back over the rocky track.

This, the first action I had seen in the desert, was a defeat. With one minor exception late in the Benghazi campaign, it was the only British reverse at the hands of the Italians that I was going to see for more than a year.

2

In the full midsummer of 1940, Mussolini saw his great chance. Now, with England preoccupied with home defence, her Mediterranean and African possessions seemed an easy prey. Conquest in Africa would elevate and enrich Mussolini at home, increase his standing with Hitler, and justify Italy to herself and the world. In Rome, then, in that romantic and grandiloquent room in the Palazzo Venezia that had seen so many Fascist chances taken and won, the Duce hatched his grand plan for the conquest of the Middle East and the enlargement of his African Empire to more than three times its size. He rode on a sudden wave of enthusiasm and popularity. Orders went out to the Italian commanders in Libya and Abyssinia to attack. In Tobruk easy-going Balbo had met his death in an air crash that may or may not have been accidental; 'Butcher' Graziani took command.

Down the escarpment came the Fascist armies, a host several divisions strong, as brave and confident as a crusade on the march. Wavell's bluff had been called. The Italians had come out at last to do battle, and there was nothing for it but to beat a retreat with the tiny British forces in as dignified a way as possible. But no one in Cairo that September knew how far and how fast Graziani was going to go. Wavell had determined to avoid serious engagement until the Italians reached Mersa Matruh, about one-third of the way to the Delta. We had been digging traps and entrenchments in the sand for months at Mersa Matruh, but would they hold? Down the escarpment came more and more water-trucks, guns, donkey teams, tanks, armoured cars. There were thousands of vehicles against

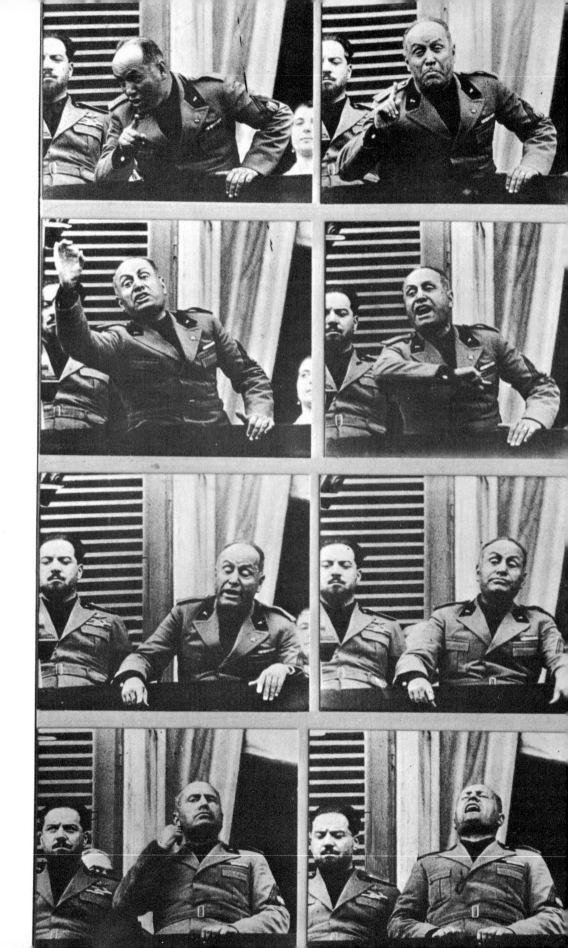

From the balcony of the Palazzo Venezia the Duce expounded his grandiloquent plans for the new Italian empire in Africa. Balbo was not included; he was soon to be killed, mysteriously, in an air crash in Tobruk.

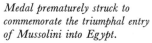

Medal prematurely struck to commemorate the triumphal entry of Mussolini into Egypt.

13

our hundreds, divisions of men against our brigades, squadrons of Savoias and Capronis against our handful of Blenheims and Gladiators. Graziani, who could hardly be called a hot-head, pulled up short at Sidi Barrani after the first sixty miles, to consolidate. Slowly, methodically and with immense labour he began to fortify and build up his lines of communications. By the late autumn he had at Sidi Barrani a sure base from which to embark on the second leg of his advance to the Suez Canal, and some hundred thousand men, all well equipped, were ready to set out in the cool of the winter.

Then in November came Mussolini's invasion of Greece. No one could have seen the disaster ahead. It was in Greece that both Mussolini and General Wavell had their major setbacks. Both started in Africa, both failed to wait until they had consolidated their African victories, both went to Greece hastily, too lightly armed and taking too little account of the differences between colonial war in Africa and world war in Europe. The only major difference between the adventures of the two men was that Mussolini himself elected to go to Greece. Wavell was later forced to it. But for the moment no British expeditionary force was sent to Greece for the embarrassing reason that there was none large enough to send; what British troops there were in Egypt stayed there to meet Graziani. They stayed there apparently doing nothing.

Week after vital week slipped by in November, and still Wavell did not move. November drifted into December, all good campaigning weather in the desert, and I began to hear criticism everywhere in the Middle East. Newspapers went as far as they could in an effort to say, 'Why doesn't Wavell attack in the Western Desert now that the Italians are tied up in Greece?'

Actually the position in the desert was this. General O'Connor, the corps commander, had placed his old armoured division as a holding force at the front between Mersa Matruh and Sidi Barrani. They had in support an Indian division including some British regiments, nearly a division of New Zealanders, and two divisions of Australians either training or simply waiting in the Delta and Palestine. There were in addition heterogeneous groups like the Poles whom it was not thought desirable to send against the Italians since Italy had never broken off diplomatic relations with Poland. Shipments had lately been arriving of twenty-five-pounder guns, new thirty-ton infantry tanks, and aircraft of various kinds including Hurricanes, Wellingtons and Long-nosed Blenheims.

On the Italian side Graziani had established one Libyan and one Metropolitan division at the front around Sidi Barrani under the command of General Gallina. Reaching inland, south, south-west and westwards in a great arc from the coast, some half-dozen fortified camps had been established: Maktila, some miles east of Sidi Barrani on the coast; Tummar East and Tummar West; Nibeiwa and Point Ninety—all more or less due south of Sidi Barrani; and finally Sofafi, deep in the desert near the Libyan border. As desert architecture goes, these camps were pretty lavish affairs. The general design was a convenient rise perhaps half a mile or a mile square surrounded with a stone wall. Inside the Italians had established messes, hospitals and sleeping quarters by scooping holes in the sand and rock, putting a stone wall round the holes and surmounting the tops with pieces of camouflaged canvas. Outside the camps they built watching-posts by digging holes in the desert. Minefields were embedded on the eastern, northern and southern approaches. Rough, incredibly dusty tracks linked one camp with another. Sidi

14

Mussolini promised the people victories.

Barrani had in addition to its ring of outlying camps two lines of fortifications where they had dug anti-tank traps and furnished niches for machine-guns, anti-tank guns and artillery. In command of the camps immediately adjacent to the central fortress of Sidi Barrani was General Maletti, a veteran of the Abyssinian campaign. He had been given what I suppose was an Italian Panzer Division. It had a special name—the Raggruppamento Maletti, or the Raggruppamento Oasi Meridionali—and there is some evidence that when the time came for the race across to the Nile, Maletti and his shock troopers were to be in the van. But for the time being he and Gallina were resting, digging in, building up supplies and waiting for their great new road, the Via della Vittoria, linking Sollum with Sidi Barrani, to be completed.

Back on the escarpment in reserve were two more divisions under General Bergonzoli—the famed Electric Whiskers—and General Berti. These had been acting as garrison troops to Corps Headquarters at Bardia and holding the escarpment. Still another division—General Giuseppe Amico's 'Catanzaro' division—was designed to act as a relief at the front. There were then some six Italian divisions—perhaps a hundred thousand men in all—available to Graziani for use as attacking troops. Facing him between Sidi Barrani and the Nile there were some four British divisions or not more than sixty thousand men. In guns of all classes, in all kinds of transport and tanks except heavy tanks, Graziani's forces enjoyed a numerical superiority of probably not less than three to one and in some cases very much more. In the air he certainly had a three to one numerical advantage. Even if his initial assaults failed, he stood—on paper—little chance of a major setback. Strong garrisons were centred at such key points as Tobruk, Derna, Benghazi, in addition to many strong pockets of supporting infantry in desert posts like Mekili south of Derna.

It was generally assumed that in all Libya Graziani disposed of some quarter million troops against Wavell's hundred thousand based around the Nile and the Suez Canal. It was apparent then that nowhere, not even at sea, did we possess equality in numbers (though both British pilots and sailors had proved in the preceding months that this was by no means necessary for success). In fact, Graziani was sitting pretty—even though he was sitting in the imponderable Western Desert which had once swallowed up a Persian host under Cambyses and brought disaster to many conquerors since then.

The general disposition of his armies was arranged with strong Latin logic. Everything fanned out exactly from a base. From Tripoli, his chief supply port where ships were then unloaded undisturbed by air raids, his lines of communication stretched east to Benghazi and far south into the Libyan desert oasis at Kufra. From Benghazi, his most vital base, the lines fanned out again to Barce, Cirene, Derna and Tobruk in the north on the coast, and in the south below the moutains to the desert fort of Mekili. Then from Tobruk the northern line reached to Bardia and Sollum and fanned south to the border desert post at Jarabub. And now he had created his latest fan stretching into Egypt as far as Sidi Barrani; thence describing an arc down to Sofafi. Every section hinged on a pivot, and the pivots were Bardia, Tobruk, Benghazi, Tripoli. Each sector fitted into the one behind it, so that the successive termini of each of the northern arms of each pivot were Sidi Barrani, Bardia, Tobruk and Benghazi. And the southern termini were the chain of desert posts, Sofafi, Jarabub, Mekili and Kufra.

16

The Italians ran a wire fence 400 miles along the Libyan frontier; armoured cars simply pushed it aside.

Doubtless other fans were planned from Sidi Barrani and Mersa Matruh until the Nile Delta was reached.

The obvious point in this grand strategy was that while you had to mass your main forces on the coast where the good roads and the ships and airfields were, yet you still had to guard your desert flank against sudden encircling inland raids. In the end it was Graziani's failure to hold this principle or realize just how far and fast an encircling raid could go that brought him to utter ruin. It was Wavell's and O'Connor's strength that from the first moment they never relaxed these encircling movements or their pressure on the desert flank. And always governing every engagement, from a siege or a pitched battle down to a skirmish, were the opposite theories of the two commanders: Wavell with his policy of light fast mobile forces; Graziani with his theory of defensive positions. Wavell stabbed with a lance. Graziani presented a shield.

The story of the Benghazi advance begins far back in November 1940. The Italians as was their custom, had not been patrolling except for occasional heavily armed parties which in a great cloud of dust toured the forward area. Our patrolling was done in small groups, sometimes a single vehicle, and nearly always at night. A lieutenant and a dozen men would drive far out into no-man's-land in the darkness, camouflage their vehicles with nets and salt-bush before dawn, and lie motionless on the floor of the desert throughout the day. More often than not, aircraft would fail to spot them, but at the first sign of superior land forces on the desert horizon they would try to identify the enemy and then quickly escape back to our lines. Thus a considerable amount of information was always coming into British Corps Headquarters. O'Connor was well aware that these fortified camps, like Nibeiwa and the two Tummars, were being built, but he did not know how many were completed or exactly where and what further forts were projected. He tried one frontal tank attack on Nibeiwa, and when some of our tanks came to grief on the Italian minefields and were met by considerably artillery fire it became obvious that these forts were of some strength. Each was reckoned to have about three thousand men with a very high rate of fire power.

But a British Intelligence colonel began to notice among the reports which the patrols were constantly bringing in that those scouts who penetrated the area between Nibeiwa and Sofafi invariably returned with no news at all. No contact was made with the enemy. Puzzled, he went out himself, just he and a driver, and lay in the desert south of Nibeiwa getting the same result. He returned on the succeeding night. And then again and again, each time going a little deeper into enemy territory. Still he struck nothing. Could it be possible that there was a gap— a considerable gap—between Sofafi and Nibeiwa which the Italians had not yet fortified nor were even patrolling? It was improbable that they would blunder like this. But there it was—over this whole area as large as the home counties in England no opposition was to be found. It was reasonable to assume that the Italians had not fortified on the inward western side of their chain of camps. After all, their own supply columns had to reach each camp from the west, so the supposition was that their minefields and anti-tank traps were concentrated on the outward eastern side. Moreover it followed that their artillery would be facing toward the British. Suppose then that this weak point, this gap between the forts, really existed? Suppose the British were to rush this gap and then, wheeling north, attack the camps one by one from the unfortified inward side? Might not then the whole Italian front be like an egg with a rotten inside? It was not impossible that we might penetrate as far as Sidi Barrani and even reach the coast behind the village to cut it off from its lifeline to Sollum. Given that, what then? Sidi Barrani could be besieged by land, sea and air. The British could push down the coast to Sollum, isolating the garrison of Sofafi to the south and forcing its members to retire up the escarpment on to Bardia.

Everything would depend on surprise. The Navy as well as the Air Force would have to be called in. Even so in November these conjectures appeared visionary and super-optimistic, so strongly were the Italians entrenched, so few were the forces Wavell had to bring against them. But the scheme was one which would have appealed to every man in the desert. O'Connor came back to Cairo and put it up to Wavell—Wavell who was very ready indeed to listen. The generals had one good card—the new infantry tanks had arrived, the famous 'I' tank. Their surprise effect would be redoubled in an important engagement. Wavell sounded out the other two services. Cunningham, reinforced from home, was agreeable. He would send some of his heaviest units ahead of the army to bombard first the outlying coastal camp Maktila, then Sidi Barrani itself, then, if need be, he would get to work on Sollum too. Longmore was less strong, but he had been reinforced also. His pilots had lately been showing a very definite superiority against the large bodies of Italian aircraft which used to come over Mersa Matruh. He also was agreeable.

At home Churchill gave support. A campaign in the Western Desert was the soundest possible way to remind the people of Britain that they were not alone, that they had outside forces fighting for them and toward them through Africa and Europe. Churchill was more than approving. He was enthusiastic. It remained now solely to choose a date and somehow keep the thing secret. That was the problem. To keep it secret in a land where gossip runs wild;

18

General Sir Archibald Wavell making plans with General O'Connor.

where enemy agents were known to lurk in every port from Alexandria to Haifa and Aden, where so many half-allies were expecting to be 'kept informed', where such arrangements as the unloading and movement of ships were plain for anyone to watch. How to get at least two divisions and artillery up to the front in the open desert without the enemy reconnaissance planes seeing them?

Wavell himself was a past master at saying nothing and appearing and acting in exactly the same way before a tea-party or a major offensive. But he was an island in a sea of garrulousness. It was as essential to keep the secret from our troops as from the enemy. There was one simple device—keep the desert and Cairo apart from one another. Communications between the desert and Cairo, as every war correspondent knew only too well, were terrible. Now while the preparations were being made in the desert no troops were allowed back on leave to the Delta where they might inadvertently spread hints and suggestions. Tickets of leave were choked off, not suddenly but gradually, so no suspicion was aroused. In G.H.Q. Wavell selected half a dozen men who had to have the exact information in advance. He swore them to silence: he ordered them to turn aside awkward enquiries among their junior officers.

But by far the most valuable aid in this campaign of secrecy was the misjudgment of the enemy. All the Fascists knew of the British Army at this time was that it had retreated before the Germans in Belgium, Norway and France, and before the Italians in British Somaliland and the Western Desert. To the Italians in December 1940 it was inconceivable that the British could really seriously attack. They were on the defensive and had been all along. Moreover there was an interior rottenness in the Italian Intelligence, something that grew naturally out of the national weakness for exaggeration. In war information becomes a commodity in itself. It has to be as exact as the corner-stone of a building or the barrel of a gun. And you could not overnight cure the individualistic Italian lieutenant and captain

19

A bush in the desert collected the papers thrown away by the retreating army.

of his boastfulness. Indeed the war had spurred officers and politicians on to still greater efforts in exaggeration. The Italian communiqués were absurd. The dangerous thing was that right through the Italian Army down to the rawest ranks a stream of wrong information was flowing. If a few shots were exchanged, the Italian private called it a skirmish and quite groundlessly claimed he had killed and routed the enemy. If a lieutenant was sent out on a raid, he expanded it in his reports to an engagement. An engagement became a major action or even a battle. From company headquarters to battalion, to brigade, to division, a supply of inaccurate details kept arriving at Italian G.H.Q. Even if G.H.Q. discounted what they heard by half, they were still left in the dark, not knowing where to draw the line between truth and fiction.

So Wavell in that first week of December might reasonably have expected some measure of surprise. His plan was simple in arrangement, simple in detail but somewhat complex at the edges. He could not possibly know how far or how fast he would go—if he went at all. So he planned his offensive first as a major raid.

If the raid went well, then his troops would be so disposed that they could pursue the enemy even as far as Sollum, if need be, or beyond—though nobody quite hoped for that. If he got into difficulties, he could again withdraw back on Mersa Matruh. The Air Force, first, then the Navy, would start the action. For forty-eight hours Air Commodore Collishaw, the R.A.F. commander in the desert, would send over almost continuous raids on to the airfields of Libya—high-level and dive-bombing and ground strafing. The object here was to keep the Italian air force on the ground until the British troops took up position and accomplished at least the first leg of their advance. The Navy meanwhile would make a dawn shelling of Maktila, the most forward Fascist post on the coastal road, and if the fort was reduced, would continue to Sidi Barrani, where the fifteen-inch naval guns were to demolish whatever they could find there. While this was going on the army would move up.

Two divisions were to be employed—the 7th armoured division under Major-General O'More Creagh and the 4th Indian division under Major-General Beresford-Pierce. The more experienced and more mobile armoured division would form the spearhead of the assault. Having gone through the gap, that unexplained but undeniable gap between Nibeiwa and Sofafi, Creagh would wheel northward sharply and attack one by one with the all-important infantry tanks the Italian camps at Nibeiwa, Tummar West, Tummar East and Point Ninety. He would also endeavour to reach the coast in the neighbourhood of Buq Buq between Sollum and Sidi Barrani, and hold a position there, thus outflanking the Sofafi garrison and cutting the retreat of the Italians, if any, from Sidi Barrani. Other units would also be sent directly upon Sofafi. Creagh's position might be a very awkward one indeed if he were not supported. Accordingly the Indian division would also plunge through the gap in close support and carry out the mopping-up operations upon Niebeiwa, the two Tummars and Point Ninety. This would bring them to the southern approaches of Sidi Barrani, which they were to attack if still able to do so. On the coast, units of the British garrison at Mersa Matruh were to emerge from their entrenchments and engage Maktila fortress which by then, it was hoped, would have been much reduced by the Navy. On the fall of Maktila the Mersa Matruh force would proceed straight toward Sidi Barrani and attack it from the east while the other two divisions were attacking from the south. Sappers would go ahead of our forces tearing up our own mines and dealing as far as they could with the Italian traps.

The weak point in the whole scheme was that somehow the armoured and the Indian divisions had to be got into position for attack without the Italians knowing it. There was no complete answer to his problem. The only course was to go ahead and see what happened. This is what happened.

On the night of December 7th when the desert air was already icy with the coming winter, the two British divisions made a forced march of seventy miles through the darkness up to points a few miles back from the Italian lines where they could still not be observed from ground level. All through the day of December 8th the thousands of men in full kit lay dispersed and inert on the flat desert. Luck held. An Italian reconaissance plane came over, but apparently neither saw nor suspected anything. No Italian patrol came out far enough to discover what was afoot. The air was busy with Collinshaw's planes passing back and forth to the Libyan airfields and they were having a wonderful time. The score of enemy

The tanks moved up to their forward positions.

aircraft damaged on the ground or caught aloft mounted from ten to twenty to the fifties. Everywhere, at Gazala, Bomba, El Adem, Tobruk, Benina and beyond, the Italian air force was being pinned to the ground. Through the night of the 8th while still the two divisions lay pressed to the desert waiting for the morning, the Royal Navy stole on Maktila in readiness for its bombardment at first light.

In Cairo at 9 a.m. on the 9th General Wavell summoned the war correspondents to his office. We were a small group of seven or eight and as we filed into the General's room and sat in a semicircle around him he got up from his chair and stood before us, leaning back on his desk. He was in his shirt sleeves. His desk was tidy; his ten-foot wall maps non-committal. He wore no glass in his blind eye and for the first time in my knowledge of him he was smiling slightly. Quietly and easily and without emphasis he said:

22

'Gentlemen, I have asked you to come here this morning to let you know that we have attacked in the Western Desert. This is not an offensive and I do not think you ought to describe it as an offensive as yet. You might call it an important raid. The attack was made early this morning and I had word an hour ago that the first of the Italian camps has fallen. I cannot tell you at this moment how far we are going to go—it depends on what supplies and provisions we capture and what petrol we are able to find. I wanted to tell you this so that you can make your own arrangements.' I asked if the weather was favourable. The General answered yes. He questioned us then to discover if any of us knew that the attack had been planned. It was important, he said, since, if the correspondents had not known, then, presumably, no one else except the authorized few had known. Not one of us was able to say he had had any hint of it. The surprise was complete.

There was a scatter then to get to the front—a full day and a half's journey away. And there began for us, on that brilliant winter morning, such a chain of broken communications and misunderstandings and mistakes that no correspondent who took part in the campaign is ever likely to forget. The press arrangements for correspondents in peace-time had been sketchy. In the face of a British victory they broke down almost entirely, though later conditions were greatly improved. It was days before we reached the front. For ever the forward troops vanished ahead of us as we sat stranded in our broken vehicles. Messages went astray for days or were lost altogether. We scraped what food we could from the desert or went without. We hitch-hiked when our vehicles broke down. Often we abandoned sleep in order to catch up. None of this, of course, was comparable to the difficulties the soldier in the line was putting up with. But it was a new kind of reporting: exasperating, exciting, fast-moving, vivid, immense and slightly dangerous. And what we had to say had such interest at that time that our stale descriptions were published fully when at last they did arrive in London and New York. It was a job that was for ever a little beyond one's reach. But I personally emerged from it two months later very glad to have been there and much wiser than when I went in.

3

THE Italian crust had been cracked already while Wavell was speaking to us. In the first sickly grey light of the morning a small frontal attack had been sent upon Nibeiwa, and it blinded Maletti to the far greater danger that was threatening him from behind. Rising up from their hidden positions, British forces began to pour through the gap with new infantry tanks in the van. These fell on Nibeiwa from the rear, while Maletti's men, rushing from their beds, were still engaged with the smaller frontal attack. Italian guns were swung upon the infantry tanks, but the tanks, carrying heavier armour than any seen before in the desert, swept on through the barrage. By now British shells were falling squarely on Nibeiwa itself, combing through the clustered stone huts, the parked lorries, the gun emplacements embedded in the surrounding wall. Maletti, a stoutish bearded man, was wounded even as he attempted to call his men to counter-attack. He retired into his tent with a machine-gun and was firing from his bedside when at last he was killed. It was all over in half an hour. The camp's thirty tanks had not even been properly manned. Everything the Italians had built through three hard months collapsed in bewilderment and chaos in that quiet morning hour when they would normally have been going about the first routine duties of the day.

Following in the wake of the army while it was hammering in the same way and at the same speed on Tummar West and Tummar East, we came on strange pathetic scenes at Nibeiwa. A cluster of broken burnt-out lorries and Bren-gun carriers proclaimed from a distance where the first British attack had fouled a minefield. Coming nearer, we found all the approaches pitted with small square holes let into the surface of the desert, and surrounding these empty cartridge cases and overturned machine-guns—the last remaining evidence of how the Italian outposts, straining their eyes through the darkness, had fired upon the approaching enemy and fled. Here and there trucks which had been carrying supplies and reliefs up to these outposts lay smashed by artillery fire beside the tracks, or were simply abandoned by the passengers who had fled back afoot to the temporary safety of the fort. Minefields were still strewn over large areas of the desert.

Cutting south and west to avoid these, and clinging closely to the tracks the heavy infantry tanks had made, we came at last into Nibeiwa itself. Here and there before the breaches in the walls a dead man lay spread-eagled on the ground, or collapsed grotesquely at the entrance of his dugout under a gathering cloud of flies. Some sixty or seventy mules and donkeys, recovered now from their shock at the noise of battle, nosed mournfully and hopelessly among the débris in search of fodder and water. Finding none, they would lift their heads and bray pathetically into the heavy dust-laden air. Italian light tanks were grouped at the spot on the western wall where they had huddled for a last stand and there surrendered. Others had bolted inside the fort itself and were turned this way and that, indicating how they had sought at the last moment for some formation to meet the attack. Maletti's body covered with a beribboned tunic still lay sprawled on the threshold of his tent, his beard stained with sand and sweat.

Sand was blowing now out of the immense ruts cut up by the tanks, and, walking through it, we went from one tent to another, from one dugout by subterranean passage into the next. Extraordinary things met us wherever we turned. Officer's beds laid out with clean sheets, chests of drawers filled with linen and abundance of fine clothing of every kind. Uniforms heavy with gold lace and decked with the medals and colours of the parade ground hung upon hangers in company with polished jackboots richly spurred and pale blue sashes and belts finished with great tassels and feathered and embroidered hats and caps. An Indian came running to us through the camp with one of those silver and gilt belts—a gaudy shining thing that the Fascists sling around their shoulders on parade. We came on great blue cavalry cloaks that swathed a man to the ankles, and dressing-tables in the officers' tents were strewn with scents and silver-mounted brushes and small arms made delicately in the romantic northern arsenals of Italy.

We sat down on the open sand and ate from stores of bottled cherries and green-gages; great tins of frozen hams and anchovies; bread that had been baked somehow here in the desert; and wines from Frascati and Falerno and Chianti, red and white, Lachrimæ Christi from the slopes of Vesuvius above Naples. There were wooden

Cement tank traps known as 'Dragon's Teeth'.

casks of a sweet, heady, fruity brandy, and jars of liqueurs of other kinds wrapped carefully in envelopes of straw. For water the Italians took bottles of Recoaro minerals—the very best in Italy—and these, like everything else, had been carted out to them in hundreds of cases across a thousand miles of sea and desert by ship and car and mule team.

The spaghetti was packed in long blue paper packages and stored with great sacks of macaroni and other wheat foods as numerous as they used to be in the shops of Italy before the war. Parmesan cheeses as big as small cart-wheels and nearly a foot thick lay about in neat piles except where some hungry soldier had slashed one open with his sword. Ten-pound tins of Estratto di Pomidoro—the tomato extract vital to so many Italian dishes—formed the bulk of the tinned stuff, which also contained many excellent stews and delicate tinned tongue and tunny fish and small round tins of beef. The vegetables were of every kind. Potatoes, onions, carrots, beans, cabbages, leeks, cauliflowers, pumpkin and many other things had been steamed down into a dry compact that readily expanded to its old volume when soaked in warm water—a fine food for the desert. We sampled one package that seemed at first to contain dry grass, but brewed itself over a stove into a rich minestrone soup.

I stepped down into at least thirty dugouts, coming upon something new and surprising in every one. The webbing and leather work was of the finest; the uniforms well cut and of solid material such as the civilian in Italy had not seen for many months. Each soldier appeared to have been supplied with such gadgets as sewing-bags and little leather cases for his letters and personal kit. The water containers were of new improved design—both the aluminium tanks that strap on the shoulders and those that one fastened to the flanks of a mule or stowed in a lorry. And over everything, wherever I went, fell a deepening layer of sand. For two days now it had been blowing, and before one's eyes one saw stores of clothing, piles of food, rifles, boxes of ammunition, the carcases of animals and the bodies of men fast disappearing under the surface of the desert. All this richness and its wreckage, all the scars of the battle and all the effort of ten thousand men, it seemed, would not prevail longer than a week or two, and soon Nibeiwa would be restored to the featurelessness and monotony of the surrounding waste.

Moving round in the sand, one stumbled on cartridge clips, rifles, machine-guns, swords and hand-grenades that had been flung aside, especially at the entrance to dugouts, in scores of thousands. These hand-grenades came to be known as money boxes or shaving sticks or pillar boxes. They were tiny things that fitted easily into the palm of your hand. They had a black cylindrical base, a rounded top coloured vivid red, and one pulled a small leather flap to explode them. I must have seen ten thousand that morning.

I went into the tented hospital where the British and Italian sick were still lying tended by British and Italian doctors. These hospitals were large square khaki-coloured tents of a good height for the coolness and fitted with ample mica windows. The stores of bandages, splints, liniments, drugs, surgical instruments and folding beds would have served this or any other comparable army ten times over. Here as everywhere there was precision and immense planning with immense quantity of materials. I sat in an operating theatre and drank wine with a soldier who had fought over the places I knew in the Spanish war. He pressed more food upon me and cases of wine—indeed it was he, the vanquished, who had everything to give and we who were tired and hungry. And somehow out of relief and boredom he had achieved a sense of fatality that had given him peace of mind. He was accepting the prospect of imprisonment much as a schoolboy will accept his lessons as painful but inevitable. Yet the Italian minded the absence of his family and his friends perhaps more than we did.

Never did an army write home or receive letters as this one did. For five miles the landscape was strewn with their letters. In the offices of adjutants I came on bureaux stacked with thousands of official postcards which expressed the usual greetings and to which a soldier had only to attach his name and address. But most preferred to write their own letters in a thin spidery schoolboy scrawl full of homely Latin flourishes; full of warm superlatives like 'carissimo' . . . 'benissimo'.

26

The theme for ever ran on children and religion. No postcard ever closed without some reference to the day when the family or the lovers would be reunited.

I read one letter which contained a piece of doggerel that, roughly translated, runs like this:

> Long live the Duce and the King.
> The British will pay for everything.
> On land and sea and in the air
> They'll compensate us everywhere.

But there was much hard common sense besides. One letter-writer insisted: 'We are trying to fight this war as though it is a colonial war in Africa. But it is a European war in Africa fought with European weapons against a European enemy. We take too little account of this in building our stone forts and equipping ourselves with such luxury. We are not fighting the Abyssinians now.'

There was the whole thing; the explanation of this broken, savaged camp. Maletti's panzer division was as tame as an old lion in the zoo. Undoubtedly they had courage, some of them. But they were living on a preposterous scale. The British brigadiers in this action had not for many weeks or even months lived as the Italian non-commissioned officer was living. In the British lines there were no sheets, no parade-ground uniforms, and certainly no scent. The brigadier dressed in khaki shorts and shirt. He got bacon for breakfast, bully stew and tinned fruit for lunch, and the same again at night. His luxuries were the radio, cigarettes and whisky with warm water. But wine, liqueurs, cold ham, fresh bread—no, seldom if ever that.

Even the Italian trucks, of which there were several hundred scattered about Nibeiwa and the other camps, carried all kinds of equipment never seen in the British lines. The field telephones, wireless, typewriters and signalling gear were far more elaborate than anything we had used. Booty, in fact, worth several millions of pounds lay here if it could only be reclaimed in time. (It wasn't.)

Sappers were at work, getting vital parts off the Italian machines so that they could keep their own vehicles on the road. We ourselves, already short of transport, endeavoured to take over one of the great green ten-ton Lancia trucks standing about. But though we inspected dozens, all had either been wrecked at the last moment by the Italians or were hit or had gear too complicated for us to start. Later many hundreds of these vehicles, together with Fiats and the S.P.A. brand, were on the road carrying British troops and supplies to the front. Indeed, as Wavell had indicated, the advance could not have gone forward without them. In guns, too, we had at Nibeiwa a foretaste of the prizes ahead. Many were of old stock and small calibre like the Breda, but ammunition lay about in great abundance.

Of the thirty-odd Italian tanks some half were fit for service and some were already being dragged off to workshops when I arrived. But the light Italian tank and the lighter flame-thrower were failures, and men asked for death in riding behind their thin armour. Curiously, in all essential things—guns, tanks, lorries, ammunition—the Italian equipment was not good. And vast numbers did not make up for the deficiency. The ten-ton Lancias ran on diesel—as did most of the Italian vehicles—but they had solid tyres which shook the vehicles to pieces after a short time among the boulders on the desert. Moreover, when a ten-ton lorry which was also a good target broke down, ten tons of supplies were held up. We preferred

'Ci rendiamo': the first Italians surrender.

to run on petrol, using five-tonners or lighter machines. If one broke down, then no more than five tons were delayed, and repacking on to a sound vehicle was easier. Nevertheless, from this moment on, more and more captured Italian equipment was pressed into service against the Italians.

Nibeiwa was our first storehouse. As I drove away from it northward in the early afternoon the blown sand cleared for a moment revealing two big desert birds that circled and twisted some twenty feet above the ground until, seeing what they wanted, they dived and settled amid the stench where an Italian mule team had gone down to death with its crew under British machine-gun fire.

Northward, toward the coast beyond Nibeiwa, things had gone with a precision and speed that outstripped all communications. After Nibeiwa, according to the plan, one section of the armoured division had branched off on the lonely desert route in the direction of Sofafi; another had struck for the coast between Buq Buq and Sidi Barrani; and the other had made straight toward Sidi Barrani, mopping up forts as it went. This last northerly column was the one I was following. Tummar West and Tummar East had gone that same first day almost as quickly as Nibeiwa. Nothing, it seemed, could withstand the new infantry tanks. Travelling only twelve miles an hour, they lunged out of the dust of the battle and were on the Italians or behind them before anything could be done. The Italians in despair saw that their light anti-tank shells just rattled off the tanks' turrets, and even light artillery was not effective against them. The whole of this advance, then, was done with this surprise weapon—surprise, not because the enemy did not know about it, but because they did not know it was in Egypt and they had nothing to bring against it.

Maktila on the coast had been heavily plastered by the Navy, and by the time the British garrison from Mersa Matruh came to attack they found many of the enemy already fled. These fugitives turned back to strengthen Point Ninety, the two Tummars and Sidi Barrani itself. But the infantry tanks rode upon them with artillery in support, and by the time I reached the battlefield all Italian forces who had managed to get away had retired into Sidi Barrani and were already attempting to escape farther down the coast road in the direction of Sollum. In spurting dust we drove past the Tummars, a richer arsenal yet than Nibeiwa. For miles on either side of the track the undulating surface of the desert was honeycombed with ammunition dumps, each dump about ten feet by eight by two feet high and spaced a hundred yards apart. These were the shells Graziani had stored against the day when he was to have advanced on the Nile. Every rise was dotted with stationary and abandoned Italian trucks and vehicles of all kinds. Notepaper flew forlornly across the battlefield in every direction, and here and there a gun stuck in the dust in a ring of empty shell cases.

A bitter artillery duel had been fought out with the Italian guns on a height near the coast. And now on the morning of the third day the British flung themselves on the defences of Sidi Barrani itself. Unwilling to delay their advantage until more artillery caught up with them, the tanks and infantry went in together against the first line. This was a series of zigzag trenches on a rise buttressed from other positions among the sand-dunes. As the fine sand whirled up in monstrous yellow clouds visibility shut down first to a hundred, then to fifty yards. The battle locked in choking heat over two miles of rocky desert. Constantly in the sand-dunes the Italians kept up enfilading fire upon the central British thrust. But by 11 a.m. at the bayonet point we had gained the first ridge and Sidi Barrani lay in view. The tanks then felt their way around east and west of the Italians, and suddenly in the early afternoon appeared right amongst them. Artillery posts were charged direct. Everywhere in the yellow light of the dust storm men were running, shouting, firing, diving for shelter. A regiment of Scots charged from the ridge they had gained earlier in the day, and though their best N.C.O.'s went down, the rest came on. Groups of Italians began bobbing up from their trenches, waving white handkerchiefs, towels, shirts, and shouting, 'Ci rendiamo' (We surrender).

The tanks now were upon Sidi Barrani itself and the infantry came pell-mell after them. General Gallina was there with his staff. They knew it was useless. Their surrender was received while still the ragged edges of the battle were sounding with rifle and mortar fire. This was about 3 p.m. Toward evening the Mersa Matruh troops, having pushed all opposition on the coast out of their way, entered the town from the east. Gallina drew the remnants of his army together and, addressing them quietly, an elderly general with a general's sweeping grey beard, he said, 'You have fought bravely.' They took him and his officers off to captivity by aeroplane.

The British now found themselves in a place of utter desolation. Sidi Barrani, was in ruins. At the climax of many heavy aerial bombardments the Navy had come and flung round after round of fifteen-inch shells upon the village. No house maintained its roof; none had its walls intact. Everything within was a mass of whitish grey rubble. Shell holes pitted the scrawny streets and twisted the barbed wire round the port. A shell seemed to have blasted each window in such a manner as to leave every wall with an aperture like a huge keyhole driven through it. Wrecked vehicles lay about, and a great quantity of petrol and crude oil drums—some of which, being hit, were burning yet and staining the sand a grimy stinking black. On the outskirts there were many guns—Bredas, eighteen-pounders and anti-tank weapons. Together with the booty at Nibeiwa and the other camps I counted over fifty captured tanks, over five hundred captured vehicles.

The troops who had swept through from the east had found the same eloquent story of surprise—half-eaten breakfasts (served with silver pepper and salt stands, china plates and cups); clothes half bundled into boxes and then abandoned. And there was the same business of bedside lights, book-racks, tents emblazoned with flags, officers' cloaks thick with decorations, quantities of freshly baked loaves, cases of chocolate, sweetmeats, coffee, jam, cigarettes, tobacco both Italian and English.

Down by the Sidi Barrani sea-cliffs an important base hospital had been established under canvas. The Italian staff in the hospital had vanished, leaving an appendicitis patient cut open upon the operating table. Instruments were still sticking in the body when it was found.

Exhausted by hard travel and sightseeing, we camped down by the hospital for the night. Savoia bombers came over and we did not wake.

Starting fresh in the morning, we came at once on to the Via della Vittoria, the new Italian road that ran straight and true to the Libyan border, over those sixty painful miles that once were strewn with deep dust and boulders. At the point where it met the British road at Sidi Barrani the Italians had erected a six-foot cement monument decorated with the fasces and carrying an inscription that declared 'despite wind and sand and the wiles of the enemy' Egypt and Libya were inseparably joined together under Fascist rule. And indeed the Italian engineers deserved praise. All through the late summer and autumn they had slaved with labour gangs at that road, and now the track was heavily metalled and waiting only for a covering of light metal and bitumen. It was banked and graded with the precision of an autostrada, and of a good width and flanked by deep ditches for the draining. Here and there culverts led off to side tracks and offered an opportunity for the heavier vehicles to turn. Steam-rollers which had come from Italy to put the finishing touches lay along the highway, and as we progressed we found more monuments that proclaimed how such and such a unit had finished a section in record time. On one crest rose a stone bust of Mussolini bearing a quotation from one of his Genoa speeches, 'He who does not keep moving is lost.' British soldiers ahead of us who had no taste for irony had bowled the head over into the sand.

Now only ten miles west of Sidi Barrani we saw signs that Creagh's dash to the coast to cut the retreat of the Italians had succeeded. Italian lorries caught unawares by British tanks lay twisted in smoking ruins on the road. Guns stood about dejectedly. All the roadside camps and storage dumps were deserted and bore signs of having been passed over by an invading army. Diesel oil drums were tumbled about, spilling their contents on the sand. Every few minutes we had to make a detour to avoid more Italian vehicles left by their drivers astride the road. Food, ammunition and oil dumps followed one another among the sidetracks, all marked with Italian direction posts. Dugout villages roofed with camouflaged waterproof sheets pitted the landscape. The Italians had dug in so completely and comfortably that this was not Egypt any more—it was a part of Italy. They had found and developed a water supply with genius. They had all but completed a pipeline from Bardia. Soon, no doubt, they would have produced market gardens in the desert. At Buq Buq, which I remembered as a Bedouin waterhole dug in the sand, there stood now a line of high pumps like those used for filling locomotives and two large underground storage tanks.

It was approaching Buq Buq that we came suddenly upon a sight that seemed at first too unreal, too wildly improbable to be believed. An entire captured division was marching back into captivity. A great column of dust turned pink by the sunset light behind them rose from the prisoners' feet as they plodded four abreast in the sand on either side of the metalled track. They came on, first in hundreds, then in thousands, until the stupendous crocodile of marching figures stretched away to either horizon. No one had time to count them—six, possibly seven thousand, all in dusty green uniforms and cloth caps. Outnumbered roughly five hundred to one, a handful of British privates marched alongside the two columns, and one or two Bren-gun carriers ran along the road in between. The Italians spoke to me quite freely when I called to them, but they were tired and dispirited beyond caring. I found no triumph in the scene—just the tragedy of hunger, wounds and defeat. These were the men of General Amico's 'Catanzaro Division', I discovered.

Soon we pieced the whole story together. Creagh had reached the coast two days before. His tanks and Bren-gun carriers had burst over the last desert rise on to the new road to find themselves confronted with the Catanzaro Division, which was then moving up on normal relief to Sidi Barrani. The Italians were smoking and singing, since none had expected action so far back behind the front. The British joined action at once, and a smart tank and artillery battle was fought out in the salt pans between the road and the sea. When their tanks failed, the bewildered Italians simply gave themselves up, and here they were upon the Via della Vittoria, marching to Sidi Barrani and away out of the war without having fired a shot.

Thousands more were clustered round the water points at Buq Buq, a more broken collection of men than I had ever seen. Many were Libyans. They sat upon their haunches in disordered groups awaiting their turn to draw water from the cisterns and receive an issue of their own cheese and tinned beef which had been gathered from one of the Italian food dumps near by. A company of British troops was guarding them—a company that could have been overwhelmed at any moment. But there was no fight in these Italians, and their fear of the waterless desert overmastered any wild idea they may have had for gaining freedom. They were confused, too, and had no inkling of the smallness of the British forces.

In the morning three Libyans approached the unarmed war correspondents' camp which we had pitched among the white sand-dunes beside the sea. They were so utterly dejected and miserable no one thought to take their guns away from them, and they sat watching us stolidly and pathetically while we finished breakfast, wanting only to be taken prisoner. We put them in our truck and drove them back to the prisoners' depot by the water wells.

Now at last we had caught up with the front. In the far south Sofafi had fallen with rich loot. It was voluntarily abandoned by the Italians before it had been attacked, and its garrison was making up the escarpment towards Bardia under

'The extraordinary sight of an entire division marching back into captivity'. December 1940.

R.A.F. bombardment. Other British troops were moving across to cut them off. Others again were pressing on Sollum and Halfaya Pass. There was artillery fire along the escarpment at Sollum, and once again I saw the cliffs curtained in smoke and aircraft battling in the sky above. Two Caproni fighters lay upended grotesquely beside the road. More and more prisoners were coming in, bringing with them many guns, tanks, vehicles and truck loads of captured documents. These last were fascinating. One of Bergonzoli's orders of the day, written just before the British attacked, read: 'The emblems of the British Army that tried to bar your way are trampled underfoot. The first steps of the march to Alexandria have been covered. Now onward! Sidi Barrani is the base of departure for more distant and much more important objectives.' Then again, how truly, 'Surprise is always the mastery of war.'

Light rain fell. There followed a wind so sharp and piercing that one could not imagine it had ever been hot in the desert. Goose-flesh pock-marked our bare sunburnt arms, our faces felt blue and bloodless, and the sand came up, stinging, icy and cruel, to bite into our bare knees and arms and stun our eyelids until we could bear it no longer and reached for towels or waterproof sheets to bind round our heads. Our food and petrol gave out, and we spent hours each day ranging round the desert in search of abandoned Italian dumps. At night six of us slept huddled in one car for warmth. When at last we made camp together we succeeded in building a fire of brushwood. On it we cooked the one good meal I can remember

of this stage of the campaign—a spaghetti stew of Italian tomato, Italian bully beef, Italian Parmesan cheese, washed down with Italian mineral water.

Standing on the top of the dunes that night we watched for an hour the R.A.F. turning one of their full-scale raids on Bardia. Looking across the wide intervening bay in the darkness, we saw it all stage by stage—the first bombs, the answering fire; the hits, the misses; the flames as the aircraft came away; drama as rounded and directional as a motion picture and watched with the detachment of a spectator in the stalls. Parachute flares with their fresh blinding light hung in the sky above the town, while bombs fell at the rate of two a minute in a regular pendulum motion—right, left, right, left. The A.A. fire in reply turned right, left, in search of the unseen raiders; then, losing contact, broke into crazy patterns over the sky. 'Like a bull fight,' someone said. 'And Bardia the bull.' Two flaring lights opened high above the town and descended straightly. Two planes gone; two picadors. Then more swerving light in the sky; more interplay of light and the counter-thrust of bomb noise against gun noise. Then the great flash as the ammunition dump went up and a slower flame advanced steadily up into the night. The bull. The surviving planes homewarding sounded over our heads. It was finished and we went to bed on the sand.

At last on December 16th—one week after the fighting had begun—Sollum fell; and with Sollum, Halfaya Pass, Fort Capuzzo, Sidi Omar, Musaid and a new line of forts several kilometres long which the Italians had built on the lip of the

33

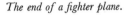
The end of a fighter plane.

There was not much danger of prisoners escaping; thirst was more deadly than captivity.

escarpment. Halfaya's old rocky track had been graded and surfaced, and as one mounted to the top the old familiar view spread out below—the sweep of Sollum bay round into Egypt; the village below and the western cliffs reaching round into Bardia. Breasting the top of the pass into the high Libyan desert, a wind of such sharpness and force swept upon our open truck that the driver momentarily was forced to stop. No one without glasses could travel looking ahead into that sand-laden wind that hit everything raised above the floor of the desert with the force of an aeroplane slipstream. British camps loomed up among the debris of the broken Italian forts.

We returned and entered Sollum where already half a dozen British warships and merchant vessels were discharging water and stores for the army. The Italians here had erected a barbed-wire compound to house British prisoners, and now it was full of their own people. In the desert, too, we found a camp exclusively for captured Italian generals, who plodded about dispiritedly in the sand. Upon every wall were scrawled caricatures of Englishmen, jibes at Churchill and Vivas for the Duce. Prisoners in their extremity were offering the equivalent of an English pound for a loaf of bread. Their units were inextricably mixed and confused, since in their flight the Italians had broken up, and many small groups had struck out for themselves in that last frantic rush to gain the safety of Bardia.

So then the first stage was ended. A rough score could be totted up. Some thirty thousand prisoners, including five generals, were in our hands. Hundreds of guns, lorries, tanks and aircraft were captured. Equipment worth millions of pounds had been won. The attempted enemy advance to the Nile had been smashed, and the last fighting Italian soldier had been flung out of Egypt. The enemy numbered their dead and wounded in thousands. Our casualties stood at the incredibly good figures of 72 killed and 738 wounded. The Italian egg had been cracked and it was rotten inside. It was largely a victory of the infantry tanks and scarcely one of these had been lost. Of the six Italian divisions that had been mustered for the capture of Egypt, less than half remained, and these, largely without guns and equipment, were crowded back into Bardia, which was even then being surrounded by our armoured forces. More than this, the Italian morale was broken and the prestige of the British Army restored. I went back to Cairo for one of the pleasantest Christmases I can remember.

34

4

ON Christmas morning I drove across the Bulaq Bridge in Cairo to the Church of England cathedral which stands, a pile of very modern yellow brick, beside the Nile a little distance down from the Embassy. After the service a great congregation streamed out into the bright sunshine. Among the brigadiers, the diplomats, the army nurses, the wives—few of these: most had been evacuated—and the soldiers, General Wavell stood chatting with his friends. People paused as they passed to gaze with open curiosity at this quiet thick-set man whose name now stood higher than that of any soldier in the Empire. He never failed to impress and puzzle slightly everyone who met him, but all the same there was nothing very much to be learned from the first meeting. His voice was high, rather nasal, and unless he was actually engaged upon some definite business he seldom said anything at all. His dark deeply tanned face was lined and heavy to the point of roughness. His thinning hair was grey, and the one good eye left him from the last war gleamed brightly from a face that was usually as expressionless as a statue.

Whatever Wavell was before the last war, he had gained from Allenby a talent for taking responsibility with suppleness and decision and for drawing others after him. In this year in the Middle East he won respect by his silence, and a good deal of admiration through his habit of confidently deputing authority to others. Wilson, O'Connor, Creagh—all of them were bound very strongly to Wavell. One other thing he had, and that was modesty. Now in his fifties, after half a lifetime of military training and planning, he had the great fortune to be able to put his ideas to the test. There was nothing very new about them—to use secrecy and surprise to the utmost, to hit hard and quickly and keep following up, to establish strong lines of communication, to be mobile—all sound military practices. But Wavell brought them to life by his own particular ingredient—a touch of daring. The troops liked him. You would often find him, just before an important engagement, sitting wearing a tin hat at an artillery observation post; he encouraged the front-line habit among his generals and liked them to stay in the field.

After the reconquest of the Western Desert, the character of the fighting in Libya changed radically. The surprise element was now gone. It was to recur only once more and very dramatically at the end of the campaign. The Italians were back on their fortified bases. They still outnumbered us, they were dug in, and they were expecting us to come on. Graziani's theory of roughly parallel lines of coastal and inland defence on set positions was coming into play. Both Bardia and Tobruk were surrounded by strong double perimeters which it had taken the Italians several years to construct. The desert bases—Jarabub, Mekili and Kufra— were remote. It was the British now who were on long lines of communications with all the problems of water and petrol supply before them. The winter, too,

LEFT: *H.Q. in a well outside Bardia. These wells were enormous, dry, and invisible from the air.*

ABOVE: *Captured machine-guns and rifles were piled in great heaps.*

had risen to a harshness that made additional hardships for advancing troops. Through the long nights Graziani could reasonably expect the arrival of reinforcements by sea at Tripoli.

The Marshal's policy was very simple—in fact it was the only one he could follow. He would hold Bardia and Tobruk, and so long as they lay across Wavell's lines of communication the British would be unable to push on. Should Bardia and Tobruk fall, then a line could be established against the invader southward from the neighbourhood of Derna to the desert post of Mekili. Here the country was riven by immense wadis and rocky heights ideal for defence. Should even this line fall, then an easy retreat over two good mountain roads could be made to Barce and Benghazi. If Benghazi was not reinforced by this time, then the whole Italian army could withdraw intact down the coastal road to Tripoli. When we were far extended there in the Libyan desert, Graziani would meet us and destroy us.

Every one of these plans miscarried. They miscarried because the tactics Wavell now put into effect were of so brilliant a nature that they must remain as a model for the reduction of strongholds in the desert. Briefly the plan was this: no matter how weak our forces were, every enemy stronghold had to be surrounded and cut from its supplies until we were strong enough to make a frontal attack. Conversely, no position was to be attacked until it was surrounded. The Navy and the R.A.F. would leave no enemy position on the coast in peace even for a single day. Thus Bardia was to be surrounded, plastered from sea and air, then attacked directly. As soon as the attack was favourably launched, the encirclement of Tobruk would start, and the reduction of the town be essayed in the same way. And so on to Bomba and Derna. Beyond that no one yet cared to conjecture anything definite.

To accomplish this, Wavell regrouped his forces with rare psychological insight. He was still going to use only two divisions—throughout the whole campaign he never had more than two divisions in the operational area. The experienced and fast 7th Armoured Division would undertake the inland swoops and the encircling movements. The India division, having well done its job at Sidi Barrani, would be withdrawn, together with the New Zealanders, and they would be replaced by most of one of the untried Australian divisions. In this Wavell aroused

Behind an Ack Ack post during a night raid.

a very definite animosity among the New Zealanders, who had been thirsting for action. They were additionally hurt when their transport was taken away from them and given to the Australians. But with the Australians Wavell's action brought him immense popularity. They had been growing increasingly, even dangerously, restive after their year's enforced idleness. Wisely now these men, already noted as shock-troops, were to have their chance while their health was at its freshest, their morale at its highest, and their aggressive qualities most eager. The New Zealanders, with their reputation of being solider and more disciplined holding troops, would be a valuable rock on which to fall back if anything went wrong. Many of the technical services—machine-gunners, signallers, railways operators and supply columns—were to be given to English or allied units. The Navy and the Air Force would dispose of equal or even greater forces than in the December advance.

Bardia as a defensive position was much stronger than Sidi Barrani. The town itself, a picturesque Fascist settlement of white-walled houses and straight streets, stood high upon the cliffs above a small, almost landlocked bay. Coastal boats of shallow draught could enter and discharge their supplies in the storehouses on the flat delta of the Wadi Gefani. This wadi effectively protected the town from the landward side and indeed left the town isolated on a spit reaching over the sea. Attacking troops had first to penetrate a ring of forts and an anti-tank trench stretching round Bardia from one coast to the other, and then cross the Wadi Gefani. It was not easy. But the armoured division was astride the road westward to Tobruk, and the morale of the Italian troops inside Bardia was not high. They numbered some thirty thousand men under the command of Bergonzoli, who had lately been carrying on a high-flown wireless conversation with the Duce in Rome, the theme of which was 'Bardia will never surrender'.

All through Christmas week Australians kept pouring up the desert road from the Nile Delta—a vast procession stretching three hundred and fifty miles from Cairo to the front. The Via della Vittoria was quickly cut to pieces, and bus-loads of troops came up on to the escarpment matted in dust, the eyes of each man two dark slits peering out of a grey mask under a steel helmet. Before New Year's Day they were in position and shelling the Italian perimeter. Patrols were nightly going into the Italian barbed wire. On January 2nd shallow-draught gunboats from the China station bore down upon Bardia's harbour, and all through that night the Navy and the R.A.F. raked the town and its surroundings with probably the heaviest bombardment of its kind that had ever been seen in the Middle East. The day, as I remember, had been full of warm, yellow, winter sunlight. Now in the evening, like flights of migrating birds, British bombers kept sliding across a sunset magnificently red. And far into the night the red fires in Bardia expanded and continued the sunset. Waiting at our camp in Mersa Matruh, we knew the attack was coming, and the desert had an almost tangible atmosphere of expectancy and strain.

At dawn the Australians attacked. They had chosen a spot in the perimeter to the west of the town, and here the sappers ran forward under machine-gun fire to bridge the anti-tank trench by blowing in its sides. The infantry tanks and the infantry were soon across, and, with this spearhead always pressing nearer to the heart of the enemy defences, the battle started along a ten-mile front around the Italian chain of forts. The effect of the British assault was as though one had tightly gripped an orange, at the same time piercing it with a fork. This went on all through January 3rd.

On January 4th the day began for me at 3 a.m., when the correspondents started from Mersa Matruh aboard an army truck. For miles along the road into Sollum we watched the final British artillery barrage being laid down along the five-hundred-foot cliffs that supported Bardia on their crest In blinding icy dust we crawled up Halfaya Pass and continued on aslant the artillery fire into Libya. Italian shells, mostly of small calibre, were crumping steadily away to the west.

Near miss on a truck carrying infantry through a gap in an enemy minefield.

At Force Headquarters, a labyrinth of underground Roman passages, a young staff officer barked laconically: 'Whole of the southern defences encompassed and we're breaking in from the north . . . ten thousand prisoners taken and God knows how many more coming in . . . four enemy schooners stopped outside Bardia, three more captured . . . enemy artillery getting weaker . . . no, I don't know where the hell the enemy air force is; we haven't seen it all day.'

We drove on along the broken border fence to the Australian headquarters, a Roman labyrinth twenty feet below the surface of the desert. The Italian gunners were getting the range there, but unevenly and spasmodically. Right and left of the camp explosions were going up in short gusty clouds of black smoke. The staff officers, deaf to it all, were diving in and out of dugouts with messages, shouting out over the telephones new orders for new positions to the men at the front about to take Bardia.

We drove on down the Capuzzo road, and there it was again, the sight I was beginning to know well—the unending line of marching prisoners with their weary, stony faces. They were herding like a football crowd into roughly-thrown-up barbed-wire compounds each holding two or three thousand men. Down the road leading to the fighting more British troops were pressing on in trucks travelling at breakneck speeds. Over Capuzzo British spotting planes ranged back and forth checking the last Italian gun positions from the white flashes that spouted up

'The stupendous crocodile of marching prisoners . . .

for ten miles along the coast. Capuzzo itself, as we drove past with the troops, was empty, more torn about than ever. Our lighter truck got on ahead of the troop-carriers as we approached Bardia. Shells were shrieking down along the whole length of the road, though never hitting it exactly as we went through. A sharp smell of explosive washed across the track in sudden bursts as each new mushroom of smoke billowed up—sometimes two hundred yards away to the left, then, erratically, far out to the right below the spot where an Australian battery was belching black fumes at the speed of half a dozen bursts a minute. Surrendered Italians were huddled on either side of the road, sheltering from their own shellfire. Others made desperate by their hunger rushed across the open to us. They swarmed round our truck in hundreds, crying: 'Food . . . water . . . cigarettes.' We flung out biscuits and they scrambled for them in a heap on the ground, forgetting the shells in their frantic hunger.

We were reaching the most forward troops now, down a road that drove through empty Italian trenches. Rifles and machine-guns were lying unmanned along parapets; dead and wounded were mingled together in ditches. Clearly the majority of Italians had surrendered as soon as their positions were invested. Over toward the coast another long line of prisoners moved across the desert without a guard,

40

. . . stretched away to either horizon'.

blindly seeking shelter, blindly looking for anyone to surrender to. In a branch of Wadi Gefani, half a mile from Bardia, the front-line Australians in full kit were awaiting the order to go over the top for the last time. They lay about in groups in the dry river-bed, smoking comfortably. You could almost trace the trajectory of the Italian shells as they screamed a hundred yards above and hit empty sand on the back edge of the wadi above us. The commanding officer limped up and took a drink from me gratefully. 'It's my birthday today,' he said. 'Just remembered it,' He was wounded.

It was 3 p.m. now and very near the end. I crawled up the Bardia side of the wadi and looked over. There it was, the white township with its church spire and the road leading in across two bridges. Just in front of the church, six hundred yards away, the last Italian gun was mouthing white flashes toward us. The final assault started just after three o'clock—British heavy tanks moving through a belt of machine-gun and even anti-tank gunfire right up to the gates of Bardia. I watched them go on spurting out shell from every gun. Crouching as they ran and calling out their war-cries, Australian infantry followed up and joined the Bren-gun patrols which had already advanced under the lee of the town in the early afternoon. I could see only a hundred or two of infantry now, and even these disappeared

41

Mussolini's desert road ran a thousand miles to Tunis.

from view as the Italian gun turned upon them. Then that last gun hiccoughed and stopped altogether. The attack swept past it and eastward from the town.

It was easy then. We grabbed a place in a line of Australian Bren-gun carriers moving in on the town, outdistanced them at the gates, and drove down the burning main street to the town hall, where the leader of the Australian company which had occupied Bardia stood wiping black sweat from his face. They had been in possession just over an hour. They had gone in in extended order through the neat right-angled streets, firing bursts into the houses. But only one machine-gun near the church hit back. All round us now Italians were coming out of caves and houses to surrender. Prisoners swarmed in every direction, and even in the light of the fires which were licking up the white walls of the houses it was impossible to distinguish enemy from friend. All they wanted was food, shelter from fighting, and a guarantee of life.

One Australian officer with eight men walked up to the mouth of the biggest cave in the cliffs. As he stood at the entrance with cocked revolver, over a thousand Italians came out into the daylight, holding up their hands. Half a dozen guards

42

were told off to get them away. Except for a few who escaped by schooner or stole across overland by night, no Italians slipped through the British net. The great majority were captured unhurt, since the Italian machine-gunners had continued firing only so long as the Australians were out of range. As soon as the Australians began to set up their own guns to retaliate, the Italians came out with white towels and handkerchiefs.

I walked down through the burning town, stopping here and there to peer into the houses. Everything had been cleared out down to the last drawer. A table was laid for ten in the officers' mess, but there was no food anywhere. We went to the harbour. Down in Bardia's lovely blue bay (where a group of naval ratings had been captured) several ships lay half-submerged and deserted. Through the clear water you could see slime already clinging to the sunken cabins and fish darting among the stanchions and sodden timbers. Thousands of tins of bully beef littered the sea floor like scattered silver coins. Birds were already nesting in the slanting masts showing above water.

The shooting and shelling stopped at last as we came back to the centre of the town. The fires in the back streets fed quietly. A little handful of us stood about in the gathering darkness, waiting for the other units of the Australian army to come up and occupy finally the cliffs and outlying forts. It was deathly quiet now after the battle. It was hard to realize we had won and it was over.

Straightway we set off on the frigid all-night drive back to Mersa Matruh, where we could send off our messages. Often in the darkness (no car lights were allowed) we swerved to avoid lost and bewildered Italians roaming over the desert trying to find their units. Many knew nothing of the rout of the Italian army. Many slept beside their guns or turned over and shouted to us in Italian for food or water or news. We picked up a wounded Italian officer and drove him along to one of the dumps where they were collecting prisoners. 'We should never have been fighting you,' he kept insisting. 'All this should never have happened.' Four of his men hoisted him shoulder-high in the darkness and carried him off to some dressing-station they knew about.

Australians, cigarettes in the corner of their mouths and steel helmets down over their lined eyes, squatted here and there among the prisoners, or occasionally got to their feet with a bayoneted rifle and shouted, 'Get back there, you,' when some Italian started to stroll away. These men from the dockside of Sydney and the sheep-stations of the Riverina presented such a picture of downright toughness with their gaunt dirty faces, huge boots, revolvers stuffed in their pockets, gripping their rifles with huge shapeless hands, shouting and grinning—always grinning— that the mere sight of them must have disheartened the enemy troops. For some days the Rome radio had been broadcasting that the 'Australian barbarians' had been turned loose by the British in the desert. It was a convenient way in which to explain away failures to the people at home. But the broadcast had a very bad effect on the Italians waiting in Bardia for the arrival of the Australians. I saw prisoners go up to their guards to touch the leather jerkins our men were wearing against the cold. A rumour had gone round that the jerkins were bullet-proof. More than anything for the defenders of Bardia the last few days had been a war of nerves. And now the Italian nerve was gone.

We drove on slowly, endlessly, chilled to the bone, past streams of ambulances and supply-wagons going up to the front where they were badly needed. By midnight we were down the escarpment. Just before dawn we were approaching Mersa Matruh, Richard Dimbleby driving to relieve our chauffeur. Six of us and our kits were jumbled somehow in the back of the tiny 8-cwt. truck, too frozen to move, but beyond sleeping. Only Dimbleby slept. The truck struck two concrete drums placed across a newly completed bridge and plunged into space over the ditch beside the road. Painfully but unhurt we picked ourselves out of the wrecked vehicle and stood beside the road.

Out of the gloom emerged an engineer who stared glumly at the wreckage for a moment. Then in a tired hurt voice he said: 'I've been working for a solid month in this bloody hole. I built that bridge. I finished it today. I was just putting up a nice little memorial to say, "Bridge begun by the 21st Company of Engineers, December 1940, Completed January 1941," I don't suppose it matters now.' Then, more bitterly: 'Or would you like to add something to the inscription? Would you like to say, "Destroyed by War Correspondents, January 1941"?' But kindly he gave us tea and we were picked up and taken into Mersa Matruh. And there we wrote and slept. We had been travelling two days and nights.

5

ALREADY while Bardia was falling Tobruk was being surrounded. Those elements of the 7th Armoured Division which had guarded Bardia's outlet to the west cut back deep into the desert once the Bardia battle had been joined. They arrived presently at El Adem, one of the Italians' three main air striking bases, just south of Tobruk. Here eighty-seven aircraft lay burnt out or broken on the ground. Several blocks of fine concrete workshops, hangars and living-quarters stood beneath El Adem's high wireless tower. Climbing it, we had a view on to the white roofs of Tobruk itself.

The machinery captured here was the first real booty that had fallen to the R.A.F., and the field itself was destined to become a valuable air junction for the British forces. But at the moment it was under shell-fire, and when I arrived there, only a handful of British troops were keeping guard over the workshops. A sheikh with seven magnificent solid gold teeth came riding out of Tobruk to meet us. The town was running short of water and food, he said, and he had had enough. He had escaped the Italians and was returning to the desert with his wives, his camels and his sons.

Keeping just beyond the point where the Italians were laying down a barrage, I drove on up to the coast to the west of Tobruk. We hit a fine road some twenty miles outside the town, and now at last the colours and contours of the desert were subtly changing. A low yellowish scrub sprouted here and there, and the overnight dew lying heavily upon the desert had brought forth thin tender shoots of grass. The colours were greyer than the Western Desert, more liquid and softer. The sun lost the edge of its harshness, and one's eyes, strained from the glare of the yellow sand in Egypt, were rested. As we pushed on westward toward Derna and Bomba, Bedouin tribesmen ran from their scrawny sack-and-kerosene-tin settlements beside the way, crying 'Sayeeda,' which means, 'May you be lucky,' or

44

'Bardia Bill', the big gun which pounded the garrison in Tobruk for many months.

perhaps 'Go with God.' The war was bringing them loot. We found they had already rifled a hospital and two roadhouses which the Italians had erected in the empty desert. This road was a wonderful thing, solidly tarred, well banked and straight, and running a thousand miles to Tunis. Mussolini had all but driven it through to the Nile. And it was a strange sensation to ride here on this sound motor-road through enemy territory, one Italian army behind us at Tobruk, another in front at Derna. Yet beyond Bedouin we saw no one, not even our own troops. It seemed impossible that the Italians should not try to rush this gap and break the siege on Tobruk.

At Gazala we judged it wiser to go back. True, the Derna garrison, immobile and undecided, was too fretful to patrol even the intervening cliffs, but the night was approaching and we had not one gun between us. To encircle Tobruk again we made the great loop southward through a desert as empty as the sea. We came only upon occasional British units that had pushed forward into the waste. These men, charged with the job of forever slamming the back door on the Italians, had all but lost touch with civilization. They had little contact with the rest of the army. They lived on bully and rationed water. They were never out of the danger zone. Nor was it possible here to tell enemy from friend in the distance, and convoys sighting one another on the horizon would manœuvre and reconnoitre like ships at sea. Once, seeing a long line of tanks descending a chain of sand-dunes to the south, we put on speed and fled. It was not worth the risk of enquiring whether they were British.

Back at Bardia we found the Australians had already moved into position for the siege of Tobruk. A great quantity of new twenty-five-pounder guns was moving up the road, and the supply convoys stretched back to Sollum where half a dozen British merchant ships were dumping ammunition and food stuffs and taking off prisoners. The problem of Tobruk differed only in detail from that of Bardia. The perimeter round the town was larger here—some thirty miles round the outer line of forts, nineteen round the inner. Tobruk itself, more than double the size of Bardia, housed a garrison of some twenty thousand, and for the first time civilians were enclosed. The town's long straight harbour was the most valuable port between Alexandria and Benghazi. Given it, we knew we could supply our forward troops from here and push on perhaps as far as Benghazi.

The fall of Tobruk;
first round to the British.

The town of Tobruk itself, like Bardia, was perched on a spit of white cliffs that formed the seaward flank of the harbour. Italian naval forces were established there, and from the half-sunken cruiser *San Giorgio* and other vessels the Italians had brought ashore several naval guns. 'Bardia Bill' had been the troops' name for the big gun with which the Fascists had pounded Sollum. And now Tobruk gunners were carrying on the tradition of Italian artillery. At Sidi Barrani and Sollum, at Bardia and Tobruk and again later at Derna, it was the enemy artillery that stuck to the end often long after the infantry had fled. The Italians used old guns, some dating from the last war. Many of their shells were duds and their precision instruments far from precise. But especially when firing upon fixed targets they showed a skill and endurance beyond the level of the rest of the Italian army.

Heavy responsibility fell upon the gunners, for from this time forward the Italian air force dwindled and finally disappeared altogether from the sky. Day after day went by and fewer and fewer Fascist airmen came against us. There was still some strafing of the troops, but now Hurricanes flying only thirty or forty feet above the ground were ranging back and forth over the whole of eastern Cyrenaica, blowing up staff cars and transports, machine-gunning troops and gathering information of the movements of the enemy. By the time Tobruk fell, the Italian air force was utterly defeated, and it was never afterwards restored to superiority. When the enemy came again in the air it was largely with German machines piloted by Germans.

Longmore's policy had succeeded brilliantly. From the first he had concentrated on damaging enemy aircraft on the ground by low-level machine-gun attacks. This put the enemy machines out of action long enough to enable our troops to come up and seize the airfields. Around Tobruk I had already seen nearly a hundred aircraft caught in this way. From the town appeal after appeal was going out to Italy for help. From Mussolini came back only promises and encouragements. Il Duce had no warships able to risk encounter with Cunningham in the Mediterranean—the tonnage he had a-plenty, but not the men. His Libyan air force had already seriously drained the air armada at home both in men and machines. Graziani, back at Tripoli, still had more than double the numbers of the one and a half divisions we were sending against him. But much of their transport and equipment was lost in Libya, and his generals, discouraged and bewildered at their

46

failures, were eagerly electing to hold a line farther back rather than sally out rashly to the relief of Tobruk.

There were good grounds for believing that Tobruk might hold. Its troops were seasoned and well dug in. They had learned lessons from Bardia. The British were extended and it was reasonable to assume that their infantry tanks would soon be forced back for overhaul. Graziani was still clinging to his theory of defensive positions. Even so, it seems impossible that he would not have come out to meet us in pitched battle if he had known how few we were. Fantastic statements came pouring out of Rome. Four hundred thousand men, they said, had been sent into Cyrenaica by the British. Cut that figure by five times and it was still a gross exaggeration. Yet is is possible that the Italians really believed they were out-numbered.

One longed to meet and talk of these things with such a man as General Bergon-zoli. He had eluded us on the escarpment. When the troops entered Bardia they found he had flown again, though when and by what route no one could say. Some believed him to be in Tobruk, where an Italian admiral was in command.

The weather now was holding a steady sharp coldness, the days tempered with sunshine, the nights starry and bitter. But toward the 20th of January a sandstorm of such violence blew up that telegraph poles were uprooted, trucks overturned, and troops huddled to the ground, wrapping their blankets over their heads. Nothing in living memory approached it, the veterans said. I tried to drive out of Bardia, but it was impossible to see even either side of the road, and we came back to the flimsy shelter of a bombed house where soon everything was deep under layers of sand. In this tempest where an enemy might come up to within ten yards unseen, the Italians at the more remote outposts in the perimeter kept firing off rounds every few minutes. Obviously they were seeing imaginary shapes in the eerie half-light. All this was excellent.

Then on January 20th the R.A.F. and the Navy were upon the town with an even greater weight of explosive than fell on Bardia. It was the same all over again. At dawn the Australians attacked. They broke the perimeter and applied the general

47

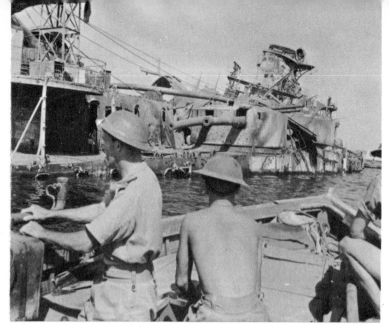

The battered wreck of the cruiser S. Giorgio, sunk in Tobruk harbour.

squeeze, English and Free French units coming in from the west. By that evening the attackers had reached every objective, and the troops in the vanguard were eight miles inside the perimeter. The attack continued under brilliant artillery fire all through the night. By noon of the following day the first troops were in the town and mopping up along the dockside.

This was our biggest capture yet. In the harbour some dozen ships lay sunken or awash, among them the *Marco Polo*, fine passenger vessel, and the cruiser *San Giorgio*, now so battered that she looked like that last photograph of the *Graf Spee* going down. On the waterfront valuable stores of water, petrol, foodstuffs and ammunition were discovered in buildings sheltering under the portside rocks. The docks and some of the heavy cranes were intact. Black trails of smoke floated from burning buildings across the harbour and the town. A lorry park was found outside, covered with more than two hundred vehicles ranging from ten-tonners to tiny 'Toppolino' Fiat touring cars. The channel of the harbour was open, and soon British destroyers were feeling their way in with stores and water to speed the army on the way. With the capture of this port we had achieved here much more than Bardia, and there was begun on that morning a tradition of the British occupation of Tobruk that is likely to emerge as one of the vital phases of the war.

The surrender was accepted in the town by an Australian brigadier. The Italian admiral commanding and his staff, all shaven and immaculate in white, and a group of four haggard generals, received him. It had been a bitter engagement. The dead were still lying out, and the wounded were everywhere. It was no time for mincing words. 'You have land mines laid in and around the town,' the Australian said. 'I will take reprisals for the life of every one of my men lost on those mines.' Quickly the Italians led Australian sappers to the mines and they were torn up. Booby traps were revealed, storage dumps opened, some two hundred guns handed over. More than fifteen thousand prisoners were gathered in for the long journey, some by sea, some by land, back to Alexandria. We had now in all some hundred thousand prisoners, but Bergonzoli had got away again. Twenty

The Marco Polo *had been a fine passenger ship.*

per cent. of the prisoners were found to be suffering from some form of chronic dysentery.

Sickness, death and wounding enveloped Tobruk. Inside the town fires blazed. Shops, homes, offices, were torn up and their furniture and household goods strewn across the roads. Walking through it, I felt suddenly sickened at the destruction and the uselessness and the waste. At this moment of success I found only an unreasoning sense of futility. The courage of the night before had been turned so quickly to decay. And now the noise and the rushing and the light had gone, one walked through the streets kicking aside broken deck-chairs and suits of clothes and pot-plants and children's toys. A soldier was frying eggs on the mahogany counter of the National Bank. A new fire leapt up in a furniture storehouse in the night, and the wine from the vats next door spilled across the road. Stray cats swarmed over the rubbish. In the bay a ship kept burning steadily. By its light the wounded were being carried down to the docks.

6

AFTER Tobruk the character of the campaign changed again. It had beeen fluid at its start, then static at the Bardia and Tobruk stage; now it was fluid again. This was desirable for the British cause, since it was manifestly to our advantage to keep the enemy on the run. At all costs he should not be given time to form a line.

Nobody expected that Derna, a hundred miles by road to the west, would be able to make a substantial stand. Nor after Derna was there any strongly fortified place before Benghazi. But the country here humped itself up three thousand feet in to the range of the Green Mountains—the Jebel Achdar—and was difficult. After Derna the road through the mountains split into two branches, one taking the more northerly route past ancient Cirene, the other in the south passing through

Again the endless crocodile of marching prisoners.

Slonta and Maraua. The two roads enclosed the rich moorland area where Mussolini had settled thousands of his model colonists. At Barce, the western junction of the two ways, the settlement scheme flowered out into a rich valley. Thence a coastal road and an inland railway ran down to Benghazi. The rains were at hand, the distance great and the dangers of ambush considerable, but already there were strong hopes that we would arrive at Benghazi.

It was resolved then to send two Australian brigades directly along the coast toward Derna. Before the town the two brigades were to split, one to take Derna and proceed beyond it to Giovanni Berta, the other to take the cross-desert route south of Derna to the same destination. At Giovanni Berta the brigades would split again, one taking the higher road to Barce, the other the lower. Then both would advance on Benghazi together. And, in fact, it all fell out better than anyone hoped: Derna fell on January 30th, Cirene February 3rd, Barce February 7th, Benghazi February 9th.

More than anything else it was a war of engineers and artillery. Sometimes the Italian gunners would stand for a day or two firing upon fixed targets along the roadway. Often their engineers would explode great slabs of the mountainsides to block our path, or demolish bridges and hairpin bends along the roads. Everywhere they could they laid land mines—I met one company of sappers which had degaused fifteen thousand, uprooting many of the metal boxes and stacking them beside the roadway. Time and again Italian labour gangs flung themselves upon some job of trench digging or building gun emplacements, only to find it was too late. The Australians advancing quickly upon them would discover nothing but freshly turned earth and equipment thrown away by the enemy in their flight.

The kilometre stones told the story of the accelerated pursuit very clearly. An Italian gang had been set the rather futile job of destroying these stones so that we should never know how far we were from the towns ahead. Outside Derna the numbers were chipped off and the stones themselves uprooted bodily and dumped across the roads as tank-traps. A few miles farther on the Italians contented themselves with merely chipping away the numbers. Then, with time getting shorter and the Australians hard upon them, they merely painted out the numbers. Finally, the kilometre stones outside Benghazi stood in their places untouched. The engineers' chisels were flung aside in a ditch.

Time was everything, and in that hectic three weeks between the fall of Tobruk

50

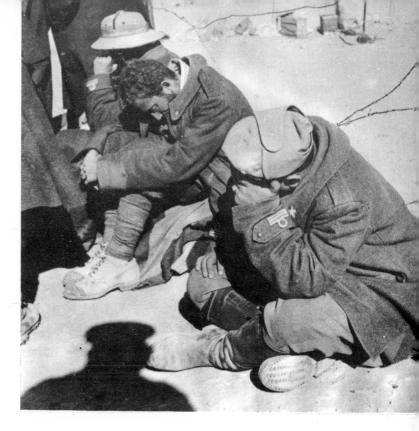

It had been a bitter fight: the tragedy of hunger, wounds and defeat.

and the taking of Benghazi the Italians were never given a moment's rest. Through every daylight hour Hurricanes were swooping on them at three hundred miles an hour, or the Blenheims were bombing. Fighting patrols with anti-tank guns were for ever running far ahead of the advancing army and taking garrisons by surprise. The Italian system of communications, always their weakness, broke down altogether, so that sometimes whole brigade staffs fell into our hands before they guessed we were within fifty miles of them.

Soon transport was the only thing that held the British back. The roads were good, but there were many detours to avoid mined bridges, and the trucks were overloaded. As each vehicle fell out, ordinance units set to work to replace it with a captured lorry. Since the majority of these captured lorries were in poor condition, the advance of the whole army was constantly checked and delayed by breakdowns. We never went a whole mile in some places without seeing a broken vehicle tossed aside in a ditch. In the end the brigade convoys, something over thirty miles in length, struggled through the mud with a collection of every type of vehicle in Northern Africa; some with broken springs and bodies lashed with fencing wire; others being towed in groups of twos and threes and even more; others which were a conglomeration of the good parts of several vehicles thrown together. Motor cycles, touring cars, road-menders' trucks and vehicles for drawing tractors and tanks—all were forced into service. In the end every able-bodied man got through.

The country the men were asked to penetrate after Tobruk was vastly different from the desert. Derna was an oasis of banana plantations and pomegranate groves, of lush vegetable gardens and leafy trees. Beyond, in the Green Mountains, you might have thought you were on the Yorkshire moors. A fresh mountain wind blew and with it came heavy rain and hailstones. The reddish-brown earth

51

Sappers uprooted the deadly landmines and stacked them beside the road.

undulated into green valleys and hilltops dotted with shepherds' flocks and neat white colonial homesteads, all built to the same standardized pattern, all modern, all surrounded with neat hedges and home gardens. The villages were trim, hygienic and attractive—if your taste runs to ordered rows of white cottages and streamlined town halls and sewerage works. All this was a great change from the desert. It relieved us of the problem of water and presented us with another difficulty—mud . . . red, clinging, loamy mud that frothed up round the axles of the cars and sent them skidding round in the opposite direction to the one in which they were going; mud that bogged tanks and stained the men up to their waists; mud that got into your food and your eyes and your hair; mud that was cold and very, very dirty.

But the first hundred miles were the best. In fair weather we rode on past Bomba toward Derna on a perfect road. Little by little the scattered bushes grew to shrubs and even at last to clumps of trees and a few palm groves. Bomba fell easily. But on Derna aerodrome, a great red plain lying above the thousand-foot seacliffs with the town below, the Italians stood and fought. Wadi Derna, a ragged valley that struck into the hills, was for a few days death to enter. A few companies of Australians charged the aerodrome above with the bayonet and made themselves masters of its storehouses and buildings. The two sides were so mingled at first that the leading Australian platoon lodging in a hangar heard Italian voices through the night. In the first light of morning they saw, not three hundred yards away, four Italian tanks. The tank crews were cooking breakfast. Scarcely daring to breathe, the Australians whispered urgently down their field telephone for anti-tank guns, and the Italians were blown up before they finished breakfast.

The aerodrome with its twenty wrecked machines was now ours, but unexpectedly about forty Italian guns firing from the other wide of Wadi Derna turned upon it an uninterrupted cannonade of shellfire.

This was a bad shelling while it lasted. And it lasted three or four days. The Italians had every building on the aerodrome registered, and the buildings were the only cover. One evening they shelled a platoon of Australians back from the open into the administrative block; then they hit the block and shelled the Australians out the back door and up the hillock behind. Once again the Italians got on to them, and the Australians were pursued with a chain of bursting shellfire across the aerodrome into another building and out of that.

*Reconnaissance among
the palms of an oasis in
the Western Desert.*

Watching from only four hundred yards away, where it was quite safe, the incident seemed funny to the rest of us. I do not think it is funny now, but it was then, at a moment when one was keyed to meet the tension at the front and the small manners of living were diminished or forgotten entirely.

One lived there exactly and economically and straightly, depending greatly on one's companions in a world that was all black or white, or perhaps death instead of living. Most of the things it takes you a long time to do in peace-time—to shave and get up in the morning, for example—are done with marvellous skill and economy of effort at the front. Little things like an unexpected drink become great pleasures, and other things which one might have thought important become suddenly irrelevant or foolish. In a hunter's or a killer's world there are sleep and food and warmth and the chase and the memory of women and not much else. Emotions are reduced to anger and fear and perhaps a few other things, but mostly anger and fear, tempered sometimes with a little gratitude. If a man offers you a drink in a city bar, the offering is little and the drink still less. You appreciate the offering and often give it more importance than the drink. At the front the drink is everything and the offering merely a mechanical thing. It is never a gesture, but a straight practical move as part of a scheme of giving and receiving. The soldier gives if he can and receives if he can't. There is no other way to live. A pity this is apparent and imperative only in the neighbourhood of death.

Derna had not yet fallen; there it lay, a thousand feet below the cliffs.   *British soldier cools his feet.*

The fall of Derna depended greatly upon the fall of a certain Fort Rudero, which the Italians were using as an observation and sniping post. In the first advance one Australian company was all but wiped out trying to take it from the seaward side, and another company attacking it from the wadi inland had to be withdrawn. The final attempt came one forenoon, when the red earth was washed and new after a heavy shower at night. The barrage had begun afresh, and a staid slow flight of Savoias—the last we were to see—had been over bombing until it ran into a lone Hurricane coming back from patrol into Libya. The Australians forgot the shelling, forgot momentarily the wounded nearby and their hunger, and raised a cheer as the Hurricane dived straight through the Italian machines and sent one dropping with that breath-taking fateful slowness to the red desert. Its bursting flames rose from behind the wreckage of the other broken aircraft on the field.

The Italian shells were falling twenty and thirty yards away from us, tearing off bits of the hangar, blasting our eardrums and raising billows of red dust from the quickly drying earth. Through the noise and blast another Australian company advanced toward us—dark little figures marching slowly with heads down in little lines across the open airfield. 'Good troops,' the brigadier had been saying back at brigade headquarters, just before this engagement, 'will never be stopped by shelling.' Yet this was hard. The Italian artillery observers could actually see them. The little lines drew level with the hangar and passed on up to the ridge, beyond which no one had yet advanced. For a moment I watched them pause in the full face of the enemy shelling on the open crest of the ridge and then they disappeared over the top of it. By the time I had crawled up to the ridge in a lull in the firing they had crossed the valley to the next rise, the one that ran straight down into Derna only three miles away.

I joined a Vickers-gun unit that was shooting at the Italian positions just ahead

54

*A slit trench
was a home
for the night.*

of the advancing Australians. The British sighted first on an enemy observation
post, silenced it, and then turned their fire on some trucks. My ridge and the
ridge on which the Australians were advancing lay parallel. The intervening valley
was filled with Italian shellfire. We gave it an hour or two and then followed. It
seemed certain that Rudero, the objective, had fallen. We went on foot, taking a
wide sweep around to the right away from the Italian positions, and came up
under the fort with a party of Australian water-carriers.

Rudero had not fallen, but there was something strange and quiet about the
place. After the heavy fighting along the beach yesterday its guns had not spoken.
We were clinging now to the side of a cliff so precipitous that it was not easy to
stand upright, and the soldiers in this sector had been here twenty-four hours without food or water. As soon as they had eaten, the company was ordered forward to
take the fort. We clambered first on to a pinnacle of the cliff where all Derna broke
suddenly into view, a thousand feet below, the most startlingly pleasant sight
one could conceive after so long a time in the desert. We were looking right into
the town as from an aeroplane. Row after row of stout, snow-white houses reached
down to the graceful sky-blue harbour. A steamer, bombed by the R.A.F. and
fired by the Italians, lay sinking at the jetty. Close by rose a high modernistic hotel
and beyond that was the main street leading to the lighthouse. One or two cars
were going along this street. A few people were moving in front of the shops. A
great grove of spreading palms made a cool green pool of colour in the centre of
the town.

While we gazed down, the Australian riflemen had gone ahead through the
barbed wire and surrounded Rudero, a rough stone pile perhaps five hundred
yards square. No sign of the enemy appeared and the soldiers relaxed a little.
Some of them made in a bunch toward the side door. Once more then the enemy had

vanished in the night. Concerned that he would miss a good picture, an officer with me, who was taking photographs for the War Office, called the men back and asked them to re-enact their passage through the barbed wire. Readily the men agreed. Twice the photographer rehearsed them through it, and then, the pictures taken, we all went up to the fort together to see what the enemy had left behind.

It was full of Italians. While we had posed for photographs fifty yards away outside, they had stood there with their rifles waiting dumbly to surrender. They lurked in the cellars and the stone passages; they stood in the central courtyard surrounded by the wreckage of our shell-bursts. They smoked, they stood packing their kits, or kneeling to get a last drink of water from a broken wooden barrel.

The Australians, recovering from their surprise, presented their bayonets and ran through every room and dugout until the prisoners were herded together in the main courtyard. They even unearthed a couple of white puppies born just before the bombardment began. Revolvers were grabbed from the Italian officers and rifles from their men. It was all done very quickly, and soon a platoon was on its way down the other side of the ridge to silence an Italian machine-gun post that was still pinging spasmodically up the hill. Farther back, six hundred yards away, I could still see odd groups of Italians on the run, but suddenly our artillery got on to them and they disappeared in clouds of blown dust and rock.

We drove back to Force Headquarters that night to send our messages. It was a strange sensation, writing dispatches away here in the blue, never knowing whether they would get back to Cairo, let alone London and New York. We had been away now so long without word from the outside world that I, for one, had lost my 'news sense'—that sense of proportion you have that tells you whether a thing is worth writing or not. Everything here to us at this minute was vital and crammed with interest. But was it interesting to the Home Guard in England, to the sheep farmer in Australia and the commuter in New York? You just couldn't know. So in the end I used to find myself putting down what I had seen and felt without trying to make a rounded 'story' of it, and without the slightest idea of whether it was worth publishing or not.

The circumstances in which we wrote were strange. We typed on the backs of trucks, on beaches, in deserted houses, in gun emplacements and tents. We hoisted our typewriters on kerosene cases, on bathtubs and rolls of kit, on humps of sand and the steps of cars, or just perched them on our knees. We wrote by candlelight or lamplight, or with an electric torch shining on to the paper. And in the end we could write anywhere at any hour of the day or night—anywhere, that is, except during a bombardment, for I tried it and failed miserably.

And now, driving through a thickening sandstorm, we groped about in the collection of galvanized huts for a place to sit down and write. We found the Intelligence hut at last, and a corner of the table there, and wrote. That night we slept in another iron shed, dignified with the name of Force Headquarters Mess. Other strays like ourselves had wandered in, and we bedded down around the concrete floor as soon as dinner was done. The wind ripped part of the roof off during the night, sheet by sheet, and rain splashed in. The banging of iron against iron was like an air raid, only more irritating. Bomba was a desolate place. We were glad to get back to the front.

Two nights after this, shortly before midnight, the Italians stopped firing. They had held on gallantly. Now their ammunition was running out. They packed

Indian troops moving down into Derna.

what they could of their equipment and escaped quietly down the coastal road in the darkness. The first Australian patrols entered the town the following morning. The road that plunged off the cliff into Derna had been cruelly blasted, but the sappers had it clear enough before the day was out, and the troops rode down.

We did not ride with them. We missed all this. It was one of those wrong decisions, inevitable sooner or later. We had thought that Derna would hold a day or two longer, and while the town, unknown to us, was actually being evacuated by the enemy, we were driving far southward across the desert to visit the Armoured Division at Mekili. It was an all-day run over a fresh rolling stretch of semi-desert in brilliant sunshine. We should have been warned that we were making a false move, for along the bad open stretch at the beginning which was under enemy observation we were not fired on. Following likely tracks, by compass and by guessing and by questioning a Roman Catholic priest who suddenly appeared across the desert, we found Mekili at last and the Armoured Division. They had had none of the spoils that fell to the men on the coast and were very short of supplies. We exchanged a couple of cases of Italian mineral water for a tin of army biscuits, and spent the night pleasantly beside the broken fort.

Next morning a signaller came casually to our truck and said: 'Derna's gone.' I poked my head out of my sleeping-bag. 'What?'

'Just heard it on the B.B.C.,' said the signaller.

We could not believe it. It seemed impossible that the B.B.C. thousands of miles away had beaten us to the news of something only fifty miles from us—something which we had waited for days to happen. We packed, jumped into the truck, took a compass bearing straight across the desert, and set off for the coast. As we drew into another British camp on the way, a wireless was blaring out across the desert: 'Derna fell last night.' It was true, then. The official communiqué, as always, had beaten us. And we had made a first-class blunder in leaving the coast front.

Miserably we drove on through the midday heat, arguing about our compass direction. I was convinced we were driving straight into the enemy lines; the

57

others thought we were headed for the Nile. This is just something the desert does to you. In the end we hit our objective dead centre—a dry water-well—and ran on at a speed that bumped our reserve petrol tins into shapeless empty lumps of metal. The silence of the coast when we got there made it all too painfully clear— Derna had fallen. We were met in the town by the other correspondents who had been there for hours. Competition among us was strong. It was, in a way, the most galling moment of the whole campaign.

7

DERNA was all that its distant view had promised. The main road wound between palms into streets of high cool buildings and spreading bougainvillaea and flowering shrubs. Big gardens lay round the hospital, and the Governor's palace stood among shaded lawns and fountains at the edge of the sea. The local Arabs had gone through the town and the bazaars, looting, the night before, after the Italians had left, and there had been a paying off of old scores in the few hours before the arrival of the Australian army. Front doors had been broken open and furniture looted and destroyed.

Everything in the European quarter was modern—modern and standardized to the nth tiresome degree. It was strange to come down from the desert into this super-suburbia where the curtains and the chair coverings came in three natty shades; where the dining-room suites in real old mahogany and three-ply were in strict neo-Fascist tradition, and china Cupids stood upon the standardized mantelpieces. Some three or four designs had been selected for the houses, and the colonist apparently just picked the one he liked best, ordered a set of furniture, and moved in. Much of the stuff was good and comfortable, but the tinsel and the regimentation broke through. Yet nothing could have destroyed everyone's pleasure in these gardens, or the luxury of a roof from the rain, and a hot bath.

We selected a white single-storey villa close to the sea, richly hung with flowering bougainvillaea, and moved in. Except for minor looting, everything had been left as it was, and soon we had good wines on the table and a fire going. I wallowed in the bath, washing away a week's dirt, and, walking naked into the next room, was somewhat taken aback to find a telephone with its owner's name let into the base of the instrument—'His Excellency Marshal Graziani'. Several soldiers tramping in long columns through the town that night slipped aside to splash a bit in the Marshal's bath, while we drank his wines and ate from his dinner service.

Old Electric Whiskers had bobbed up again. He was in command here, they said. But once more he had vanished.

For three nights we slept in Derna on made beds. We lived luxuriously, and friends would drop in to taste our cooking and selection of wines. Two officers driving up from the rear left cards on us, and we sent them a couple of bottles of the Marshal's better brandy. Each day we would drive out to the front that kept

The writing on the wall at Derna. To believe, to obey and to fight was not enough.

eating steadily into Cyrenaica. Since we had come down off the cliffs we had to ascend them again outside Derna, and here the Italians had chosen to blow three large holes out of their fine road that wound up the mountainside. Once over those we were well on our way to our rendezvous with the other brigade at Giovanni Berta.

And so it went on after this, the Italians for ever seeking somehow to delay and harass the steady oncoming lines of tanks, lorries and guns. Giovanni Berta fell, and the two brigades rode on again. Tert on one road offered nothing against us; nor did Abragh on the other. Luigi di Savoia collapsed, and we came into Cirene, once a place of a million Romans and the birthplace of the man who went to the help of Christ on the Cross. Nobly still its ruins rose out of the hillside, the marble tinted pink when I saw it in the late afternoon. Below lay Roman Apollonia on the sea: all this valley was rich in antiquity.

Graziani had lately made his headquarters here in the cumbersome hotel that stood massively on the hill beside the delicate Roman columns. Here, as everywhere, there had been much looting. The Arabs had turned at last on the Italian settlers left defenceless by the retreating Italian army. In the gap before the arrival of the British they had cut loose to pillage and burn and loot and destroy. With tears the Italian settlers implored us everywhere to stay and guard them. Even their women were not safe, they said. They brought us gifts of fresh eggs and loaves and fruit and cheese and wine.

The whole problem was presented neatly to us here in Cirene. In the barracks on the hill above the modern village we came on two Italian gendarmes still armed. They had rounded up some twenty Arab looters and locked them in barracks without, so far as one could discover, food or water. For days the Arabs had been confined there with these guards watching them. And now what to do? We had no guard to leave. Manifestly men could not be imprisoned without food or water. Nor could enemy soldiers be left at large with their rifles. The choice of action was not mine to take, but I did not agree when the British officer in charge took the rifles from the gendarmes and liberated the Arabs, who immediately ran delightedly across the compound, shouting: 'Viva Inghilterra!' This treatment

59

could have been interpreted by them as no other than licence to continue their looting, and I suspect they were already at it before we left the village.

But at this moment the problem was secondary, and we were concerned only to push on. Slonta fell, and Maraua, and now every man knew that it was Benghazi itself that was our object.

I was travelling with Clifford of the *Daily Mail,* and Captain Geoffrey Keating, our conducting officer; with our driver, a lad from South Wales, we ran on again in our Morris truck to the head of the column travelling down the southern road. For a time we kept with the Bren-gun carriers, scouting on ahead, and as prisoners were being roped in, we acted as interpreters. The danger of mines ahead was the chief concern, and when one prisoner protested to us that there were neither mines nor opposition of any kind between us and Barce, the Australian colonel commanding said: 'All right. Tell him to get into that ruck and drive two hundred yards ahead of us. Tell if he tries to make a bolt for it we will machine-gun him.'

We told him. The man was haggard and very afraid, but he had no choice but to obey. And if we had taken a hint from the wisdom of the colonel, then Clifford and Keating and I and our driver might have been more comfortable that night. But at that moment a major of the Armoured Division suddenly appeared with a fighting patrol of armoured cars. He had cut across from the open desert to the south. And now this major offered to patrol ahead of the Australian army, and we were invited to go along.

Steadily the tracks of the retreating enemy got warmer along the road. An Italian colonel and staff officer who were trying to round up their utterly disorganized forces were captured. Then we came on whole bunches of Italians. They said the road ahead was clear for some miles at least. Hurricanes had just passed that way, making a frightful wreckage on the road where they had caught and overturned several lorries full of men. The vehicles were uprooted bodily from the track, and the unwounded passengers frantically waved white handkerchiefs at us as we passed by. The road now in the early evening turned into wooded undulating hills.

And then at last we were on the enemy. A group of Italians in green uniforms were laying mines in a bend in the road. They dropped the mines and fled into the bushes at the sound of the leading armoured car and our truck following next in line. There were two more armoured cars following immediately behind us. We could still see and hear the Italians in the bushes, but, having seen so many surrender already, it did not seem worth while giving them a burst of machine-gun fire. British officers and men jumped out of the vehicles and began tearing up the mines to make the road safe for the Australian troops now advancing up the road some miles farther back. As they worked, the Italians, about half a dozen in all, emerged on to the road a little higher up and stood watching us. It was strange they did not surrender. 'Give them a burst,' someone began to say, and then from the hill ahead a long whining scream of bullets came at us down the roadway. We were ambushed. The enemy were in force. Breda guns, two-pounders and mortars crashed their shell dead among us. Clifford and I made for the wooded bank on the left, but it was hopeless—the enemy were firing almost at point-blank range, two or three hundred yards away. The rest of the British patrol also tried to make for cover, some of them shooting as they ran. One Breda-gun burst set the armoured car next to ours ablaze, killing the men inside. I heard the muffled scream of another

Cirene, once a place of a million Romans.

man, hit half a dozen times in the legs, being gallantly dragged back along the gutter by his comrades. The enemy's tracer-bullets made long criss-cross sheaths of light down the road.

Our driver had been cruelly hit on the arm by an explosive bullet as he had leaped from the truck. I ran over to him, tearing off a bandage from a sore on my knee, but he was huddled crookedly in the shallow drainage gutter, quickly drenching in his blood. Then a piece of shrapnel struck Keating in the forearm, while a bullet tore a ragged hole in his leg. He fell forward softly upon the driver in the shallow trench. By now the line of cars was blazing, and although the enemy could see Clifford and me alone, trying to bind up the wounded men, they concentrated all their fire upon us. Forcing the driver to his feet—he was in great pain, but trying very hard to help us—we crouched and dodged from bush to bush. All this was at dusk, and as we crossed each open space the Italians unloosed their fire again. Three hundred yards back in a ditch we were forced to stop and dress the wounded men again. Then with my arm round Keating, and Clifford's supporting the driver, we began a long bad walk back to our own lines. The shelling eased slightly after a few minutes, and soon our only concerns were whether we would make the distance and whether or not we would be fired upon

Indian riflemen advance through the noble ruins of Cirene.

by our own troops. But with a rush of gratitude I heard English voices in the darkness, and, raising our voices, we got an answer.

Even as we hoisted the wounded on to a Bren-gun carrier, Australian patrols were coming up to encircle the hill and take it. We went back next day when the hill was won, to salvage what we could from the wrecked truck, but it was next to nothing. Smashed cameras and typewriters, bedding rolls riven with bullets, suitcases battered into shapelessness, lay strewn about. Even our fine Parmesan cheese was pitted like a Gruyère, and a tin of army biscuits had all but reverted to its original flour. Razors, glasses, compasses, revolvers, water bottles—everything was smashed.

We had no food now and practically no clothes. Apart from my greatcoat, all I was able to salvage was the uniform of an Italian sailor—stuff I had got at Tobruk—and in that uniform I stayed until the end of the campaign.

We were sitting forlornly there among our wreckage when the other war correspondents arrived, and we clambered aboard their vehicles. There was no time to lose. The advance was going very quickly now.

Barce, when we first sighted it, was erupting with a series of heavy explosions. The Italian rearguard, working with time-bombs, were smashing the waterworks, the electric-power plant and anything else they could lay hands on. Smoke, black, white and red, billowed up in great mushrooms over the neat white town. It did not seem to matter to the Fascists that the thousands of Italians they left behind would have no water, light or heat. Across Barce's wonderfully fertile valley that might have been anywhere in Dorset or Devon, the colonists' trim white houses were stretched in rows to the horizon, all of them sheltering little groups of frightened, anxious people. The steep road before us winding into Barce had been blown at many places and sown with mines. Half-finished anti-tank trenches made scars across the mountainside.

An Australian officer and six men went down afoot and restored order to that lovely valley. Settlers escorted them to the town's best hotel for a hot dinner, and soon the hastily reformed town council was getting the life of the town back to normal. The rest of the Australian army, who would not wait for the repair of the coastal road, cut inland over earth tracks beside the railway running directly into Benghazi.

We came to the railway in the darkness and pouring rain, and groped along it until we got to a deserted railway station. An Arab boy with a lamp lit us through the empty ticket-office and upstairs to the bare stone-floored rooms, where presumably the stationmaster had lived. His reports showed that the last train had gone through at 3.10 p.m. two days before. The telephone to Benghazi was still working, but when we tried to ring through there was no answer—just a confused buzzing on the line. We built fires in the house to make tea and a stew.

As we ate, more troops came in—about half a dozen of them. They were in high spirits. They had been generously served with wine by the peasants, and now they were determined to go on to Benghazi by themselves without waiting for orders. They had picked up an ambulance somewhere in Barce and now they wanted petrol from us. One of the men was festooned with captured Italian revolvers. He was full of good noisy humour, and he twirled the revolvers round and round on his forefingers. We gave them a little petrol, and the ambulance set off crazily in the darkness. Amazingly, we saw it still going the next day.

Deep in the night I woke and heard a loud tearing noise on the railway outside. Some of the others heard it too and sat up. It was a heavy rumbling in the rain, and whether it was a runaway truck or some ghost-train in the night I do not know —we were too sleepy to care.

A kind of frenzy possessed the Australians now in their utter determination to have Benghazi at once. I cannot conceive that anything would have stopped them from that Wednesday night on. But now hail and rain came that turned the countryside into red mud and slush. Every few kilometres the tracks were blown away by the Italian rearguard, which was fighting only for time and still more time in which to organize and make a stand. Australian engineers slaved at the head of the column until men in their ranks were forced to drop out through sheer exhaustion, while others came forward to take their places. Soon it developed into a contest between the engineers and the squads of Italian minelayers and dynamiters. All that first day after Barce, while the storm still gathered force, the Australians kept flinging boulders into craters along the roads or breaking open new roads along the goat tracks. Kilometre by kilometre—yard by yard sometimes—the troops moved forward. It was a forty-mile-long column of vehicles that crashed over tank-traps and plunged headlong into valleys and across ruined gaps in the railway line. Nowhere could the Italians destroy the way sufficiently to hold them more than an hour or two.

At El Abiar, where the Delmonte Division used to be quartered in barracks nearly half a mile square, we came on the brigadier in command bolting cold poached egg and toast, while he kept on issuing the same order to every officer who came in: 'Push on. Push on.' I lunched in the officers' messroom on hot rum and cold bully beef. The room showed every sign of panic-stricken flight—swords flung away, meals left on the table, shaving things strewn about. An Italian orderly was protesting: 'I don't know what has happened. They have all gone off and left me.'

We went on again. All the way down the track vehicles were fighting with the mud. Prisoners began to pass by, cold and weary men, utterly confounded by the débâcle, who stared in astonishment at the convoys of British vehicles that appeared suddenly out of the driving rain. At Regima we were held up again for an hour on an icy hill. Everyone's nerves were strained now as the end of this interminable thousand-mile journey from Cairo was in sight. We bumped on again past two blown-up railway yards, and round by a goat track, and suddenly a burst of cheering went up from a gun-crew travelling ahead of us. Benghazi lay in view.

It stood there clearly, a long line of white rooftops by the sea, a cloud of smoke shot with flame rising from the centre of the town. Nearer on the coastal plain were the red and grey roofs of Benina—Benina, through which Mussolini for a year past had provided most of his bombers and fighters with their ammunition for the destruction of Egypt and the Army of the Nile. All of us had been bombed by aircraft from Benina. Now that whole airport was deserted and in ruins. Through glasses I counted twenty-two wrecked aircraft on one end of the airfield alone. A water-tower had been blown bodily out of the ground by the R.A.F. Half a dozen hangars, each large enough to accommodate a goods train, were shattered and savaged into a state of uselessness.

In the airport's living-quarters, where we slept for a few hours, Italian pilots had lived well with their private baths and neat dressing-tables equipped with double mirrors and scent-sprays. But all was in wild disorder by the time we got in. Electric light, heating and water had been sabotaged only thirty hours before. While we rested here Italian couriers came posting out from Benghazi to beg for a parley. The emissaries followed—the Lord Mayor, a Roman Catholic bishop and a few police officers—and the Australian brigadier, known from his vivid red hair as 'Red Robby', received them in a draughty airport building. The Italians came to offer the complete submission of the capital, of the naval base and of all military establishments, of the Italian, Arab and Greek populations of all the surrounding country, and anything the British chose to regard as theirs. The Italian Army, Navy and Air Force, they said, had fled. The brigadier sent them back with promises of protection. The carabiniere, he said, could retain their rifles to keep the peace and prevent looting.

It hailed and rained, and even the red mud itself seemed to be flying in the wind that night. A bleak windy morning followed and we drove into the town, Benghazi. It was, in the end, the unsung soldiers of the line who had the honours that morning. While it was still very cold and grey they got down from their trucks in the streets—just one company—and marched into the square before the town hall. They were unkempt, dirty, stained head to foot with mud. They had their steel helmets down over their eyes to break the force of the wind. Some had their hands botched with desert sores, all of them had rents in their greatcoats and webbing. They had fought three battles and a dozen skirmishes. They had lost some of their comrades, dead and wounded, on the way. They had often been cold, hungry and wet through in these two months of campaigning in bitter weather. The townspeople crowding

64

Benghazi, first time through.
British enter the town
in January 1941.

round the square had half-sullenly expected brass bands and a streamlined military parade. Instead they got this little ragged group of muddy men. They hesitated. Then a wave of clapping broke down from the housetops along the pavements and across the square. One felt like clapping oneself in that highly charged moment. The applause was thinnish and no doubt would have greeted any other conqueror who had come in. But at least it was spontaneous and unasked for, and an earnest that the people would peacefully accept British rule.

The troops stepped out into the centre of the square and swung round with a full parade-ground salute as the brigadier drove up and alighted on the town hall steps. The Mayor of Benghazi, wearing a tricolour sash across his chest, was waiting for him, surrounded by civil guards, officers and the bishop. They listened tensely while the brigadier issued orders through an interpreter. 'I reappoint you and all civil officers in their present positions. You will continue with your normal work. Get the people to reopen their shops and businesses. Your civil guard will act in conjunction with my own garrison troops.'

In five minutes it was done. As I came away from the square a tobacconist was pulling down the shutters from his shop. Everywhere people saluted my khaki cloth cap. I walked down to the Albergo d'Italia and ordered coffee with a roll of bread. Someone put half a lire in the café music-box. And then it came again, that same feeling of unreality and futility. Suddenly I felt very tired.

I went upstairs to a room with a bed and clean sheets. There was a hot meal waiting—a meal I had not prepared myself in a ditch by the roadside. And it all seemed very uninteresting. More than anything I wanted to get away quickly and to see and hear no more of the campaign and the fighting and the booty.

The quietness and peace of Benghazi were extraordinary. Fifteen days ago the newspapers had stopped publishing; the banks had closed and most of the businesses had shut down a week since. Three days previously the buses had stopped running. A Fascist gunboat had cleared out, and some thousands of civilians, their cars stacked high with household goods, had fled toward Tripoli. Benghazi's garrison had followed hard on their heels. The small force left behind had started blowing up oil stocks, burning papers and wrecking instruments too cumbersome to take away. Refugees had begun pouring down the road from Cirene, Barce, Tolmeta and Tocra, and wild rumours had spread through the town about the British advance—rumours that were all too true. Some had panicked then and rushed their women and children into the country. One passenger plane that was not airworthy had tried to make a getaway and crashed, killing forty people.

65

Sunken ships in Benghazi harbour.

Yet there was little damage in the town at that time. Many of the portside houses bore marks of shrapnel bursts, but the civilian quarter, including the Arab markets spreading a square mile, was intact.

I went down to the Hotel Berenice where I had stayed just before the war. Graziani had used it as a headquarters. Like most of the other principal buildings in the town, its corridors had been faced with an additional stone wall as a protection against bombing. Little remained there to show how the Marshall had worked for his abortive campaign against Egypt. The cathedral just behind the hotel was safe, but in the harbour, noisy then with its thunderous surf, I came on two sunken Italian destroyers that were hit on the day of the R.A.F.'s first long-range raid on the town the September before. Half a dozen other vessels, small supply ships mostly, lay about at their moorings, either beached or awash. In the town, water and light supply was working—an unbelievable luxury to men who had had weeks on a gallon of water a day and had grown used to seeing by the stub end of a candle at night. Here and there posters of Mussolini had been defaced. A group of Arabs had hastily stitched together a crude Union Jack, and were parading it through the town while they gave vent to a weird and horrible victory chant. The churches and monasteries continued placidly.

I lingered on for a day or two aimlessly waiting for transport back to Cairo. I was determined not to face that journey of a week overland. When I did leave, I left by air in strange circumstances and with a feeling of intense relief. But there was first another job to do. When we were in Benghazi we got word for the first time of the battle of Beda Fomm, which had been fought by the Armoured Division while we were coming along the coast. Now we drove south to see what had happened.

8

UNKNOWN to us, while we had been following the Australian Army, a manœuvre that was destined to alter the whole character of desert fighting and put an effective end to the campaign had been carried out by the British armoured forces inland. It had been foreseen by Wavell and O'Connor that the mere occupation of Benghazi would not mean the destruction of the still very strong forces which Graziani had under his command. These would simply escape down the coastal road toward

Tripoli to fight another day. So it was resolved that an attempt should be made to cut them off. This would involve a forced march of some two hundred miles at speed straight across an open desert that was largely unmapped, in circumstances so unfavourable as to be almost prohibitive. No army had ever crossed this wasteland south of the Green Mountains before. Even the Bedouin seldom attempted it. The camel tracks led nowhere. The surface of the desert was rough in the extreme. The vehicles were already badly strained, and it would be necessary to steer by compass, carry all supplies without hope of replenishment, and leave the rest to luck. And all had to be done against time.

But the generals were encouraged in their resolve to go forward when units of their armoured forces made contact with the enemy at the Beau Geste fort of Mekili, fifty miles south of Derna (where I had met them during the fall of Derna). A squadron of British tanks there came unexpectedly upon a large force of Italian tanks and mechanized infantry, and, unwilling to wait until reinforcements came, gave battle at once. Some twenty Italian tanks were destroyed in the running engagement that followed, but the main body of the Italian Army slipped away before it could be encircled. This was galling. It had seemed at Headquarters for a moment that the battle of Cyrenaica might have been settled there and then. Now there was nothing for it but to risk this adventure across the open desert.

It seemed obvious that this, the main effective striking force left to the enemy, would return to Benghazi through the mountains, perhaps interfering with the advance of the Australians on its way. If all went well for us on the coast, however, it was reasonable to assume that the Italian commanders would not stay to fight but would make back towards Tripoli, where they would have time to form an effective line. The only real question at issue was, 'Could we get to the coast in time to stop them?'

On February 4th two columns were ordered to move out on the big march from Mekili—one to strike toward Soluch, thirty-five miles south of Benghazi, and the other toward Beda Fomm, close by near the coast. The trucks were stacked to capacity, the men's drinking water cut down to the equivalent of about a glass a day, and the regulation halts for food and sleep reduced by half or more. There was only one order of the day: 'Get to the coast.'

The wind blew shrilly and bitterly at first. Then a storm of full gale force sprang up against the last convoys. While the forward units were often battling against fine sand that reduced visibility sometimes to nothing, those that followed on were faced with frozen rain that streamed down in front of the wind. Standing in their trucks like helmsmen, the commanders of vehicles had their fingers frozen clawlike around their compasses. Through day and night the long lines of tanks, armoured cars, Bren-gun carriers, trucks, ambulances and guns bumped onward. If a vehicle fell out, that was just too bad: its drivers had to mend it or jump aboard another vehicle and press on. The going was the worst the men had known after a year in the desert—bump over a two-foot boulder, down into a ditch, up over an ant-hill into another boulder—and so on, hour after hour.

They travelled bonnet to tailboard in the darkness, and spaced out again for protection against air raids in the daylight. O'Connor's own car broke down when he came out to urge them on. At places it was impossible to do more than six or seven miles an hour. The drivers, muffled up to the ears and strapped in leather jackets and goggles, became unrecognizable under a caking of sand or mud.

'*Smoking steel carcasses on the sand.*'

Several times they had to deploy and fight against Italian outposts. Yet they did it in thirty hours. Two hours later would have been too late. The Italians would have slipped through.

On February 6th the report that the two columns had reached their objectives was followed by the dramatic news: 'We have contacted the enemy on the coast. Three large columns are moving south from Benghazi.'

The road from Benghazi, in fact, was packed with enemy vehicles. It was the last of Graziani's forces, escaping with all his eight senior generals, and with some 130 tanks, 300 guns of all calibres, more than 20,000 men and many hundreds of lorries and trucks. The British were outnumbered five to one in tanks, five to one in men and three to one in guns. They were up against a fresh and desperate enemy.

At midday the British opened the battle along a broken desolate stretch of the coastal plain, some ten miles in length. The tanks swept forward and all three columns were engaged. The artillery deployed and opened fire. For the last time

A British minefield hurriedly laid in a forward position.

the Italians turned and fought, fought out of desperation more fiercely than they had ever done since the war began. This in fact was the only time they honestly gave battle, battle to the death or surrender.

The British commanders, meeting under shell fire, hastily made their plans, and, since there were some hours of daylight left, those plans were simply to go straight ahead, cut the enemy's retreat in the south, and smash him in the centre. In the southern sector thirteen British cruisers gave chase to the main body of Italian tanks and destroyed forty-six of them. Mines were laid in the southward path of the remaining enemy formations, and as they ran upon them they were attacked again.

In the centre the Italians were themselves attacking fiercely. But British artillery had got the range on the coastal road from which the enemy were operating. By nightfall burnt-out tanks, trucks and guns were lying everywhere, just great smoking steel carcasses on the sand.

Twice the British tanks exhausted their ammunition and had to go back for more. All night the shelling continued, while one after another Italian field-guns were registered by their flashes, straddled with shot, and finally hit. General Tellera was in command of the enemy. He turned, as every Italian general had done before him, and looked for some loophole through which to escape. 'I cannot believe,' he told his staff before he died, 'that the full strength of the British has got here so soon, or that they can have blocked us to the south.'

But he was wrong. In the darkness the British regrouped for the final crushing blow. One section spun fanwise round his north flank and reached the sea. Another, rushing south, straddled the road to Tripoli. When the morning came with the threat of heavy rain these jaws began to close. The Italians counter-attacked then. Their infantry still remained confused, undirected, inactive, and much of it still embussed. But their artillery spoke out violently, and a charge of such resolve was made upon the British that one tank succeeded in reaching a brigade head-quarters before it was shot up.

Then the jaws shut. Bofors and twenty-five pounders raked the sea plain from one end to the other. Everywhere the Italian attack was fought to a standstill and broken up. There was carnage in the centre of the battlefield. British machine-gunners and light units went in to support the tanks. They picked off one target after another, until for ten miles the road was littered with upturned smashed vehicles that had crashed into one another or upended themselves grotesquely in the air.

All through the second night the mopping up went on along the beaches and the marshy plain. White handkerchiefs began appearing as the Italians in thousands came out of hiding in the rocks. General Tellera was hit by a bullet and died on the field (his body was given full military honours later in Benghazi). General Cona took over. He had a more forlorn hope than ever Weygand had in France. The fighting had been carried with grenade and rifle and bayonet into the sand-dunes. It was there that the British found Bergonzoli at last, and many other generals and staff officers. The rejoicing message went back to headquarters: 'Bergonzoli in the bag.'

By Friday morning it was all over, and the British were sweeping on to occupy Agedabia and Agheila, nearly two hundred miles south of Benghazi. Only a few Italian tanks and a few score vehicles had escaped the battle of Beda Fomm. And now we had in our hands seven generals and their staffs, about twenty thousand more prisoners, 216 guns, 101 tanks and vehicles in hundreds. And Cyrenaica was ours. In all this fighting, here and on the coast from Sidi Barrani to Beda Fomm, the entire British casualties had not exceeded three thousand in dead, wounded and missing. It was complete victory—even though the world never had time to realize it before the reverses set in.

Graziani's army of Cyrenaica was destroyed for ever. Of the quarter million Italian troops in all Libya something more than half were either killed or in our hands. At least two-thirds of his equipment in ships, aircraft and land weapons were destroyed or captured. Nineteen Fascist generals were prisoners. An area of land as large as England and France had been lost by Italy. The Suez Canal had to a great extent been removed from the war zone. The morale of the Italian soldier was broken. Wavell and his men had been lifted to immense prestige at home and in America. All this had been done in precisely two months.

And the fall from power to weakness, from bravado to humility and despair, was displayed with brutal clarity in a mean little farmhouse in the mean village of Soluch where I found my way after the battle. Pushing through the thousands of prisoners who stood about aimlessly in the mud, I went past the guards about the farmhouse door, and there, squatting in the unfurnished corridors or standing in the shoddy yard outside, were the captured generals, the brigadiers and the full colonels. I went from one to another—General Cona, the Commander-in-

Bergonzoli
in the bag.

Chief; General Bignani, leader of the Bersaglieri; General Villanis of the artillery; General Negroni, Chief of the technical services; General Bardini, head of the motorized division; and General Giuliano, Chief of Staff to Cona. In the yard outside, sitting in the back seat of a car with a rug wrapped round him, was Bergonzoli. He was ill; I stood outside and saluted him, and he opened the door and leaned forward to speak to me.

'Yes, I had supposed you would want to know how I kept on eluding you since last December,' he said. 'The others asked me that. Well, I walked out of Bardia on the third day of the battle. I saw it was hopeless, and with several of my officers we set off, walking by night, hiding in caves by day. It took us five days to reach Tobruk. We passed right through the British lines. We were so close we heard your troops talking. We saw their watch-fires and smelt their cooking. My staff major, a heavy man, was forced to drop out through exhaustion and I suppose he was captured.

'After Tobruk fell, I flew out aboard the last remaining plane to Derna. Derna was in some ways our best stand of all, but when at last many of our guns were out of action and we had no more ammunition I got my troops away at night and with them drove off in a Toppolino car down the coastal road to Benghazi.

'We had no time to prepare defences outside Benghazi. In any case, it was an open town. We had no wish to expose the women and children there to any more misery. We decided to leave with our army for Tripoli. You were here too soon, that is all. Your forward units found us on the coast on Wednesday morning when we were in an exposed and dangerous position. But we gave battle at once.

Our tanks and artillery and men were tired and at a considerable disadvantage on the coast, but they came quickly into position and gave battle magnificently. We launched two counter-attacks that were very nearly successful. Our tanks against superior numbers broke right through the English lines. Our second attack was made when our forces were largely decimated and our ammunition almost exhausted. And always, here as everywhere else, we were grossly outnumbered. So when our second attack was unable to prevail we had no choice but to make an honourable surrender.'

All this was spoken in Italian through an interpreter, but when the interpreter translated, 'I ran away,' Bergonzoli snapped in English, 'Not ran away, drove away.' I have compressed here all the pertinent things he said in answer to the correspondents' questions, and this was the theme of it—'We were outnumbered.'

Poor little Bergonzoli. I had expected a blustering, piratical sort of general. But here he was, a soft-spoken little man with a pinched swarthy face that had aged unbelievably since his great days in Spain. His famous 'barba elettrica' was a neat, bristly beard parted in the centre. A large diamond flashed on his left hand as he waved it for emphasis. He wore a plain, undecorated green uniform. Among the Fascist generals, he was certainly the bravest of the lot. One could not help perversely wishing that after so many risks and chances he had got away in the end.

He was taken the next day to hospital in Benghazi, as it was thought he was suffering from appendicitis. But the day after that they brought him to the aerodrome at Berka on a stretcher, and lifted him into a Bombay transport plane. Then, with the six other captured generals and myself squatting on our luggage on the floor of the aircraft, we took off for Cairo.

We flew on for four hours non-stop over the territory we had conquered—past Barce and Cirene, Derna and Mekili, Tobruk, Bardia and Sidi Barrani. As the Pyramids showed through the mist, one or two of the generals turned listlessly in their seats to look at this green valley where they had dreamed they would arrive as conquerors. But they seemed to care little about it any longer.

9

In the spring, at the moment of his triumph, Wavell was forced to decisions more difficult, more dangerous and more important than any he had faced before. After the first rosy glow of optimism had passed, it was seen that the capture of Benghazi had not reduced British difficulties in the Middle East, but multiplied them.

The first decision that had to be taken, and taken quickly, was whether we should advance to Tripoli. Tripoli was another good seven or eight hundred miles by land, and nearly all of it desert. The men who had reached Benghazi were tired, and many of the vehicles and weapons altogether worn out. Benghazi was already being mined and bombed so heavily by the newly arrived German aircraft that it was untenable by the Navy and unsuitable for the time being as a supply port.

True, units of another armoured division were now arriving in the Middle East,

Anthony Eden and Sir John Dill at the British Embassy in Cairo. They were optimistic.

but the men were untrained in the desert, and in any case the campaign against Italian East Africa had already been launched and materials as well as men were needed there. Then again, of what use these extra eight hundred miles of desert coastline? Benghazi as an invasion or air striking-point was almost as near Italy as Tripoli, and both were farther off than Malta, which we already held. It would require a large garrison—a larger one that we could spare—if we did seize the rest of Libya.

Those were the main points against going on—points that were thrashed out by O'Connor and his generals as they studied their maps in the damp and gloomy bedrooms of the Hotel d'Italia in Benghazi, and by Wavell in his office by the Nile, and by Churchill and the War Cabinet in London.

But there were two big advantages in continuing the advance at once—first, the Italian army was in poor condition to resist even at the gates of Tripoli, and would probably collapse against any sort of opposition; and, secondly, we should prevent the Axis from landing reinforcements and coming on again.

There remained the political factor, and that probably tipped the balance against continuing. Greece, though still attacking, was wearying, and the Germans were preparing to march against her. Greece, in fact, sent an urgent request for help the moment Benghazi fell. Once in Greece, an expeditionary force might prop the whole tumbling structure of the Balkans. The mountains of Greece were high. We had held a line there in the last war. Could it not be done again?

Neither Wavell in Cairo nor the War Cabinet in London alone were competent to decide. So Mr. Eden and Sir John Dill got in an aeroplane and flew to Cairo to thrash it out. They talked to Wavell, Cunningham, Longmore. They flew to Ankara and sounded out Sarajoglou and the Turks, they went on down to Athens. Then they came back to Cairo, well pleased with what they had seen and heard. Little by little the opinion grew that we could risk this adventure, that we could organize another and better Gallipoli in the Balkans. It was not one man's opinion. It was certainly not Wavell's, but Wavell naturally was the man who would have to carry out the job.

And so, while the Middle East was still mellow with its victories and optimism still glowed in the arguments of the generals and the faces of their soldiers, it was decided that we should march out upon Germany in the battlefield of Europe.

Through March Egypt hummed with activity. The Greeks had asked for at least six divisions. Very well, then, we would give them five, anyway, and the help of the Fleet and twenty squadrons of aircraft and food and oil. Sixty thousand men were ordered to the ships—Australian and New Zealand infantry, British gunners and technicians and mechanized units. In contrast to the opening of the Benghazi campaign, there was no secret about the expeditionary force to Greece. The Egyptians were gossiping about it in the bazaars.

The troops themselves knew all about it. They had been mustered at Alexandria and Port Said and were looking forward to a change from the eternal desert. New soldiers had arrived from England and were eager for the fight on the romantic soil of Greece. They had good weapons. There was talk of advancing through Europe to the relief of England. Courage and hope ran high. Wavell alone was non-committal.

Three weeks later Belgrade was in ruins, and most of Cyrenaica was lost. Six weeks later the swastika was on the Acropolis, and what was left of the British expeditionary force was evacuating on a bombed sea. Nine weeks later the Germans held Crete.

Against that Addis Ababa was ours. Tobruk held. Sections of the German forces had been decimated. And the German plans, whatever they were, had been held up and disrupted. These were some consolations. But, it might have been added, had you never gone to Greece you might still have had Benghazi and Crete too.

There were a dozen, a hundred 'mights.' Rising out of the welter of mights was only the courage of the men who had fought for Greece and Crete and the desert. It was that courage that in the end lifted the Middle East out of the despondency caused by the Greek campaign. That and the holding of the Russians in Russia.

Now, after the event, it is clear that there were one or two major misapprehensions ruling in the spring of 1941. First we did not even then know that the Italians were so weak or the Germans so strong. We underestimated the ability of the Germans to reinforce Libya and advance across Cyrenaica. We, perhaps deliberately, overemphasized the danger of the invasion threat to England. Politically we misjudged Turkey. Militarily we underestimated the German dive-bomber and the power of his airborne divisions.

The German offensive in the Middle East followed the most careful political planning and the most exact military preparation and timing. The German design was force and overwhelming fire-power applied in restricted areas. The chief interest of the enemy lay in dispersing Wavell's already widely divided armies to the utmost. And in some measure this scheme succeeded. Undoubtedly extra reinforcements that would have gone to Greece were retained for the protection of the Nile after Cyrenaica had fallen. The British forces in Cyrenaica had been stripped to the bone. Australia was compelled to divert troops to Singapore, and we had to land Indians at Basra.

The presence of the Germans in Libya was not altogether a surprise. It was well known that Badoglio and the other Italian generals were removed to make

HAPPY FAMILIES:
LEFT: *Rommel and his wife and son.*
BELOW: *Wavell and his wife and daughter.*

way for the new commanders sent down with troops from Germany. It was known that the Luftwaffe had occupied the air striking-bases in Sicily, and their bombers and fighters were appearing in increasing numbers over Malta and Benghazi with much more resourceful tactics than the Italians had ever shown. Our own R.A.F. kept reporting the continued and increasing arrival of troopships at Tripoli.

There were several brushes between the Germans and our patrols in the desert between Benghazi and Tripoli. Agheila fell, and Agedabia. And then General Erwin Rommel, the Nazi commander, with his one German armoured division, supported by the residue of the Italian forces, put Wavell's tactics into reverse. One section of his army fell unexpectedly upon Benghazi; the other crossed the desert south of the Green Mountains from west to east and engaged the British at Mekili. It was the sort of military coup a commander can expect once in a lifetime.

The British in Benghazi had reduced their garrison to a skeleton. Most of the fighting vehicles were back in the Delta being repaired. For a hundred miles they had little or no support. And the suddenness of the attack spread confusion. Light British tank forces that went out to engage returned to their base near Benghazi only to find that while they were out the petrol dump had been exploded—in error. The tanks without fuel had to be abandoned.

Round Benghazi there were no defensive lines at all. There was nothing for it but to blow up equipment and munitions that could not be got away, and retire in as good order as possible until we had time to make a stand and discover the

75

German photograph of General Erwin Rommel (left) in the desert.

strength of the enemy. But the supply convoys that were toiling up that wearisome road from Tobruk and Egypt could not be turned about in a moment, nor could the troops suddenly be regrouped for defence. The British forces were still stressed for advance, not defence. Communications broke down. Units became isolated.

General O'Connor and General Neame sent their immediate staffs and their baggage back by the main road and themselves followed a short-cut. They found themselves blocked by a long convoy. A squadron of Nazi motor-cyclists, far in advance of the main German army, drove up. The British driver who first saw them was shot dead at point-blank range, and the German motor-cyclist who had shot him was in turn killed outright. But the other motor-cyclists closed in, and travelling up the line of vehicles they came on the generals' car. It was the worst possible luck. With tommy-guns pointing at them through the car windows, O'Connor and Neame were compelled to surrender, and were promptly taken back to the German lines. Only a few days previously O'Connor had been knighted. No army could easily afford the loss of so shrewd a tactician, and this little Irishman, with his energy, his quick forceful manners and his charm, was loved in the desert. It was a bad blow.

While the British on the coast and in the mountains were still giving ground and seeking to get some cohesion into their command, the Nazis' desert column arrived suddenly at Mekili, where the British garrison under General Gambier-Parry was in no condition to receive them. Gambier-Parry was taken in his tent, and Mekili collapsed.

It was now seen that no line could conveniently be held short of Tobruk, and on Tobruk now the Empire forces converged. From Egypt itself what reinforcements there were available were hurried up to meet the enemy on the escarpment. The Germans and the Italians, in the full tide of their success, flung themselves headlong on Tobruk. They were flung back. The Australians and British with their backs to the sea had recovered from their surprise. They manned the long outer

perimeter and fought with that desperate and deadly accuracy that was soon to become memorable in Greece and Crete.

Shaken but not yet rebuffed, the enemy left a containing force round Tobruk and swept on easily to Bardia and the escarpment. But the advance had now spent itself. Indeed, some units had outrun their course, and prisoners in groups of some hundreds began to fall to the British. Rommel, hardly expecting so quick an advance, had not equipped or provisioned his men for a long drive into enemy territory. No food or water convoys could keep up, and soon his advance units were in desperate need. Provision-carrying aircraft were not enough. Germans were captured in a state of near insanity for lack of water.

Upon Tobruk, then, Rommel turned the full power of his considerable force of Stukas, Heinkels and Messerschmitts, and there began a series of violent raids which in the next three months reached the amazing total of one thousand. Heavy guns were drawn up to pound the outer perimeter. Heavy tanks and eight-wheeled armoured cars were turned upon the perimeter itself. Cut off, short of water and food, lacking sleep and many of the crudest amenities of life in the field, the Tobruk garrison fought back. Attack after attack was launched against it, and though one penetrated a little distance into the outer perimeter, making a blister in the British line, every onslaught was halted.

At the end of a month the enemy abated their direct attacks. At the end of two months they were abandoning their heavy dive-bombing raids and were resorting to shelling. They began digging in themselves. Unable to make a surgical operation upon this angry ulcer in the side of their lines, the Germans decided to seal it up.

At the end of three months the 'rats of Tobruk'—Lord Haw-Haw's description—were taking the offensive with nightly fighting patrols. Nor was Haw-Haw's other description of them as 'the self-supporting prisoners' quite accurate. Tobruk pegged the German advance. Always it lay athwart the enemy's lines, restless, threatening and defiant.

77

The Rats of Tobruk.

Inside the garrison the men lived a strange restricted life without liquor or women or picture shows or amusements of any kind. They had no fresh vegetables. They were pestered by heat, sand and flies. They had no ice. They were bombed every day and every night. The ships that brought them supplies of bullets and bully beef were sometimes sunk in the harbour. But they learned to make a life out of this confinement. They played cricket on the sand. They swam. The cooks and orderlies and batmen amused themselves by collecting old pieces of Italian pre-war cannon and ammunition. These they rigged up as best they could on bits of rock and concrete. Having no precision instruments, they poked their heads up the barrels of the guns and sighted them that way before the charge was put in. They achieved elevation and direction by removing or adding another rock to the base of the cannon. And in their spare time they banged away at the enemy, alongside the modern twenty-five-pounders—banged away so effectively that the Australian general in command was forced to give them official recognition and an honoured place in the firing line. Anti-aircraft guns were lacking, so the garrison turned small arms upon the raiders, and one officer alone brought down six with a Lewis gun. Never was a more timely stand made; never one more vigorously continued.

Of many good stories of Tobruk here is the one I like best. A tiny Greek freighter was loaded with German prisoners in Tobruk harbour and told to proceed to Alexandria. Three knots was the speed of the freighter and three knots was her absolute utmost. Dive-bombers attacked the vessel, and though an escorting British minesweeper did what she could, and the German prisoners rushed on deck waving white towels and tablecloths, the little freighter disappeared beneath tons of exploded water. When the raid was over, the minesweeper drew near again. Smoke was belching from the funnel of the Greek—from the funnel and the ventilators and the bridgehead. And she was doing nine knots.

78

Benghazi, second time through. Italian troops tour the town.

It is ridiculous of course to assert that the Germans in the course of a few days regained all that Mussolini had lost in two months in Cyrenaica. Even a juicy morsel of the desert like Cyrenaica is of little value unless one destroys armies there. That Wavell had done with a vengeance. Our retreat cost us under three thousand men and fewer vehicles. Nevertheless, the loss of Benghazi was a bitter surprise.

*

BY July 1941, the first phase of the war in the Middle East was done. It had actually ended on June 22nd when the Germans marched upon Russia. Just as the R.A.F. had saved England until the help of the United States arrived, so Wavell had stood in the Middle East until the imponderable Russian army rose to fight with us. It had been a big and tiring year. From next to nothing the Army of the Nile had risen to half a million men, despite its reverses—English, Australians, New Zealanders, South Africans, Indians, Poles, Czechs, French, Palestinians, Cypriots, Sudanese, Belgians, Ethiopians, East and West Africans. And at last they were being armed from the United States as well as from England and the Dominions.

As the Russian war rolled on into the late summer, and one peaceful week succeeded another in the Middle East, it began to become clear that something had been done here to earn this rest and prepare the way for bigger offensives. Something like a quarter of a million Italian soldiers were safe in concentration camps in Egypt, India and South Africa. Ethiopia had been won back, and two other Italian colonies were conquered. Berbera was recovered. The Western Desert and Tobruk held strongly. The Canal was open and secure. But by far the major achievement had been in the sphere of our reverses—the sphere that inevitably will be the centre of argument. Whatever were the demerits of our tactics and planning in Greece and Crete (which were the cause of the Benghazi reverse), it could not be denied as the winter of 1941 set in that our campaigns there had delayed Hitler's plans for the Middle East and perhaps baulked them altogether.

Admiral Sir Andrew Cunningham and Air Chief Marshal Sir Arthur Longford.   *General Morshead commanded Tobruk.*

I for one was deeply sorry when at the close of this hard year's fighting the papers came out with the announcement that Wavell was going.

The war correspondents went down to G.H.Q. to say good-bye. The general was in his shirt-sleeves again. And for once he was full of words.'We have had some setbacks, some successes,' he said, and he went on to sum it all up. It wasn't a particularly good summing-up. The theme was 'More equipment'. But I saw suddenly how sincere he was, how hard he had tried—tried, fought, organized, argued and held on. There went out of Cairo and the Middle East that afternoon one of the great men of the war.

10

T HE lull in the Middle East was, of course, no lull. The two opponents had simply drawn off from one another in order to re-equip and fling themselves forward again more violently than ever before. There was tremendous activity behind the lines. Wavell had gone to India and his place had been taken by Auchinleck. Stemming from this, immense changes were taking place right through the Army of the Nile. The Army became three armies—one the Eighth in the Western Desert, another the Ninth in Syria and Palestine, and the third the Tenth based on Baghdad and territories to the east.

The lifeline to besieged Tobruk; stores being unloaded in the harbour.

A spate of new people came in from England and India, bringing with them new machines, new tanks and guns, and one or two fresh ideas. Air Marshal Longmore had gone, and his place at the head of the Middle Eastern Air Force was taken by Arthur Tedder who had been second in command. Under Tedder the R.A.F. was doubling and tripling itself with Beaufighters and Bostons, Wellingtons, Hurricanes, Marylands, Tomahawks.

At sea Andrew Cunningham still had command, and new warships were sailed to him from England to replace those he had lost in his great actions off Crete and in the Ionian Sea. The time of the big naval sweeps through the Mediterranean was finished now. Against increasing and unremitting opposition from the Luft-waffe, the Navy was getting supplies into Tobruk and Malta and sinking the Axis convoys that slipped out of Naples on dark nights and made for Tripoli by way of the Tunisian coast.

Only the isolated garrison of Tobruk was seeing real fighting and this was for the most part a matter of shelling, offensive patrols and bombing. It is good to remember the garrison as it was this August during the great days of the Tobruk tradition. The town and its thirty-five-mile perimeter were manned by British tanks, artillery and infantry, and by the 9th Australian Division, all under the command of Major-General Morshead. German and Italian forces were encamped right round the perimeter and several divisions of enemy troops lay on the Egyptian frontier. Although the main part of our desert army was little more than a hundred miles away from Tobruk, it was impossible to send fighter support to the garrison or maintain British aircraft there. An experiment was made in landing Hurricanes on Tobruk airfield, but they were sighted at once and shot up within a few minutes of landing. No flares could be lit to bring in aircraft at night. Morshead had to rely solely upon anti-aircraft fire to hold off the German bombers that were coming over every day on their five minutes' run from El Adem field just outside the perimeter. Our men holding the perimeter could actually hear the German aircraft warming up to take off from El Adem.

Tobruk itself was a maze of broken, tottering buildings though still they gleamed

The two Cs-in-C: Wavell—'one of the great men of the war'. Auchinleck—'something of a mystery.'

white and clear in the sun. Shells fell constantly among the wrecks in the harbour. All that dusty and ravished plain reaching up to the minefields, trenches and barbed wire of the perimeter was under enemy fire, so that reliefs on the front had to be carried out at night. Even the food of the front-line men had to be cooked near the town and taken up to the trenches in the starlight. The men who had lain all day in the sun facing the enemy would crawl through the trenches to the dugouts where the bully stew and brackish tea was served out. And they would relax there for an hour or two at night to smoke, talk and read. Before the morning came they would walk back to their posts. By any standard they were very fine troops. They were the Rats of Tobruk.

All these men—some twenty-five thousand—were maintained solely by the Navy and the merchant fleet. Destroyers crammed with men and stores would steam out of Alexandria and Matruh and make the quick dash through the night into the treacherous darkness of Tobruk harbour. Only a narrow channel was kept open through the sunken ships and the entrances to the harbour were mined.

Landing crews—and these included a little band of picked Indian troops—would be waiting on the improvised docks and lighters. They worked feverishly through the midnight hours getting ashore the shells, tanks, spare parts and boxes of food. The reinforcements came off silently and under the spasmodic glare of bombs and gun-flashes they marched off somewhere into the darkness. Then the wounded were carried down to the ships and borne off into the open sea before the morning broke. At sea the ships were often followed and bombed by the enemy until they reached port in Egypt.

In all this there was none of the stir and excitement of the battle action. There was no thrill of closing with the enemy, of seeing the torpedoes go out and the big guns straddle their targets on the horizon. Seldom, if ever, were the men on the Tobruk run able to see that most terrible and exhilarating sight on the ocean—an enemy warship that billows suddenly into flame and casts up its stern for the long dive to the seabed.

All this was stealth, speed and essentially defence. Yet still I carry a photographic picture in my mind of the dark harbour of Tobruk. Over on the right somewhere lies the wreck of the Italian liner *Marco Polo* and another vessel that by some freak of the weather or high explosive had edged a good twenty feet of its bows on to the yellow cliffs on the southern side of the harbour. On the left lie the broken buildings of the town rising tier on tier up to the crest of the promontory which binds the harbour on its northern side. In between is the heavy darkness of the harbour itself. All around is the noise and sharp light of gunfire.

The dockside labourers straining their eyes can just make out the low hulk of a moving ship. It is probably no more than a triangular shadow weaving in and out of the wrecks, until it comes alongside. The decks are crowded with men in full kit. No one smokes. There is an exchange of shouted orders from the destroyer's bridgehead and answers from the quay and then the men begin filing off. The winches are moving before the gangways are down.

Thousands of men have stood on Tobruk quays watching this scene while they, too, waited in full marching kit for the order to go aboard, to go aboard and leave Tobruk and get a spell of rest and quietness and good food back in Egypt or Palestine. While they pondered on cool beer and how it would be to see women again and trees and gardens, many have thought, 'Will there be room for me?' There always was room.

It is a notable thing in seafaring that through this period I have called a lull, nearly the whole of the 9th Australian Division was taken off Tobruk and replaced by two English brigades and a brigade of fighting Poles. The casualties in the change-over were almost nil. The Australians left their trucks and guns behind and the new troops simply move into the perimeter and took up the struggle. It was done so secretly and quickly the enemy never knew of the change-over until it was completed. Even if this manœuvre lacked the excitement of a battle, it had the importance of a victory.

Meanwhile on the frontier Rommel was doing little more than digging in. He was mounting entire turrets he had taken off captured British infantry tanks. They were embedded in concrete on the high points of Halfaya Pass, overlooking the British forces that were sprawled across the Egyptian desert below, and down across the road to the sea. There was shelling, minelaying, patrolling. But not much else. Rommel had his plans for the winter and so had we.

II

GENERAL AUCHINLECK, the man who had succeeded Wavell as Commander-in-Chief of the Middle East, up to this time had been something of a mystery. He had slipped quietly into this job from India, and for some reason through a long career he had escaped or avoided the publicity which clung so relentlessly to the other generals like Gort, Ironside and Wavell.

His record did not promise genius. His had been the most regular of all regular army lives. He was even born at Aldershot, the vatican of British soldiering, and his father was a gunner. They said—inevitably—that as a boy he used to dig trenches round the family orchard and that he drilled his younger brothers and sisters. He went, of course, to Sandhurst, and one might almost guess the rest—the commission in the 62nd Punjabs in India at the age of twenty, the fighting against the Turks in the Middle East through the last war, the lonely soldier home on leave during the early nineteen-twenties when everyone wanted to forget soldiering, the marriage with the pretty girl he met in France, the return to the India of polo and rhythmical promotion.

Up and up he went, with a never a move out of character. There was the fighting on the North-West Frontier, the term at the Imperial Defence College in England, that nursery of generals, then back to rising commands in India. Colonel, Brigadier, Major-General, Lieutenant-General. This war had brought him a brief command in Norway, a brisk administrative job preparing the south of England after Dunkirk, and then finally that ultimate goal of every regular officer in the Empire Army —Commander-in-Chief, India.

No, none of it was very exciting. It was believed in the Middle East, with reason, that something more than an efficient but average general was wanted to restore our losses and take the offensive. Wavell's personal magnetism, which seemed to survive every setback in the war, had made it very difficult for a successor to step into the Middle East command. The sudden removal of Wavell to the India command was not liked in Cairo, or the desert.

The man who stepped out of his aircraft one hot morning in June 1941 to take command in Cairo was, of course, utterly different from his reputation, or, rather, different from what everyone expected him to be. But when people had got over their first surprise at finding him so different, and Auchinleck had taken his two defeats in the desert, it was again fashionable to point to his prosaic career and say, 'He lacked new ideas, drive, initiative.'

Both views—the early reaction in his favour and the subsequent tendency to regard him as just another regular soldier—were hopelessly mistimed and misinformed. This book is no defence of General Auchinleck. But it is an attempt to describe his two campaigns in the desert and explain how they went wrong under the direction of this vigorous and intelligent mind.

There is a strange contradiction in nearly everything about Auchinleck, and this in the end is probably the reason why success was always snatched away from him just at the moment when it seemed secure. He had extraordinary charm and gentleness in conversation, and he could be utterly ruthless. Half a dozen times he sacked some of his closest associates who failed—sacked them overnight so that one day they were in charge of a sector of the battle in the desert and the next on their way to England and retirement. In each case he maintained a bigoted loyalty to these men until they made their major mistake, and you might argue from this that he was no chooser of men.

For a man who had been ridden by British army drill and discipline for forty years, Auchinleck had a mind of quite exceptional freshness and originality. He would seize on every new idea and explore it at once. He was ready to meet everyone and anyone. He brimmed with ideas himself. He was very easy to talk to. With all this he was still scarcely known to his men or the public. That curious psychology by which everyone in the Middle East felt that they knew Wavell personally never operated in the case of Auchinleck. With all the instincts of a social and gregarious human being, he had never learned how to make contact with the world at large. He loathed public speeches as much as he enjoyed private conversation. He almost never broadcast. He avoided social engagements.

He believed that he could control the battle from Cairo, and that it was possible to galvanize his men with a stream of advice and encouragement sent out from

headquarters. In the light of the last two campaigns, it is apparent that the desert is not geared to remote control. Things move too quickly on an open front like the desert. It was not until after the fall of Tobruk in the midsummer of 1942 that Auchinleck at last accepted this fact and went down to the front to take personal command. Rommel had been at the front the whole time. Often he was in a tank and directing his men 'in clear' over the radio telephone. He was stopped only when Auchinleck took up a similar position on the opposite side of the line.

It is only fair to say here that Auchinleck had an amazing run of bad luck with his generals. There had been in the desert since the outbreak of the war a number of young commanders of exceptional ability and toughness. One after another they were killed, usually in accidents, or captured through some trifling unforeseeable reason. Air Marshal Boyd and Lieutenant-General Carton de Wiart were shot down near Italy on the way out and captured. Lieutenant-General O'Connor, who led that first fantastic march south of the Jebel Akdar and annihilated the Italian Army at Beda Fomm, was very nearly the ideal desert commander, but he took a wrong turning on the way back from Benghazi and was picked up by the Nazis with two other experienced British generals.

There were two brigadiers, Russell and Gott, who were outstanding leaders in Wavell's first campaign, and Gott through his brilliance and tenacity and personal courage was becoming a legend in the desert. Both were killed in aircraft. Tilly, another general, contracted pneumonia and died as soon as he reached the desert.

Pope, an expert in armoured fighting, crashed in the same aircraft as Russell. Jock Campbell, a sort of Francis Drake of the desert, the man with the greatest daring and enterprise on either side, died on the Sollum escarpment when his car overturned. Young veterans like Coombes, O'Carroll and Garmoyle were killed or captured at critical moments in the fighting. Other irreplaceable men like Freyberg, Gatehouse, Briggs and Lumsden were wounded by Stuka bombs or stray bullets when they were most needed.

This total of nearly twenty commanders goes beyond mere coincidence or the normal fortunes of battle. The loss of O'Connor, Gott and Campbell alone was a far more serious disaster than the loss of Benghazi or even possibly of Tobruk. When they and the others went, it meant that Auchinleck simply did not have the men to lead his troops in the desert. Even those who had failed—half a dozen or more—had been sent home or to other jobs, and could not be recalled.

However, during September 1941 most of these misfortunes lay ahead, and all we knew of Auchinleck was that he was working with great urgency and speed in G.H.Q.

His personal appearance and address had made a great impression, for he was a strikingly handsome man, looking at least ten years younger than his fifty-eight. Many senior officers went to his room with some misgiving, for it was rumoured that a purge was about to start among the staff. They went in like lambs and came out like tigers. Auchinleck, they found, was a pleasant, amiable fellow. He had friendly blue eyes, thick reddish hair, a strong vigorous face with the usual faint military moustache. Physically he was a fine sight, a tall distinguished officer who had no affectations. He wore the shorts and shirt which had now been adopted right through the ranks. There was no stuffiness about him. The new general was feeling his way carefully. The purge did not come until later.

I went down to the desert to see this new Eighth Army which Auchinleck was creating. It was some time since I had been in the desert and I cannot say I was very enthusiastic about going back. The road down from Cairo to Alexandria was just the same except that there was more traffic on it. We turned left outside Alexandria and drove along the coast road as I had done so often— past the fig plantations and the wonderful turquoise sea at Alamein, where the sunlight strikes the white seabed and is reflected back to the surface so that the water is full of dancing light and colour. Then over the bad bumpy part of the road that takes you into the supply base at Daba, where there always was and always will be a sandstorm. Daba had a restaurant now with paper flowers on the tables and bacon and fresh eggs on the menu. That was something quite new. After Daba we got into a traffic jam which was a wonderfully encouraging thing to see. It went on and on for many miles—tanks, heavy lorries and twenty-five-pounder guns, staff cars, transporters and signal wagons, anti-tank guns and anti-aircraft guns, travelling workshops, water wagons, ammunition trucks and still more tanks. This procession reached all the way to Cairo, two hundred miles away, but it had thickened here. Everything was moving forward to the front.

Beside the road, at places like Fuka, I saw many squadrons of new aircraft, new tent cities, new dumps for petrol, spare parts, food and general stores. There were a couple of new prisoners' camps. Many aircraft kept sweeping by overhead. That little piratical force Wavell had sent to Benghazi had become a great army. The war correspondents' old camp at Bagush I simply could not recognize. It

RIGHT: *General Cunningham commanded two army corps.*

FAR RIGHT: *General Ravenstein commanded a Panzer Division.*

was like coming into an hotel. An officer met us, took our names, allotted us to tents —*tents*, we never had tents before—and our bedrolls were carried off for us. They said dinner would be ready in an hour, and if we did not want a swim we could go into the bar. This was the first time anyone had cooked a meal for us, and as for bars, those were the sort of things one talked about nostalgically and never saw.

There were enough new vehicles for everyone; enough petrol, enough rations, enough maps. The only thing lacking was war. It was dead quiet at the front, a day's run farther on. The enemy seemed very distant, and the fact that their patrols did occasionally come exploring only added a sense of mild excitement to the other sensations of remoteness, of quiet and of deep peace.

It was the last time I was to see the desert at peace for nearly a year. The old days of small piratical raids had gone. The desert was filling up with thousands upon thousands of armed men. Two great armies, as mobile and heavily armed as any in Russia, lay camped within half a day's distance of one another. As more and more guns and tanks were pressed into the desert, the days of peace were running out rapidly. The new battle when it came would no longer be a border skirmish but a full-scale test of strength between the Germans and the British.

Little by little, as I moved around the desert, I began to piece together the dispositions of both armies and weigh the chances of success. On our side General Sir Alan Cunningham, who had done so well in Ethiopia against the Italians, had two army corps of roughly three divisions each. In the extreme north opposite Sollum and Sidi Omar lay the Indians and the New Zealanders, and they had a

General Gatehouse briefs
men of the Armoured Division
the day before the battle.

division of South Africans in reserve. In the centre were three newly equipped British armoured brigades with supporting artillery. In the south, the line was held by another division of South Africans and more Indians—these last based on Jarabub. In addition there were about twenty thousand British and Polish troops in Tobruk with something up to one hundred infantry tanks.

In all, Cunningham could call upon about one hundred thousand men, eight hundred tanks and nearly one thousand aircraft of all kinds.

Rommel had somewhat more men. Spaced mostly around Tobruk were the following Italian divisions—Brescia, Trento, Trieste, Pavia and Bologna. These were infantry, some of them motorized. The 90th Light Germany Infantry with more Italians held the frontier bases, Bardia, Sollum, Halfaya Pass, as well as positions round Tobruk. The Axis armour consisted of the German 21st Panzer Division under the command of Major-General Ravenstein, the 15th Panzer Division under Major-General Neumann-Silkow, and the Italian Ariete Division. In all Rommel could count about one hundred and twenty thousand men, four hundred tanks and somewhat fewer aircraft than we had.

Both commanders were planning to attack about the same time. Rommel proposed to bring the main weight of his armour and guns upon the south-eastern sector of Tobruk perimeter and take the garrison by assault. On the border he proposed to do nothing more than hold for the time being.

Cunningham planned to contain the enemy garrison on the border by running a horseshoe formation round it—the Indians to hold the eastern arm, the New Zealanders to hold the western arm. The British armour, supported by the South Africans, was to go through the wire fence at Fort Maddalena in the centre and hunt for the enemy armour. They were to force the Axis tanks to fight by running a cordon round them—a cordon reaching from Maddalena to the outskirts of Tobruk. While the tanks were engaged, the Tobruk garrison was to sally out in

88

the south-east as far as El Duda and there link hands with the New Zealanders coming along the coast through Gambut. In the far south the Indians were to make a diversion by sending out an expedition to the desert post of Jalo south-east of Benghazi. Once the German armour was destroyed—and this was paramount—the whole army was to sweep on to Benghazi and beyond to Tripoli if possible.

The British were to attack on the morning of November 18th. The Germans proposed to start their assault of Tobruk about November 23rd. Neither side was quite sure of the other's plans, though each had a pretty shrewd idea. We would not have attacked on the 18th if we had known definitely that Rommel proposed his Tobruk adventure for a few days later. It would have been pleasant to have allowed Rommel to get his main forces stuck into Tobruk and then to have taken him in the rear. On Rommel's side, it is evident that had he known of our zero hour he would have shelved his Tobruk attack and disposed his forces differently.

12

GENERAL SIR ALAN CUNNINGHAM, the brother of the admiral, and at that time in command of the British Forces in the desert, called the war correspondents into his concrete dugout at Bagush on the night of November 16th. He was a blue-eyed, ruddy-complexioned man with a soft voice, and he smiled a good deal. He looked more like a successful business man than a general, even when he said to us, 'I am going to attack the day after to-morrow . . . everything depends on how the battle goes.'

We trooped up and out into cloudy night. There were no stars and Matt Halton and I stood still for a moment to accustom our eyes to the darkness. Then we began to move slowly across the sand-dunes to our camp. We were too pre-occupied to talk much or watch where we were going. Out in front of us a hundred thousand men lay camped in the sand, British, Germans and Italians, and others like the Poles who had drifted into this arena by the haphazard course of war. No shot was fired. All around us men were asleep. The sea moved easily and quietly along the beach. The one irresistible thought that filled my mind was that within thirty-six hours all these placid, sleeping men were going to rise up and start killing one another. Nothing could stop the battle taking place. All the orders were given, the guns placed, the tanks grouped and ready, and the empty beds standing row on row in the field hospitals. It seemed a calculated cruelty. The inevitability of the battle was the hardest thing to accept. I kept perversely remembering one night nearly two years before when I had stood hour after hour on the cobblestones outside the prison in Versailles waiting for the murderer Weidmann to be beheaded. They had erected the guillotine, tested it, roped off the crowd, backed the hearse into the square and then with the utmost punctuality they had brought Weidmann out at dawn and cut off his head. Now it was not one man but a hundred thousand.

I began to say something about these morbid ideas to Matt and we fell into argument: he saw the colour and the movement of the battle. In the end we agreed that the inevitability of a catastrophe—the actual knowing of the zero hour— was the hardest thing to take. It was easier to be left in doubt.

By this time we were hopelessly lost and we roamed about for an hour by the sea before we reached our camp where the others were finishing off the last of the beer. There was an air of nervous excitement as we marked our maps and made our plans to move up to the front at dawn.

It took us all next day. We ran down the good coast road beyond Mersa Matruh and then turned deep into the open desert down the Siwa track. Clifford, Richard Busvine of the *Chicago Tribune*, a little Scots conducting officer and myself rode ahead in a Humber staff car. Our two trucks filled with bedding, water, petrol and provisions followed on behind.

It rained in squalls of bitter sleet that night. Like artillery, the lightning came rushing from the Mediterranean and, as we lay awake and watching in the open, the water seeped through bedding, blankets, ground-sheets—everything. Men crouched against the sides of tanks and guns in the futile struggle to keep dry. The infantry sat numbly in their trucks with their greatcoat collars turned up over their ears. No aircraft could take off from the sodden sticky sand. It was a cold, miserable and disheartening start for the battle. Bedraggled and wet, we trailed on in the wake of the soldiers. Every track we took was the wrong one. Somehow the great lumbering Eighth Army had got itself into motion, and there were hundreds upon hundreds of vehicles all bumping across the sand in different directions. The general trend was west into Libya, but no one seemed to have a clear idea of what was happening or where we were going. Sometimes for hours we coasted along with South African supply convoys, and then, giving that up, we turned aside to chase a few stray guns on the move or paused miserably to brew a cup of tea and make some new plan for getting where we wanted to go—the front where the tanks were in battle.

Still that night we had seen no action and we camped a few miles east of the frontier wire near Fort Maddalena. A cold fierce wind had succeeded the storm. In the morning it was better. We passed the ruins of Fort Maddalena in the early sunshine, and the sky now was full of British fighters and bombers passing on to the front. A great part of the southern part of the army had swept through this break in the wire at Maddalena, and now we began to catch up with it. There were remarkable mirages in the desert that day. At times you could see on the horizon a towered city that floated on a lake and undulated as you watched like a stage backcloth blown in the wind. Small bushes looked in the distance like great trees, and each truck was a two-storied house passing through the dust. Often we saw groups of castles on the horizon. As we approached, these turned to battleships and then at last from a mile away they resolved into the solid shapes of tanks. We were getting up among the fighting troops at last. But still no one could direct us to Corps headquarters, and when we did find the location it was too late— Corps had moved on. Again in the evening when we were tired and angry and had seen nothing, we were still embroiled in the endless and meaningless cavalcade of lorries. Once a stranded tank crew had prevented us from driving straight into the Italian lines. We had heard firing then, and there was talk of forty Italian tanks having been knocked out, but we could get nothing definite.

Unknown to us, much of the army was in the same condition as ourselves. The tanks, guns and lorries had poured helter-skelter into Libya and at first no enemy was to be found anywhere. There was a very good reason for this. Rommel, incredible as it may sound, had been taken by surprise. He was far behind the front when scouts came rushing to his headquarters with the news that the British Army was on the move and that it was no 'reconnaissance in force' but a full-scale offensive. Hurriedly Rommel had called off the Tobruk affair and, with that sure instinct of his for organization, had begun bunching his tanks together. A large body of these German tanks now came scouring down the border fence to test the strength of the invaders.

By this time Cunningham had succeeded in laying his various layers round the Axis forces. The Indians were entrenched with their minefields east of Sollum and had approached Sidi Omar farther to the south on the frontier. The New Zealanders had rounded the German frontier positions and were making up toward Sollum, inside the German lines. The three British armoured brigades, a band of steel in these soft layers of infantry, had strung themselves in a shallow arc from Maddalena to the outskirts of Tobruk, and south of them the sprawling mass of the South African division lay in support.

The other two British moves were also in operation—the garrison at Tobruk had begun to sally out toward El Duda, there to await the arrival of the New Zealanders coming along the coast; and the diversionary column from Jarabub had set out on its long forced march to Jalo, south of Benghazi.

The whole British plan seemed to be based on the assumption that the Germans once surrounded would be forced to fight from inside while their dumps and lines of communication lay outside. But you cannot isolate a force in the desert. We were committed to the policy of getting behind the enemy and forcing him to battle. It was like penning a savage bull in a hencoop.

Although we outnumbered the enemy in tanks and guns, the forces were far too small to surround him. In the attempt to carry out the manœuvre that ancient and fatal error of desert warfare was committed on a mammoth scale—the three British tank brigades were divided. The first of these, the 4th Brigade, under Gatehouse, consisting of the fast light American tanks, stayed in the east. The newly arrived 22nd Brigade, with its Valentines, was placed in the centre in the direction of Bir Gobi, and the 7th, with the support group under Brigadier Jock Campbell, was sent up to Sidi Rezegh on the outskirts of Tobruk. There we were—like a pack of wolves sitting around a lion waiting for the kill.

These forty-eight hours must have been a time of puzzlement for Rommel. Overnight he suddenly found the desert—his bit of desert—overrun for hundreds of miles. Now cautiously he had moved his tanks southward near the border to see what it was all about. Late in the afternoon of the second day they bumped into Gatehouse and his American Honey tanks, and by the merest luck I saw the action from a distance.

My party had blundered into the British armoured division headquarters and the first officer I saw there was the welcome figure of Colonel Bonner Fellers, the United States military attaché. Bonner Fellers was often in the desert. He liked to gather his facts at first hand. In the Wavell campaign we used to see him buzzing round from place to place in an ordinary civilian saloon car. And now here he was again looking quizzically across to the east where quick heavy gunfire had suddenly broken the quietness of the afternoon.

I called across to him, 'What's happening?' He just had time to answer, 'Damned

These light Honey tanks had never seen battle before; they had come straight to the desert from the steelmills of America.

if I know,' when we had to duck for shelter as two Messerschmitts came over ground-strafing. Then, clambering on top of our trucks, we saw the opening of the strange confused battle that began in the evening light of November 19th and finished in almost the same spot some eight or nine days later.

Dark rainclouds were pressed solidly on to the eastern horizon. Against this backcloth a line of grey shell-bursts flared up, and soon there were so many of them that a series of twenty or more were hanging together on the skyline. As the battle joined more closely these bursts grew together and made a continuous curtain of dust and smoke and blown sand. This was the battle of the guns reaching its climax—German guns on our tanks, our guns on the Germans; the range perhaps five thousand yards. Then came the tanks.

What a moment it was. These light Honeys with their two-pounder 37-milli-metre gun, their ugly box-shaped turrets, their little waving pennants, had never seen the battle before. They had come straight from the steel mills of America to the desert, and now for the first time we were going to see if they were good or bad or just more tanks.

Gatehouse, with this heavy head, his big hooked nose, and his deep-set eyes, sat on his tank watching the battle, estimating the strength of the enemy, the position of the sun, the slope of the ground. Then he lifted up his radio mouthpiece and gave his order. At his command the Honeys did something that tanks don't do in the desert any more. They charged. It was novel, reckless, unexpected, impetuous and terrific. They charged straight into the curtain of dust and fire that hid the German tanks and guns. They charged at speeds of nearly forty miles an hour and some of them came right out the other side of the German lines. Then they turned and charged straight back again. They passed the German Mark IVs and Mark IIIs at a few hundred yards, near enough to see the white German crosses, near enough to fire at pointblank range and see their shell hit and explode.

92

I saw nothing of all this infighting. I doubt if anyone saw it at all clearly. Dust, smoke, burning oil, exploding shell and debris filled the air. From a distance it was merely noise and confusion.

Fires on the battlefield delayed the early winter night a little. But by six o'clock it was too dark to see any more and one after another the guns hiccoughed into silence. Both sides drew off.

Through the sharp cold of the night the Nazi recovery units crept forward on to the battlefield and they were not unkind to our wounded lying there. They handed hot drinks to the men who lay helpless beside the smoking wrecks of their tanks and threw blankets over some of those who would otherwise have died of exposure before morning. Working at speed, they hitched up the partly damaged vehicles, both British and German, and dragged them off to repair shops. They seized on all the food and clothing left about in the mêlée of battle and bore it off.

A few miles away my little party had gone into a protective leaguer for the night. In the last light we had cooked and eaten our bully-beef stew. The 'soft' vehicles—those that had no armour—had lain dispersed about the desert all day to minimize the danger of air attack. Now we drove these together into a compact group for the night, and a ring of tanks and armoured cars lay about us on guard against surprise attacks in the darkness. But neither side reopened the fighting through the night, and I was woken half an hour before dawn by a burst of Bren-gun fire. This was the signal for the leaguer to disperse again and drive on to a new stretch of desert lest our position had been plotted by reconnaissance aircraft the day before.

As we came to rest in our new base the darkness began to weaken under the red glow of the coming sun. Visibility extended first a few yards, then a hundred, then two hundred, and the formless silhouettes of a few hours before resolved into tanks and trucks and guns. A few miles off the battle began again at the point where it was broken off the night before. Gunners and tank crews, straining their eyes through the mist, now suddenly caught sight of the enemy again and put their gloved hands to the frozen metal of the guns. At some places Germans and British had lain right alongside one another through the night and the men opened up with machine-gun fire as they scrambled for cover. Then for a brief hour the firing ran in bursts along the eastern horizon, and once again the men on the tank radio link could hear the tank commanders shouting at one another in the thick of the battle —'There they come, Bill . . . half right, two thousand yards, six of 'em . . . right, let them have it, the bastards . . . Christ, that was a beauty!' Scarcely before the sun was over the horizon the Nazis drew off, and turning west avoided further engagement.

All this time—through the engagement the previous night, during the night itself, and now again this morning—the battle arena had been cut off from the rest of the world. No one at headquarters had any clear knowledge yet of how our experiment had gone forward or of how the Honey had behaved in its first encounter.

But now some of the crews, young English boys, began coming back, and they had remarkable information. It seemed that the German tanks with their heavy 50- and 75-millimetre guns had opened up an effective barrage at ranges of up to fifteen hundred yards. At this distance the Honey's two-pounder was quite unable to reply, and Gatehouse had accordingly ordered his men to charge forward until they were within shooting distance—about eight hundred yards. To cover that terrible seven or eight hundred yards under continuous enemy fire, the Honeys had zigzagged back and forth across the sand and to some extent had thrown the German gunners off. The great speed of the American tank had helped, and once they had got well up to the Germans they had done great execution. But some thirty of our tanks had been lost in the process of getting into battle—some of them had not even had a chance of firing a shot. The German losses were unknown because so many of their tanks had been salvaged in the night.

This first day of battle then had revealed the two grave disadvantages which were to handicap the British for the whole of this campaign and for many months to come. It was known on this first morning that all our tanks were out-gunned, and that however many vehicles the Germans lost they were going to get a far greater number back into action than we could because of their efficient recovery system. Their huge tracked and wheeled tank-transporters were actually going into battle with the tanks themselves. Even while the fighting was still on, the men in the transporters were prepared to dash into the battle, hook on to damaged vehicles and drag them out to a point where they could start repairs right away.

Rommel, on his side, was finding out that he was up against a very much more numerous enemy than he had reckoned with. He had broken off his engagement with the Honey tanks in order to regroup nearer to his main forces about Tobruk, but as he went west and north he continued to bump into British armour. In the south-west at Bir Gobi, the Italian Ariete Tank Division had had a brush with the British 22nd Armoured Brigade and also been forced to withdraw. These Italian tanks now began to slide along the southern side of the British armoured line trying to find a weak spot while the Germans were doing exactly the same thing in the inside of the British ring. And so both German and Italian tanks fetched up together at the north-western extremity of the line at Sidi Rezegh just below Tobruk. Rezegh airfield had been surprised and won by Campbell's support group and the 7th Armoured Brigade the day before.

Rommel now decided to fling the bulk of his armour on to the British at Rezegh and so force a gap out to the west. Rezegh became the decisive battlefield of the campaign. All day the 7th withstood the full weight of the Panzer Divisions while they waited for the other two British Armoured Brigades to come to their assistance.

General Gott himself was at Rezegh and I saw one of his messages come into divisional headquarters in the late afternoon. It said: 'We are all right, but we would like to know when the other brigades are arriving.' Gott had begun the action on Rezegh with over one hundred tanks. By the end of the day, when help at last arrived, he had barely a dozen serviceable vehicles left.

Both the 4th and 22nd Brigades were late in arriving—the 4th because it had delayed to attack a large soft convoy of German lorries, the 22nd because it was a new brigade sent far too hastily into the desert and some of its elements got temporarily lost. There were already large numbers of inexperienced British troops wandering about the desert uncertain of their direction.

So now the battle of annihilation on Sidi Rezegh began. I drove with Edward Ward of the B.B.C. and one or two others into that spit of flat land we were holding just above the Tobruk escarpment. It was ringed with fire. In the east the Germans were counter-attacking the airfield and Jock Campbell was like a man berserk. He led his tanks into action riding in an open unarmoured staff car, and as he stood there, hanging on to its windscreen, a huge well-built man with the English

General Jock Campbell, V.C.

officer's stiff good looks, he shouted, 'There they come. Let them have it.' When the car began to fall behind, he leaped on to the side of a tank as it went forward and directed the battle from there. He turned aside through the enemy barrage to his own twenty-five-pounder guns and urged the men on to faster loading and quicker firing. He shouted to his gunners, 'How are you doing?' and was answered, 'Doing our best, sir.' He shouted back, grinning, 'Not good enough.'

They say Campbell won the V.C. half a dozen times that day. The men loved this Elizabethan figure. He was the reality of all the pirate yarns and tales of high adventure, and in the extremes of fear and courage of the battle he had only courage. He went laughing into the fighting.

From El Adem in the north and the rocks of Tobruk escarpment the enemy was attacking too. I saw his guns ranging on our forward tanks in the north and they stood like knockovers in the shooting gallery of a country fair. Like an endless chain of artificial ducks, British vehicles passed across the horizon, and every now and then a shell burst, belching black smoke, would fall among them.

Then in the third sector, around to the west, more enemy were pushing forward. As the darkness came in Very lights spurted up from every direction. These were the signals of the Germans showing where their forward troops were closing in. We had at this time just this narrow promontory of territory reaching up from the southern desert toward Tobruk—the British armour in the end of the promontory at Rezegh and the mass of South African infantry forming the stalk and base.

The airfield fell, and as my party struggled back in the mud and darkness I saw the enemy's Very lights creeping rapidly around us. They rose, a series of reds, greens and yellows, to the east, north and west and then they began to close in on the south. That meant we were surrounded . . . at least temporarily. On this night the firing did not cease, and the broken burning tanks glowed fitfully and grotesquely across the damp sand of the desert.

In the morning we left Ward behind and made a bolt southward to reach rear headquarters. Even as we bumped along the uneven track German armoured cars came in again from the west and east driving in front of them, like stampeding cattle, hundreds of British lorries, ambulances and supply wagons.

At divisional headquarters we had to pack and run quickly, and we went back to Corps to write our messages and spend one quiet night out of the battle.

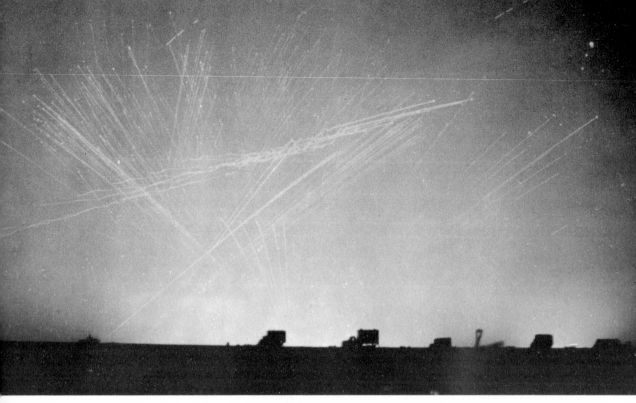

British vehicles passed across the horizon like a chain of artificial ducks.

I was strolling in the sun at Corps and the others of my party were lazily washing in the open when the enemy break-through came. We were in a slight hollow lightly studded with camel thorn and salt-bush—just fifty or sixty vehicles dispersed about with a few armoured cars to protect us. Into this hollow about a hundred British trucks suddenly burst in a whirl of dust. We looked up wondering. Some convoy perhaps with urgent supplies? Then from another direction several hundred more vehicles, tanks among them, came flying pell-mell across the desert, racing past our stationary vehicles without stopping and covering us in great billows of fine sand.

This was no organized convoy. The others got the idea at the same time as I did. As I raced back toward our trucks Clifford and Busvine were already flinging the bedding, the cooking pots and our clothes into the back of the trucks. Everyone was packing at speed. The big three armoured vehicles which housed the Intelligence, Operational and Signalling staffs were being warmed up. One of our officers, shaving-soap on his face, came over when he saw us packing, and enquired with all the confidence of ignorance, 'What's the flap? Ops will tell us if we have to get out.'

'Take at look at Ops,' said Clifford briefly. The Ops crew was flinging aboard beds, maps, cases of food and everything they possessed.

Another great swarm of vehicles rushed through the camp and now shells began to fall among them. It had been a bright early morning, but now the churned-up dust had blotted out the sun and visibility became reduced to two hundred yards or less. In this semi-darkness and confusion thousands of vehicles got hopelessly mixed so that men and vehicles of entirely different units travelled along together, and since many of the drivers had no orders they simply rushed ahead following anyone who would lead them.

My party stuck to the Signals vehicle, but unknown to us the young officer

96

inside had jammed his hand in the door and was semi-unconscious. His driver simply went on as hard as he could in the direction away from the firing, which was south-east, and we followed blindly. Twice we stopped and while men ran from one vehicle to another asking for orders and trying to find out what was amiss, more shells came over the horizon. We were being followed—and fast. So the hue and cry went on again. Occasionally vehicles around us ran on to mines or were hit by shells or were simply fired by their bewildered drivers who believed the enemy to be upon them. Once when we paused on a rise—an odd collection of tanks, cars, lorries, light guns and command vehicles—a squadron of British aircraft came toward us flying low. Everyone ran to their places and the stampede began again.

All day for nine hours we ran. It was the contagion of bewilderment and fear and ignorance. Rumour spread at every halt, no man had orders. Everyone had some theory and no one any plan beyond the frantic desire to reach his unit. We were just a few hangers-on of the battle, the ones who were most likely to panic because we had become separated from our officers and had no definite job to do. I came to understand something of the meaning of panic in this long nervous drive. It was the unknown we were running away from, the unknown in ourselves and in the enemy. We did not know who was pursuing us or how many or how long they would be able to keep up the pursuit and whether or not they would outstrip us in the end. In ourselves we did not know what to do. Had there been someone in authority to say 'Stand here. Do this and that'—then half our fear would have vanished. So I began to realize, sitting there in the swaying car, how important the thousand dreary routine things in the army are. The drill, the saluting, the uniform, the very badges on your arm all tend to identify you with a solid machine and build up a feeling of security and order. In the moment of danger the soldier turns to his mechanical habits and draws strength from them.

On the battlefield the individual vanishes. Men turn with absolute trust to one another; they need one another as they seldom do in the even time of peace. The leader should be the product and best expression of the system; not an individual experimentalist. The system should be flexible and inspired enough to throw up the best men into leadership so that when the leader comes to take a daring decision it will be just the decision all his men would have taken. And this must be still more true of guerrilla fighting and the partisans, even though the trappings of the military machine are missing there.

These matters, I suppose, should have been obvious enough, but I personally only began to see them clearly during this ignominious retreat back into Egypt. I wanted badly to receive orders. And so, I think, did the others.

It was a crestfallen and humiliated little group of men that finally felt its way towards the frontier wire fence as dusk fell. We found a gap in the wire and as we plunged through it with a feeling of relief—even a fence between us and the unknown pursuer was something—a British major came up in a truck and began to organize us and knock some sense in us. We stopped and grouped the vehicles in three close-packed lines for the night. Lights and gunfire were still showing a few miles to the north and men came forward to act as sentries. Food, water and petrol were portioned out. Cigarettes were forbidden. Once or twice through the night we heard tanks—ours or the enemy's—rumble past, but when the morning came, grey and damp, the desert was clear. So we rode on into our own rear lines.

The War Correspondents' base camp was at Cunningham's headquarters and we were the last party to get in. Our colonel, Philip Astley, was waiting for us anxiously. We could give him no news of Eddie Ward or Harold Denny of the *New York Times* or Godfrey Anderson of the Associated Press, or half a dozen South African correspondents. Later we heard that they had been overrun the night before and were last seen standing in the prisoners' lines being searched by Nazis.

Two others had run their truck on to a mine, a third had been lost at sea, one or two more were simply missing. The correspondents had taken a bad beating and the loss of Eddie, with whom we had so often gone campaigning, was more than an ordinary distress to Clifford, Busvine and myself.

We shaved, washed, ate breakfast and slept, and presently began to sort things out a little more coherently. It had been a bad reverse for the Eighth Army but not nearly so bad as we had imagined. While the tanks were still locked in this bloodiest of all battles in the desert Rommel had decided upon a gamble that had the elements of genius and the wildest possible folly. He had detached a part of his tanks and armoured cars and flung them straight across the desert through the British lines of communication. A tank among the unarmed lorries is like a shark among mackerel. In a spectacular night attack, the German panzers had almost entirely overwhelmed the 5th South African Brigade and then they had plunged straight into Egypt and attempted to rejoin their infantry forces left on the frontier. British soft transports had scattered before them and confusion more deadly than shellfire spread everywhere. And now lost groups of men roamed about, passing and repassing through the enemy lines. Convoys of vehicles were scattered over 100 miles of desert, not knowing where to go. Batteries of guns and groups of tanks were left stranded in the empty desert. Men who believed they were holding the end of a continuous salient suddenly found the enemy behind them. And north of them and south of them and all round them. Then the enemy in turn would seek to carry off his booty and prisoners only to find that his own base had vanished and that he was in the midst of a strong British formation. Prisoners became gaolers. Men were captured and escaped three or four times. Half a dozen isolated engagements were going on. Field dressing stations and hospitals were taking in British and German and Italian wounded impartially, and as the battle flowed back and forth the hospitals would sometimes be under British command, sometimes under German. Both sides were using each others' captured guns, tanks and vehicles and absurd incidents were taking place. A British truck driven by a German and full of British prisoners ran up to an Italian lorry. Out jumped a platoon of New Zealanders and rescued our men. Vehicles full of Germans were joining British convoys by mistake—and escaping before they were noticed. Generals themselves were taking prisoners and corporals and brigadiers were manning machine-guns together. On the map the dispositions of the enemy and ourselves looked like an eight-decker rainbow cake, and as more and more confused information came in, intelligence officers threw down their pencils in disgust, unable to plot the battle any further.

It seemed indeed that Rommel had achieved a master-stroke. Cunningham had little hestitation in pointing out that the wisest course was to retire his army out of Libya to re-group. Most of his tanks appeared to be lost. He was out of touch with a great part of his army. The New Zealanders had succeeded in making contact with the Tobruk garrison at El Duda but only for a few hours. The

General Neil Ritchie took over from General Cunningham. Here he is talking to the other Coningham, the Air Vice-Marshal.

Germans had surged forward, broken the bridgehead, and now Tobruk was again, a beseiged fortress with barely forty-eight hours of twenty-five-pounder ammunition left. Of the two British Corps headquarters, one, the 13th, had bolted into Tobruk and was besieged there and the other, the 30th, was split up and out of touch. Among the South Africans alone we appeared to have lost an entire brigade —more than two thousand men.

At this grim moment Auchinleck exhibited a touch of brilliance and moral courage that was the high-water mark of his career. He flew to the desert and opposed a final and absolute 'no' to the proposal for retreat. He refused to acknowledge that Rommel's spectacular breakthrough had disorganized the Eighth Army. He argued vehemently that it was only a matter of sticking to what positions we still held and that the enemy must break and give way. He said finally that in order to maintain our stand the last man, the last gun and the last tank in the Eighth Army would be sacrificed. The Eighth Army would go through or never come back.

In this hour of great crisis Auchinleck cast about for any expedient that would delay the enemy until we could return to organized attack. He found it in the Jock Column. Brigadier Jock Campbell had previously spent some time in the desert organizing small fighting patrols. Each was just a handful of vehicles— perhaps a troop of armoured cars, two or three troops of guns and a company of lorried infantry. They were provisioned for a few days or a week or more and the command handed over to a young lieutenant who knew the desert. Each commander's orders were simply these—'Get out and behind the enemy. Attack anything you see.' It was an order that had a peculiar attraction to a certain type of young Englishman. The elements of the Drake and Raleigh tradition were in it. Piracy on the high sands. Where the British Army still bungled hopelessly in massed fighting, there were still the individuals who fought brilliantly in small guerilla groups, who had the inspiration of feeling free and the taste for quick and daring movement.

So the partisans of the desert were born. As fast as they could be put together

Auchinleck rushed them out into the desert. Within a few days he had twenty or more groups behind the enemy lines, burning, looting, shooting, cutting in and running away, laying ambushes in the wadis, diverting enemy tanks, breaking signal wires, laying false trails, breaking up convoys, raiding airfields, getting information. It was a make-shift while the Eighth Army worked desperately to reorganize itself, but it began taking immediate and heavy effect.

Returning to Cairo Auchinleck drove to his house on Gezira and late at night wrote the letter to Cunningham which removed him from his command. There was no time to consult Churchill or the War Cabinet. Auchinleck himself had to take the decision to depose the man he had sent for so hopefully only a few months before. The letter was handed to Major-General Neil Ritchie, Auchinleck's deputy chief-of-staff and Ritchie flew down to the desert the following morning to take command.

Already now in the last days of November the situation was righting itself slowly—righting itself for the last great onslaught of Sidi Rezegh. It had turned out that the fighting troops at the front had not been shaken nearly so much as the soft transport behind Rommel's breakthrough. The breakthrough itself had petered out to nothing after the first wild dash—the enemy tanks had come within five miles of our main dump and missed it altogether. They had not touched our railhead. General Gott and all the troops north of the breakthrough had simply driven northward and carried on the battle from the coastal area. The Indians were successfully attacking Sidi Omar in the centre. The Germans and Italians bottled up in Halfaya, Bardia and Sollum were trying to send out some of their men but ineffectively. The New Zealanders under Freyberg, the finest infantry division in the Middle East, were still defending the coastal ridge about Gambut. Tobruk still held. More tanks were coming up and the broken loose ends of the army in the central desert were being brought together. In the far south the Indians had reached Jalo and overwhelmed it.

My little party flew back to Cairo for a day or two to refit. What an exquisite pleasure it was going back to Cairo. The first hot bath, the first cold drink, the good meals and the clean clothes: these were the things that made the war suddenly fall away and become unreal.

But it was no time to stay eating and drinking in Cairo. Refitted, refreshed and reprovisioned Clifford, Busvine and myself set out with Randolph Churchill for Sidi Rezegh to see the tank battle that was going to decide everything for good and all.

We reached Gatehouse just as he was going into action. His headquarters had been overrun and he had lost all his possessions. He had a Scottish plaid rug wound round his waist and fastened by a leather strap. He had an arm-chair strapped to the top of his tank and he sat there directing his men. The tank was blasted and pitted with shell holes, but Gatehouse was uninjured. All but five or six of his original Honeys had been destroyed but he had reinforcements. He had been in almost continuous action for nearly a fortnight and he was feeling good.

'You better keep close behind me,' he said, and off we went into Sidi Rezegh. The battlefield now was a scene of extraordinary desolation. Several aircraft had nose-dived into the ground and stood upended grotesquely. I recognized the one that had attacked us the previous week. About thirty Stukas and Messerschmitts had come along the British column making their slow graceful dips to the earth and

A Scottish soldier and his officer were buried together, their tin hat and balmoral hung on their upturned rifles.

shooting upward as the bombs sprang downward and burst. Then one Messerschmitt had peeled off and come after us about twenty feet above the ground machine-gunning. The air hummed and screamed with bullets. I was wearing my blue Italian sailor's jacket and I remember thinking as I pressed into a wheel rut, 'He can't help seeing me.' And as I had glanced up I had seen the white taut face of the German pilot. A young South African sergeant close to me had stood up to him with a Lewis gun and in a daze I saw the machine falter in its course, lurch to the sand and erupt into a streaming plume of black smoke. I had seen the pilot's face in the second of his death and it had showed no fear or hate or excitement— just intense concentration. Death had leapt on him too quickly to be felt. Now we passed by the blackened aircraft and the grave.

Every few hundred yards there were graves—the dead man's belt or perhaps his helmet flung down on top of the fresh earth and over it a cross made of bits of packing case: 'Cpl. John Brown. Died in Action.' Then the date. This scrawled in pencil.

LEFT: *An Australian who died in Tobruk.*

BELOW: *Every few hundred yards there were graves.*

Sometimes there were mingled German and British graves as though the men had gone down together, still locked in fighting. Sometimes the dead were laid alongside the blackened hulks of their burnt-out tanks. The tanks themselves still smouldered and smelt evilly. Their interior fittings had been dragged out like the entrails of some wounded animal, for you would see the mess boxes, the tooth brushes and blankets of the crews scattered around together with their little packets of biscuits, their water-bottles, photographs of their families, hand-grenades, webbing, tommy-guns, mirrors, brushes and all the mundane ordinary things that fill a soldier's kitbag and are a part of his life.

Empty petrol tins, the flimsy and khaki-coloured British and the stout black German ones, were scattered everywhere. Like great lizards, the broken tracks of tanks were sprawled across the sand with their teeth gaping upward. One tank newly hit was fuming and spluttering with interior explosions and every few seconds ignited Very lights would burst through the overhanging coils of black smoke. Its petrol tank crashed open in a sheet of flame. Nobody seemed to take much notice. The ground itself was criss-crossed a thousand times with the deep crenellated ruts of tanks and these, with indifference, had smashed rifles, bullets, machine-

RIGHT: *The dead lay alongside the blackened hulks of their burnt-out tanks.*

W: *The battlefield was ours; only rman helmets were left.*

guns, tins, boxes, papers and even human beings, into the mud. Muddy water was seeping steadily into shell and bomb holes. Over everything hung the same bleak winter's sky. Across this wilderness, made doubly a desert by the past week's fighting, the British tanks went forward once more.

We had barely reached the lip of the airfield when Gatehouse, still sitting in his arm-chair, suddenly swung his tank about, and began looking with his glasses towards the spot where the sun was setting among a knot of dark clouds. It was usual for the enemy to attack in the evening with the light behind them and now some eighteen or more of their tanks were coming on to our rear.

Speaking into his mouthpiece, Gatehouse turned his forces about, sending some of his Honeys out to the west, some to the north. He had with him a battery of twenty-five pounders of the Royal Horse Artillery that day and these he posted in the centre close to his own tank. The twenty-five pounder was never intended to be used as an anti-tank weapon. For one thing it is a gun-howitzer. For another it has to be towed, then uncoupled and swung about before it can be brought into action. It cannot be retired or shifted as quickly as an anti-tank gun should be. But the short range of our two-pounder gun had forced Gatehouse to bring twenty-five-pounder artillery right into the front line to cover the Honeys until they got into range.

I could just see the dark dots of the enemy tanks against the sunset light as the R.A.F. came in and laid a stick of bombs across their path. One bomb fell far short and killed one of our gunners, but his comrades worked on in the face of the enemy fire. It all happened within the space of twenty minutes. I saw two tanks ablaze on either flank and a doctor's car racing out towards them. The crews were leaping from the burning hulks like sailors leaving a sinking ship. Then the twenty-five-pounder troop posted in front got the range—three thousand yards—and the plain lit with their shell bursts. Still the Germans came on through the barrage and I heard the artillery major shorten his range down to fifteen hundred yards, then one thousand. By this time the enemy was very close, firing straight out of the battle clouds toward us. The forward artillery ceased fire, hitched up their guns and came careering back. As they came, the rear troop took up the barrage and they in their turn fought the enemy down to a thousand yards before they were forced to retire. Then again the original troop was ready to take up the fight from a position farther back. By this time our tanks were near enough to open fire from either flank and all Sidi Rezegh was raked back and forth with their shell. It was beautiful timing and wonderful coolness considering that if the enemy tanks had got through, the guns and their crews could not have escaped.

In the last light of the day the Axis tanks drew off and this time the battlefield was ours. Such skirmishes were going on at several other spots around that same flat stretch of ground which both sides had decided should be the final testing place. As I came away, I began to sense something new in the fighting. No longer

From a German Propaganda Booklet: 'English students at Cambridge under the shadow of war' . . . the German students were given leave to work.

Englische Studenten unter dem Ein-druck des Krieges in Cambridge . . .

. . . und ein Kriegsbild aus dem deutschen Heidelberg

Das deutsche Heer hat zahlreiche Studenten beurlaubt, damit sie ihr Studium in der Heimat abschlie-ßen können.

the Very lights closed around us in the darkness. The enemy opposition was getting weaker.

Freyberg meantime was reopening the way into Tobruk with the bayonet. His men had withstood two tremendous charges of tanks and anti-tank gunfire and now they were coming forward again. Far back on the frontier Sidi Omar had fallen to us. The guns of Tobruk were still spouting their barrage from the sea. It was very near the point where one side or the other must collapse through sheer exhaustion. Some five or six hundred tanks had fought one another to destruction or impotency. Just a few were left on either side. The fact was that the hard armoured coating of both armies was destroyed. The softer, slower infantry was exposed at last and left to decide the battle. The Eighth Army had come out of its mortal crisis, and had gathered its second wind. Most of its original tanks were gone. Many of its dead lay in that torn stretch of ground reaching along the coast from Tobruk to Bardia, then south along the frontier to Sidi Omar, then east to Bir Gobi and so back to Tobruk.

The first stage of the battle was over. No one could say clearly yet who had won. British, Germans and Italians lay around Tobruk too exhausted to go on, almost too tired to pick up the spoils of war. As December came in, the coldest month of the year, the semi-quiet of utter weariness had settled over the front.

13

CAIRO was going through all the spasms of despair, hope, exhilaration and back to despair again. A myopic and confused propaganda was trying to sublimate all these moods and at the same time keep track of this most incoherent of all battles. Little or nothing had been allowed out about our losses or the German gains. A new British victory had been served out to the world's press and radio each day. The breakthrough had been ignored. Newspapers were encouraged to come out with such headlines as 'Rommel Surrounded,' 'Rommel in Rout,' 'Germans desperately trying to escape British Net.'

Now, in early December, the amateurs controlling propaganda began to see what a bogey of over-optimisn they had raised. Before the battle had fairly begun they had told the world that we outnumbered the enemy in guns and tanks and so any future victory of ours had been discounted in advance and any setback made to appear doubly severe. And now all the guesses and easy prophecies were coming home to roost. People all over the world were beginning to suspect that Rommel had been overlong in a state of rout; that just possibly something had gone wrong. Each day a new estimate of the number of enemy tanks destroyed had been made and now people with mischievous minds began to add up the total and find out that each German tank appeared to have been destroyed at least twice. Somehow now the facts had to be given, and given in such a way as to maintain morale and not disturb the public's faith in the news they had already received.

The men who were in charge of propaganda had not yet graduated to the realization that the public of both America and the British Empire was quite able to accept the news of defeats and delays; what the public disliked intensely was having its hopes raised high only to be plunged into the disappointment of reality later on.

There was no need either before this campaign or any other to raise the hopes of the people. A tremendous disservice was being done to the fighting soldier. His problems and difficulties were being misunderstood. He was being applauded for victories which he had not won and his real successes were being overlooked in the backwash of disappointment and disillusion.

So now, when the Eighth Army, by a moral triumph of its general and by the fighting stamina of its men, was about to move forward to a victory, there were few to applaud, still fewer to understand how it was done. The earlier glowing heroics had soured into cynicism and boredom.

Feeling a little as though we had been cheated, Clifford and I went down to the desert again. We had to take that appalling Mersa Matruh train and it was on our first night out that we got the news of Pearl Harbor, of the *Repulse* and the *Prince of Wales* and the entry of America into the war. We set out, a caravan of three vehicles, for Gambut and the coast.

From the outset it was clear that the shape of the battle had altered. At Gambut we came on the wreckage of many Nazi planes—Stukas, Messerschmitts, Dorniers and Junkers. Then as we rode along the coast road the news came through that Tobruk was released at last. Such of the enemy who were not locked up in the Sollum area were heading westward. It was the break at last. Worn out, short of supplies and badly short of armour, Rommel was clearing out. We stopped beyond Gambut and turning off the track ran down to the sea where a German workshop had been established. The place was lying exactly as the Germans had left it when they had hurriedly turned to escape, and there in these tents and bivouacs lay the private life of an army. It was like some Doré etching of a forgotten and spellbound village, a place that reminded one of the mystery of the sailing ship, *Marie Celeste*, which was found intact upon the ocean without a man on board.

The tents were equipped with concrete floors and electric lights. They had tables and chairs, canvas baths and alarm clocks. There were tables covered with a confusion of little comforts which had apparently been issued to each man in the Afrika Korps—highly coloured boxes of bakelite filled with buttons and cotton and thread, endless bottles of mouthwash, eye lotion, body powder, toothpaste, liquid soap, water purifiers, headache powders, ointments, hair oils and shampoos, even a special chocolate that was supposed to 'pep you up' according to the label. (I tried some; nothing happened.) A year before during Wavell's advance I had seen how lavish the Italian camps and equipment were. But whereas a good deal of the Italian equipment had been showy ornament, all this stuff was ingeniously designed and must have greatly lightened the burden of living in the desert.

The Nazis had neat little cooking stoves with telescoping pots and pans and little blocks of white concentrated methylated spirit with which to boil a pot quickly and easily. They had those electric torches you pump with your hand, and varieties of camp lights and other gadgets. There were many cigarettes, many tins of British bully beef they had captured earlier in the year. The field kitchen was stocked with sacks of fresh potatoes, onions and lemons, and there was evidence they had been getting fresh meat up from Benghazi and Tripoli. In a clothing dump I came on thousands of pairs of woollen gloves and underclothing, stockings, sweaters, shirts, tunics and caps. There was no shortage of anything. It was a profusion the people of Germany had not seen for years and although much of the stuff was ersatz it was warm and well made.

The tank workshops eclipsed anything we had in the forward areas. Bedded in concrete and under canvas were big lathes and a heavy smithy. Cases of tank precision instruments worth many thousands of pounds lay about. One was full of periscopes. Several huge boxes contained new 50-millimetre guns which apparently could be fitted to damaged tanks in this place. There were sheets of armour, new tracks and tyres, a mass of woodwork and steel parts. It almost seemed that they could have built a tank here in the desert by the sea.

The richest prize was about thirty tanks of all kinds which the Germans had left lying about. These tanks had been brought in for repair and when the retreat was ordered, they had been set on fire. Some still smouldered. At the same time German officers had run down to the sea and cast many of their maps and papers into the waves. But these had been thrown up again by the high tide so that we were able to gather some of them. One was a large coloured sheet showing the uniforms of all the British forces for identification purposes. The artist had drawn his models with strong virile faces—a slight but interesting point. Unlike us, the Germans in their domestic propaganda never underrated their opponents.

In one tent we found little bags of real coffee which a soldier had been parcelling up as Christmas presents for his family at home. Clifford, of course, dived for the letters and correspondence lying about. He translated revealing extracts from the letters the men had received by a fast bi-weekly airmail from Germany. One German wife wrote: 'You must insist on leave. It has been ten months now since you were sent to the desert and others who arrived in Africa after you have had leave.' Then there were passages like this: 'We have no news of Hans, but we think he went to the Russian front. Rudolf has gone there too, and there were some others from the village whom you knew. But we have no news from any of them.' The soldiers had apparently been complaining of the conditions in the desert for there were many letters from mothers commiserating with their sons over the dust and the heat and the flies. All the letters referred to Russia and spoke hopefully of success there. For some reason the writers insisted that the fall of Leningrad had taken place. (Rommel at the height of this campaign had officially circulated the news that Moscow had fallen.)

In most of the official papers we saw that the general motive seemed to be the suggestion that the Germans on the other fronts were doing exceedingly well and that it would be a humiliating thing if they were let down by the Afrika Korps. Good propaganda that. Even units in the Afrika Korps were set against one another in friendly rivalry.

At various places in the camp stone and concrete monuments and emblems had been set up. They bore such inscriptions as 'We Germans die but never surrender.'

We loaded our truck with some of the excellent dried vegetables and fruits the Germans used and packets of rusks and black bread covered with silver paper. I picked up a couple of their tidy little green bivouac tents, and we drove on to Tobruk. As we left Bedouin were roaming through the camp, looting. A German major who had fallen asleep just before the British arrived sat miserably in the back of a truck with a guard over him. A gleam of hope had come into this officer's eyes when Clifford went up to him and spoke in German. 'You're a German, aren't you?' said the major. He hoped that he had met a fifth columnist.

It was a memorable moment driving down into Tobruk. Coming from the east, you do not see the town until you are right upon it. Then, as you wind down from the El Adem cross-roads, the scarred white village breaks suddenly into view. On this day it had the appearance of utter dreariness and monotony as though the very earth itself was tired. Every foot of dust was touched in some way by high explosive. The sand was full of shrapnel and broken bits of metal. Countless thousands of shells, bombs and bullets had fallen here among the rusting barbed wire, the dugouts and the dust-coloured trucks. You could distinguish the men of Tobruk from the other soldiers. Their clothing, their skin, and especially their faces, were stained the same colour as the earth. They moved slowly and precisely with an absolute economy of effort. They were lean and hard and their lips were drawn tightly together against the dust. They seemed to fit perfectly into the landscape and it was impossible to say whether their morale was good or bad, whether they were tired after so many months of bombing and shelling and isolation—or merely indifferent. They had become identified with their underground and dusty existence. Certainly they were not exuberant at their release—it had been too hard and grim a business for that, and the realization of it would only come after weeks or even months. The base troops were still going about their normal duties as though nothing had happened. They stood patiently in queues at the water points and the food dumps. They talked laconically about the things they had talked of for months—the weather, last night's raids, the quality of the rations. Of the high excitement and heroism that had held this place for nine months there was no sign whatever. There were no flags, no bands, no marching men. The war seemed to have reduced nearly everything to a neutral dust. Except for the lines of crosses in the cemetery and an occasional passing ambulance there was not even any suggestion of pain. Tiredness and boredom governed this place where no green thing grew, where everything had been designed for death for long over a year of warfare.

The Germans and Italians were forming a new line about forty miles farther on— the Gazala Line. We joined General Kopansky and the Polish Brigade just a few minutes before they went in to break the northern sector of this line. The Poles had burst out of their confinement in Tobruk with the exuberance of Red Indians and now, as their infantry deployed under shellfire, their Chief of Staff said to us

108

with no intention of being funny, 'It makes a nice change for the boys. A very nice change indeed.'

It did too. They went into battle as though they were buccaneers boarding a fifteenth-century galleon. Zero hour was at 3 p.m. At ten to three the barrage went over our heads on to the enemy and the anti-tank guns slid forward on either flank. At three precisely the horizon about a mile to the north-west of us suddenly sprouted a line of men and this line began to tramp forward straight into the enemy fire. Without glasses I saw the shells bursting among them and as the smoke hung on the desert for a minute you would be sure that that sector had been wiped out. But when the cloudburst cleared there they would be again—the fighting Poles, still going forward and shooting as they went. The quick staccato noise of machine-gun and tommy-gun fire came ringing along on the bleak wind as the Poles closed right in and covered the last few yards to the enemy positions with the bayonet.

On our left flank the New Zealanders and Indians were going forward as well. It was mainly an infantry fight now. That night the German Gazala Line was broken and Rommel gave up Cyrenaica. He gathered what was left of his Panzer Divisions and, abandoning Derna, Barce and Benghazi, he cleared right out for three hundred miles along the desert route south of the Green Hills. It was only fair after so many British reverses to remember that this was the second time that the Axis had bolted from the desert—their own desert.

Many Italians were left behind to be captured. I sat on Gazala cliffs that night looking down on the coast road some hundreds of feet below. Through the glasses I could see a group of British Tommies going forward on foot up the road toward a bluff that blocked their view to the west. From my perch I could see a platoon of Italians marching toward the bluff from the other side and it was obvious that they wanted to surrender.

It was like watching an early Mack Sennett comedy. The Italians and Tommies reached the bend in the road at the same moment. The Italians at once threw up their hands. The Tommies, intent on gathering some loot beside the road farther on, marched straight ahead. The Italians ran after them and threw up their hands again. The Tommies waved them away. The Italians began to argue—I longed to be closer so that this silent movie would turn itself into a talkie—and some of them threw down their guns to make their intention absolutely clear. At last one of the Tommies jerked his thumb back in the direction of the British lines. Dejectedly the Italians picked up their arms, formed into a double file and trailed off down the road again, seven soldiers in search of a captor.

The drive into Derna was like a recapitulation of a day in the Wavell advance in 1940, except that the enemy did not defend the place this time. Eight or nine German troop-carrying Junkers full of soldiers who had not yet heard the bad news came down on to Derna aerodrome just at the moment when our forward Indian platoons were occupying the place. The Indians laid low while the big planes swooped slowly round and settled into their landing. Then the Indians blew them to bits. Only two of the Junker pilots managed to get into the air again.

Then the British troops scrambled down the steep thousand-foot cliffs into Derna. Derna was still a lovely village. But in that interval between the departure of the Italians and the arrival of the British, the Arabs had cut loose. They had gone through the township looting and destroying, paying off old scores by firing the shops and warehouses. The streets were covered in broken glass. A number of British wounded lay in the hospital and the Arabs had gone shouting and looting through the wards. They set fire to the west wing of the hospital in order to obtain more light by which to loot. The sick British patients struggled out of bed and fought the fire through the night and drove the Arabs out.

When we entered the town in the morning the wounded men were lying exhausted among their dirty sheets. Some, too tired to get up, were on the floor among the puddles of water they had used to fight the fire the night before. The stench of sickness was awful.

All night these broken men had watched the hills above the town, hoping and praying that the British Army would come and rescue them. In the early morning they had given up hope. In utter weakness and despair, they had abandoned the vigil and slumped down into sick sleep or a coma that served as sleep. The major who led the first British troops into the town thumped heavily on the door of the hospital and shouted: 'Any British here?' There was no answer. The wounded prisoners lay there like cattle, uncomprehending. Some raised their heads and stared at the smart figure in the doorway and it meant nothing to them. Again the major shouted, 'Any British here?' Suddenly a young R.A.F. pilot, less badly wounded than the others, jumped up and yelled hysterically, 'It's all right. It's all right. It's all right. It's the British.'

Fresh bandages, food and doctors were rushed to the hospital.

When we captured Derna the previous year we had found wine in the town and fruit, butter, eggs and chickens. This time there was little except the good clean spring water. We stayed again in the Governor's house by the sea but it was only a shell and its polished woodwork was scarred by the boots of young Nazi soldiers. Even the banana groves and the pomegranates seemed to have gone sterile. Yet still the place was a green pool of colour in the desert and it was pleasant to walk through the shaded courts and know that the Axis soldiers had been here only a few hours before.

Beyond Derna lay Giovanni Berta, the first of the Italian settlers' villages in the Green Hills. We approached it by the back road above the cliffs. Everywhere the British Army was in hot pursuit. Columns of vehicles thirty and forty miles long were coasting along the red mud tracks and we wound on steadily up into the green slopes where flocks were grazing on the first natural grass we had seen for many months. An occasional three-engined Savoia kept darting out of the low rainclouds to spring a bomb on the long procession of British vehicles. By this time my party was reduced to the conducting officer and myself travelling in the forward car with a driver and Clifford following on behind with the truck and another driver. One of the Savoias made a dead set at Clifford on a lonely stretch of the road. We stopped our car and looked back just in time to see the big unwieldly machine leave the clouds and two black bombs leaped out of the undercarriage. Clifford and his driver were like two animated Walt Disney figures. They sprang straight out of the truck into the air and landed neatly on top of one another in the ditch beside the road. The bombs burst harmlessly a few yards away.

Up in the air sprang Clifford and his driver again in search of safer cover; and down they went again as another bomb landed beside them. Until these things turn to tragedy they seem really very funny at the front. When the bomber had gone Clifford came up and found us still laughing. He stared at us coldly.

'The frontier crouch'.

At a brigade headquarters they told us Giovanni Berta was already occupied, so we passed on to the front of the column and went ahead until we were in clear view of the sparkling white township only a mile away. A stray shell went overhead and through the glasses I could see Indian troops moving forward to a group of old Roman pillars that dominated the township on the south. There was something strange about the Indians, but I could not think for the moment what it was. They crouched as they walked. They moved up the slope with hunched-up shoulders. Where had I seen that walk before? I was still idly trying to puzzle it out as we drove up to the pillars and there was a quick urgent shout from someone— 'Get those vehicles in here. Get them in here quick.' We drove under the cover of a shed and got out in front of a bearded Indian doctor. He was saying excitedly, 'Where the hell have you come from? Down that road? There has been no vehicle along it yet—it's under fire.' So Berta had not fallen. We asked where the enemy were shooting from. 'Come on,' said the doctor. We went on foot up to the three Roman pillars. Now I remembered what it was. It was, for want of a better description, 'the frontier crouch.' Unconsciously as a man goes up toward enemy machine-gun positions he stoops and falls into a sort of animal lope. Stooping in this way we got to the crest of the rise and looked over—straight into the enemy four hundred yards away. They were on the rise of the opposite side of the valley. As we watched, British artillery raked the slope from one end to the other, and like hunted rabbits the Italians ran blindly hither and thither. Alongside me some Indians were firing mortars and shells. They made a fussy whistling and screaming, arched over the valley, and fell at the mouth of a cave where I could see a number of Italians were hiding. There seemed to be an argument going on in the mouth of the cave. One Italian was holding a white flag on a stick and the others about him kept preventing him from hoisting it aloft.

Then the Indians got the order to creep forward and take the position by assault before the darkness closed in. The British shells were landing in a regular rhythm now. It was all very confused. Machine-gun fire was snapping right along the floor of the valley. Grey ranks of Italians began to break from cover all over the place and advance toward us. They carried no white flags. They were getting nearer and nearer—only three hundred yards away now. A counter-attack then? An

Indian soldier went racing past us and an officer shouted to him in Hindustani, 'Are they counter-attacking?' The soldier shouted something over his shoulder that we interpreted to mean 'Yes', and at that we bolted down the slope. It was not until we got to the bottom that we saw the Italians coming in without their arms to surrender. It had been a nice hundred yards sprint we had done all the same.

So Berta fell, and we motored on past the villages of Savoia and Tert and on to the ruins of Cirene. Not far from this spot ten months before, we had been caught in that Italian ambush. Now we drove down the road together to the same place to get to the head of the British column. It was absorbing to see the approaches to the place again, and I was saying rather fatuously, 'It's like doing a Cook's tour of the battlefields after the war,' when Preston Grover of the Associated Press came up and said, 'You can't go any farther. There has been an ambush.' It had happened all over again in exactly the same spot except that we were not in it this time. The poor devils in the leading armoured car had been caught by cross-fire from the undergrowth.

We slept that night in an Italian hospital at the front. Its priceless equipment—surgical instruments, bandages, drugs, beds and bedding—had been strewn through the mud by looting Arabs and the rain soaked down steadily. The ambush was cleared on Christmas Eve and we drove down into Barce. This lush valley was once a thriving dairy settlement and its white homesteads and creameries were among the finest in Africa. The barren moorlands had been made to give out fruit and flowers and all the rich things of modern farming. Four armies—Graziani's, Wavell's, Rommel's and Auchinleck's—had crossed the valley in advance and retreat. They left a curse upon the place. The fences were broken and the doors of the homesteads flapped open admitting the wind and the rain. The crops grew rank and the fields were falling back into the morass of their original mud. A few settlers lingered on and they stood in their doorways staring vacantly and without comprehension. When the soldiers called to them only one or two of the younger girls answered and then automatically and without smiling. Over everything was

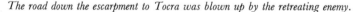

The road down the escarpment to Tocra was blown up by the retreating enemy.

that same air of neglect and decay and utter weariness. This final catastrophe in the valley was too much. Nothing here now was able to struggle against the war any more. Rain poured through the dilapidated roofs and it was no longer worth the effort to make repairs. Ploughs rusted in the fields and cattle mooed in anguish for someone to milk them. The fight to maintain civilization here was too unequal, too disappointing, too hard.

The valley was simply given up. Under our eyes the land was returning to its old sterility.

At Tocra the retreating Germans had blown away part of the cliff on to the road, so we had to spend the night at Barce. One of the correspondents had captured a couple of turkeys in the cellar of the hotel and we badly wanted to eat our Christmas dinner in Benghazi. We debated whether we would stay at the Hotel D'Italia there or one of the other places. We promised ourselves hot baths and clean sheets and some urgent shopping through the town.

Early on Christmas Day we set out. The Arabs were friendly as we ran into the suburbs and we hastened on, hoping that the best rooms in the hotels had not yet been taken by the leading British patrols. Then gradually as we drove through street after empty street, the realization came on us—Benghazi, too, had collapsed. It was no longer a city. The plague of high explosive had burst on the place and left it empty, apathetic and cold. The shops were shuttered, the markets closed and ruin succeeded ruin as we drove along. The facade of the Albergo d' Italia where we hoped to stay, bulged outward sickeningly. The Berenice by the sea, where the Luftwaffe headquarters had been, was burnt out, and all that was left inside were the cords from which the valuable silk parachutes had been cut away. Blasts had pockmarked every building, direct hits had ploughed the waterfront and dashed the anchored vessels on to the seabed. For nearly a year the R.A.F. had gone on and on, night after night, and here we were looking at the scoresheet—a ravaged, ruined city.

We found a block of flats fairly intact where two scared Christian Brothers alone remained. While I cleaned out a couple of rooms in the flat of the chief of police, three of our party went down to the Berenice which had the only decent sized stove in the town. Somehow they cleared the cinders from the kitchen, killed, plucked and cleaned the turkeys and basted them with hot fat as they sizzled on top of the stove.

We all felt so forlorn that day that we had decided to abandon any real idea of celebrating Christmas. Then in the midst of our depression everything went well. The turkeys were a miracle of tenderness and flavour—even though they had to be rushed half a mile in a truck to our flat. Out of someone's kit came Christmas puddings, brandy, wine, chocolates, raisins, and a tinned ham. Others brought more wine, whisky and liqueurs. Cigars and nuts appeared. I found a dump of Italian mineral water and Chianti and someone gave me a bag of fresh oranges.

Outside in the harbour the Germans were dropping delayed action mines. The wind leapt against the windows, and flung beams and broken bits of plaster on to streets. We were horribly dirty after the long thousand-mile journey from Cairo. But here we sat on this Christmas night eating, drinking and singing, and beyond any other Christmases it will be a time for me to remember.

Boxing Day we scoured round the desolate flats to the south of Benghazi as far as Magrun, Soluch and Beda Fomm, the scene of last winter's great battle. But the action flagged. The Axis troops had retreated fast to beyond Adjedabia and at this point we were not strong enough to harry them strongly or cut them off.

We turned to the long drive back through the rain and mud. At Bardia I paused briefly to watch de Villiers launch his assault on the Germans still holding the border positions. By the time Bardia had fallen I had reached Cairo and the second stage of the campaign was done. It was New Year's Day.

14

RAIN fell. The people in Western Cyrenaica declared they had never seen such rain before. You might have expected them to say that since the weather is always believed to be worse in war-time—probably because the people are more exposed to it. Even so this was exceptional. Day after day heavy grey stormclouds hung over the Green Hills and drenched the countryside. Great hailstones came down, an almost unprecedented thing, and away to the south near Adjedabia the front-line troops reported they had seen flakes of snow on the desert.

The rain began in the neighbourhood of Derna and beyond Derna it engulfed one village after another—Giovanni Berta and Slonta, Cirene and Barce, Tocra and Benghazi. Everywhere the troops stood about huddled in their greatcoats and every spare bit of clothing they could lay hands upon. Some protected their faces with woollen balaclava helmets; others draped captured bivouac tents about their shoulders and went foraging through the deserted houses in search of firewood.

Convoys of motor vehicles crawled along the roads to the front, with painful, agonizing slowness—the slowness that Lord Milne meant when he spoke of war as consisting of short periods of intense fear and long periods of intense boredom. They started out from the dry desert of Egypt and made an immense and dusty tour around the Halfaya positions where the enemy garrison was still holding out. When they regained the road again in Libya they ran into the rain and the cold. The roads were jammed. For hours the vehicles stood still, thousands of vehicles, and there was nothing to do but sit and wait in the pouring rain for the blockage to be cleared. Wherever the enemy had blown the road engineers and road gangs worked in the knee-deep red mud easing the vehicles through one by one over temporary bridges and half-finished by-passes. No one on the road had any news. No one seemed to know what was going on at the front. The journey from Cairo lengthened from four days to a week to two weeks and still the front line lay somewhere out in the remote and elusive horizon of the wet desert.

Near Tocra, where the plateau suddenly spills into broken hills and cliffs, the vehicles were being pushed along by hand over a dangerous blowout. It was no use going round. We tried it. We drove for hours along a sodden track and every so often our big station wagon would pitch and slither into the green underbrush, and we had to tug and heave until we got it out again. The country here behind Barce still held enemy refugees and wandering Bedouin but the war had driven them into the cover of the hills. Even above Barce itself where the enemy

Convoys moved with agonising slowness through the knee-deep mud.

had hastily thrown up a series of tank ditches and side roads, the war had forced the people away. Farmhouses, orchards, cattle, sheep, crops—everything—were abandoned to the rain and the mud and the invader.

In the desert south of Benghazi it was far worse. Red mud stretched interminably across the dreary landscape. I went out to the airfields of Berka and Benina—those two key fields that were going to be the springboards of our next great air sweep through to Tripoli. Inch by inch the grounded enemy aircraft were sinking into the mud. There were scores of aircraft, all useless. Those which had not been wrecked or broken up at the last minute by the Luftwaffe were falling to pieces in the wind. The rain did the rest. All morning I splashed through the muck and wet, and it seemed to me then that no aircraft would use these fields for weeks to come.

A Valentine tank badly bogged in a soft salt flat near the coast.

As though to prove it, a light British reconnaissance plane came down. It bucked and bounced away as it touched down. The wheels skidded madly, flinging the wet earth over the fuselage, and the machine finally came to rest in a pond. There it stayed immovable; after that no aircraft attempted to take off or land.

It was the same at Barce and Maraua, at Magrun and Soluch. Only Msus was left as the one available field in the forward area that could be used. There was no question of supplying the troops by air, even if we had the transport planes, which we hadn't.

But it was vital to get supplies to the troops. So long as this problem was unsolved, everything else had no importance. The British tried the sea. They loaded ships in Port Said, in Alexandria, Mersa Matruh and Tobruk and set sail for Benghazi. Given Benghazi as a port the rest became fairly easy. But Benghazi could not be used as a port. Within an hour of my first going into the town on the heels of the leading patrols, it was being bombed and mined. When I came away it was still being bombed and mined. The Germans came over in waves from Sicily. Their mines lay on the seabed in the narrow confines of the harbour and there was no equipment to deal with them, no means of spotting where the danger lay. U-boats lay in wait outside. The docks and the railways leading to the docks were a chaos of exploded stone and steel and concrete. There were no lighters to take off the cargoes, no cranes to lift the boxes of ammunition, no pumps to draw off the petrol from the tankers. A tangle of wrecked steamers blocked the channel through the bay. Benghazi was no use. Only the land route was left. And the land route was choked.

The Eighth Army was like a healthy plant that had suddenly been denied water. The young leaves at the top suffered first. Around Adjedabia the troops first went short of tinned fruit and vegetables, then jam and cheese. Finally they had bully beef, biscuits and tea, and not much else. Little by little all the supplies fell away. Petrol was the most serious. The men could keep going on bully and biscuits, but until the petrol came they were unable to move. All over the desert I saw parties out scouring for enemy fuel dumps. Squadrons of new tanks which had toiled all the way by train and road to the front found they could do nothing.

For hundreds of miles isolated groups of men were strung across the wet desert with no orders and no notion of what to do. The sap was being drained out of the Eighth Army, not by the enemy, for Rommel had withdrawn around the Gulf of Sirte, but by the desert and the weather and the distance.

The ancient law of the desert was, in fact, coming into play. Once more the British had proved that you can conquer Cyrenaica. Now unwillingly they began to prove that you cannot go on. It had been the same for both sides. Tripoli and Cairo were equidistant from Cyrenaica. The enemy had shown that he was capable of sallying out of Tripoli, of crossing Cyrenaica and digging his nose into the Egyptian desert. But there he stopped. And now coming in the reverse direction, here were we stopped at Adjedabia. The trouble was that the farther you got away from your base, the nearer the retreating enemy got to his. Consequently as you got weaker, the enemy got stronger.

Four trusted and able generals had tried to disprove that rule. In the summer of 1940 the Italian, Graziani, had advanced as far as Sidi Barrani in Egypt, and there he stuck. In the following winter Wavell had driven through to Adjedabia and he could do no more. In a few days Rommel had reconquered all that lost Axis territory, but he, too, collapsed in exhaustion at the Egyptian border. Now, finally, Auchinleck had swung the see-saw back the other way and his army was already floundering in the mud.

Auchinleck would not give up. Despite everything he was determined to go on to Tripoli. While still the rain swept across the Cyrenaican waste through the early days of January he kept pushing his generals to make haste. They must get Benghazi open. They must clear the roads. They must speed the unloading at Suez. There was no fighting to speak of—just the long dreary struggle against inefficiency and delay in the great problem of supply.

The most urgent thing, of course, was to wipe out the enemy garrison at Halfaya. It was blocking the coast road and putting an extra one or two days on the journey from the Nile Delta to the front. Bardia had fallen on New Year's Day after a brief struggle, but still the enemy gunners were able to lob shells on the coast road from Halfaya. At last, in the middle of January, Halfaya fell and the route was clear right through to Benghazi.

The news was received in Cairo with a good deal of exitement and pleasure. Now all Cyrenaica was in our hands and the fall of Bardia and Halfaya had yielded us 13,500 prisoners, as well as a large quantity of war material. A rough check showed that in all the enemy had suffered somewhat less than fifty thousand casualties. Clearly it was a victory. The conquered territory and the long lines of prisoners were there for anyone to see. But still there remained the fact that the bulk of Rommel's army had escaped clean out of Cyrenaica and even in retreat it had made many sudden and damaging forays against our vanguard. And still the rain came down in the desert.

Rain never really falls on Cairo. The place is bathed in perpetual sunshine and at this time of the year it is just strong enough to take the chill out of the air and make the climate ideal. Men back on leave flooded the bars and clubs of the city. The movies were crammed. There was no shortage of anything. Prices were leaping up but then the men in the desert had nothing to spend their money

General Gott being driven round Benghazi by General Jock Campbell V.C.

on except their leave. Cairo was gay and secure. Each day at the Turf Club I used to see the ticker machines typing out the non-committal news from the front. It seemed to be a stalemate, nothing more. There was no need to worry. The breaking open of the bottleneck at Halfaya had released many damaged tanks and vehicles and these were being hurried back to the delta workshops as fast as possible. There were hundreds of tanks in the workshops. Soon all these would be ready for the great new drive on to Tripoli. True, there was a good deal of stuff now being diverted from the Middle East to Singapore and Java and India, but still new American aircraft were arriving for duty in the desert. It was machines we wanted, not men. Just a few more machines and we would be set to go again.

Only very few in the High Command saw the dangers ahead. I lunched one day with Auchinleck and afterwards, as we walked back and forth through his rose garden, he traced the history of the campaign for me step by step. He made me see how much he had been compelled by events to do what he did do, how impatiently and emphatically he had urged his men on to certain courses of action only to find that they were baulked or diverted by the weather or by some move of the enemy or some mechanical thing that happened unexpectedly. He revealed how often a general has to shift his ground and change his orders because the situation is never static. He saw the mistakes all too clearly. I found him modest and direct and extraordinarily clear-sighted that day. He had no rosy pictures of the future. There was his determination to go forward at all costs and he clung to that through all the fog of mishaps and delays and setbacks that were constantly going on. This was his one hour of leisure through the day and he kept pacing back and forth hunting for new ideas, rearranging the old ones, analysing and comparing the things that had happened.

Nor did Gott or Willoughby Norrie, the two most active generals in the field, seem to me to be particularly confident. Norrie, in fact, was hurrying down to the front, for already there were signs that things were going wrong. Gott turned over to me his maps and papers on the campaign at his Cairo headquarters. He said that he wanted me to use them in the writing of this book and I found them fascinating. He emphasized the necessity for good supply, the necessity for always keeping your supply line in the desert at a right angle to your front so that it would present the smallest possible target and ensure the quickest delivery.

All Gott's theories on supply were being ignored at that very moment. This was not so because the men in command were ignorant or pigheaded. It was happening because the Eighth Army was simply incapable of overcoming the physical difficulties of distance and time. It was too far away from its base. Nor was there cynicism in the ranks about the generals. Gott in particular was loved. I had seen him in Benghazi just a few days previously. He had come in from the front, dirty, unwashed and tired. He drove through the shattered streets to the hospital which was still intact and full of British wounded who had been left there by the retreating enemy. As I stood in the doorway I heard the whisper go round the ward, a filthy evil-smelling place, that Gott was coming in. And with him was Jock Campbell. Gott and Campbell together were a remarkable sight, both of them very tall and heavily built, both soldiers who fought at the front alongside their men, both, as far as one could guess, indifferent to any form of high explosive. The sick men heaved themselves up on their elbows and grinned as the two leaders went down the ward. It was, in some ways, a pathetic little thing, that currrent of enthusiasm that swept through the hospital and I do not know why I remember it so clearly. Still, there it was—the men still had their leaders and they were willing to fight their way on to Tripoli if they could get there.

The trouble was that they could not even get to the front. As one vital day succeeded another the most the British could get into the Adjedabia region was two brigades. A full brigade of new Valentine tanks had arrived in Suez and these, after a painful journey, did reach the firing-line in addition to the other two brigades. The 4th Indian Division was posted as a garrison for Benghazi, and scattered back along the recent battlefields were South Africans, British, New Zealanders, Poles and Fighting French—about five small divisions in all. They could hardly be called a co-ordinated force. They sprawled across 300 or 400 miles of desert and only that small group around Adjedabia was in actual contact with the enemy.

There was another and entirely separate British force—the Long Range Desert Group. Their numbers were so tiny that they could never seriously affect any

The Long Range Desert Group; their safety was the vastness of the desert.

TOP: *On a clear hot morning the LRDG set out.*
Often they had to dig their vehicles out of the soft sand.

Petrol was calculated to the last spoonful.

battle one way or another. Yet their exploits about this time had become so famous and they were so successful that they were a factor in the fighting. The Long Range Desert Group was a collection of young men of the commando type. They were volunteers and trained men. They had their headquarters in the caves of Siwa Oasis and from there they used to set out on incredible journeys many hundreds of miles inside enemy territory. Their safety was the vastness of the desert. They struck unexpectedly by night and got away.

Their leader at this time was a young New Zealand major, whom I had met at Siwa one day when one of the most daring raids was being carried out. Just a handful of men had set out in ordinary army trucks. They had measured out their water and petrol to the last spoonful. Every spare pound of weight had been given to machine-guns and bullets, grenades and flares and dynamite. On a clear hot morning they set out into that part of the southern desert where no one, not even the Bedouin, ever penetrates. For many thousands of square miles the country has

The LRDG ate on their feet.

been scorched into a useless waste, entirely waterless. For the first few hundred miles they knew they were safe enough. No enemy patrol would venture down there, no aircraft was likely to reconnoitre so far south.

As usual they rationed themselves to a cup of tea in the morning and another at night. Another cupful of water was enough for washing. They did not shave but instead grew beards that matted with fine dust as they went along. They travelled slowly—on the good stretches about ten or twelve miles an hour. Often they would have to get down and dig their vehicles out of the sand. One or two of the trucks broke down and, since to abandon the trucks would mean abandoning their crews to death through thirst, the whole caravan waited until repairs were made. Inch by inch and remote from all the world they edged their way across the map. There were no tracks in this desolation and they were guided by compass.

Five days out they came on their objective—a secret Axis airfield, so far behind the front that the usual guards were not stationed around it. Leaving their trucks a few hours' drive away, the men went forward afoot to reconnoitre. Creeping over the sand in the half-light of the evening, the saw a squadron of German bombers lying dispersed near a group of tents. Many camouflaged vehicles were standing around and there were dumps of petrol and bombs spread about near the aircraft. Everything depended on their taking the place by complete surprise.

That night they attacked. Some ran to the German mess tents and sprayed the enemy officers with tommy-gun fire. Others attacked the aircraft with crowbars and hand-grenades. They smashed the instruments in the cockpits and set fire to the fuselage. One after another the petrol dumps went up. It was very quickly done. The Germans ran wildly about among their tents not knowing from what quarter they were being attacked or by how many. Machine-gun bullets were spitting across the airfield from a dozen different directions at once.

As soon as the enemy aircraftsmen ran across to one fire, another started somewhere else. Flares went up over the weird scene and in the yellow light men fought one another with pistols and bayonets. When most of the aircraft were smashed and confusion in the camp was complete, the British commander drew off his men. Driving several prisoners before them, they tramped off to their trucks and drove at full speed into the empty desert. It had been a heady and exciting night, brilliantly successful, but there still remained the long journey back to the British lines.

Enemy aircraft picked up the British car tracks the next morning. They were bombed that day and again the next and again after that. But somehow all came back. Incredibly dirty, tired and dishevelled, they drove into their base bringing their prisoners with them.

There were many raids like this. Sometimes several occurred at the same time. Through the winter they had paved the way for a strong British column that crossed the desert to the tiny oasis of Jalo not far from Adjedabia, and in the middle of January Jalo was still in our hands.

All this time Rommel had been planning his counter-attack. It was not done quickly. Among the marshes of the Gulf of Sirte coastline, near El Agheila, he decided to make his stand and prepare. Tanks, guns and men were sent across to him from Italy. Some were landed on the beaches close to the front. Others were dropped off at Tripoli and brought around the coast road. Rommel was only two days' hard drive over a good road from his supply centre at Tripoli and every kind of material began flowing up to him at a time when the supplies in the British frontline were running short.

In the middle of January, he began with a series of flanking raids on the British vanguard. These were not serious affairs but they gave Rommel the information he wanted and they forced the British to keep using their ammunition and fuel. Soon he felt strong enough to attack. His air reconnaissance had shown him the disposition and size of the British frontline. He knew that if he could once get through the front he could fan out inside the British line and create havoc among the soft transport on the supply lines inside. Beyond that lay Benghazi, and Benghazi never was defensible. Neither side had ever attempted to use it as a battleground. The sea-cliffs receded at this point of the coast leaving the town on an open exposed plain. The roads leading northward up the cliffs are bottlenecks and so make retreat difficult. Rommel had abandoned Benghazi on his retreat, and given a first success he could reasonably expect to retake it now.

There is not much to tell. In open pitched battle the heavier German tanks fell on the Valentines near Adjedabia. Some of the Valentines ran out of petrol before they were engaged or had to be abandoned on the battlefield. Others lost contact with the supporting anti-tank guns and so faced the German barrage alone. Others again were lost because the Germans overran the British petrol and ammunition dumps.

Communications seem to have failed badly almost from the first moment. Hard-pressed infantry could not get support and reinforcements either lay idle

The desert railroad was pushed ahead at the rate of a mile a day.

or when they attempted to reach the threatened quarter found their path blocked by the enemy. In three strong columns then the Axis forces streamed straight into the British lines. They fanned out and it was the same old story—isolated British groups being mopped up one after another. In two days the British cutting edge was gone. In three days the British advance had definitely turned into a retreat.

One after another the bases south of Benghazi fell—Adjedabia, Saunu, Antelat, Soluch, Ghemines. There remained only the important operational point at Msus where the British had built up their main supplies. After a confused series of skirmishes Msus fell and then there was no hope for Benghazi. The British garrison had to act quickly. Demolition squads set to work on all those priceless supplies which had been dragged with such pain and difficulty to the town. Once more Benghazi was ringed with fires at night and big explosions towered up from the cliffs. Two of the Indian brigades were safely got back up the coast road in the Green Hills. A third brigade was cut off in the Benghazi area. It was a bad moment.

When Rommel had driven Wavell out of western Cyrenaica a year before he had ignored the coastal route and cut straight across the desert to Mekili south of Derna. This time he ignored the desert route and instead cut the road leading out of Benghazi. The commander of the trapped Indian brigade rose to the crisis and provided the only really satisfactory British action in the whole engagement. He fought his way out of the German ring. He not only fought his way out but he gathered a number of prisoners and brought them with him.

After that some order was got into the British retreat. A defensive line was thrown up at Gazala, reinforcements were hurried with the hurry of desperation from Egypt and the retreat was ended. For many days after, well into February,

The lifeline to Malta; a convoy which got through.

British troops kept drifting back to the Gazala Line from Benghazi and all that area we had held so flimsily and vainly for a few weeks.

This, then, was the bitter end to the winter campaign that was to have carried us to Tripoli. On balance we still had the advantage—we had relieved Tobruk, we had destroyed one Axis tank force and taken a respectable number of prisoners. And we had conquered half Cyrenaica. But still it seemed an inconclusive and unsatisfactory end to the adventure, and one could not avoid the conclusion that there had been a straight fight and the Axis Army was better than the British Army. There were no tricks, no great inequality in numbers, no exceptional runs of luck, and no surpassing genius anywhere. The cold fact was that somehow the British had to build a better army. And build it quickly. In the meantime it was a stalemate. The Axis forces were as exhausted as were the British. Too weak to strike, they stood watching one another warily across the Gazala Line while they gathered their strengths again. They were to stay like that until high summer.

15

In February Singapore and then Rangoon fell, and I was sent off to India to report on the situation there, and on the Stafford Cripps' mission. It was not until May that I got back to Cairo.

The desert baked in the midsummer sun. For fourteen hours every day the sun sat there in an unclouded sky, and long after nightfall the rocks were still warm to touch. The nights were too short to bring much relief from the glaring heat and it seemed that one day followed another almost without interruption. When the soldier woke in the early morning the sun was in his face and long before the day was over he was longing for the moment when it would go and the night close over. The sandstorms always stopped in the evenings. Sometimes a light dew fell and a man waking in the night would feel a cool dampness soaking his sleeping-bag on the sand. By the sea a light breeze sprang up occasionally and it was like taking a long, cool drink. The troops sat in the open turrets of their tanks and let the breeze go over their dark, leathery-skinned faces. Inevitably one man fried an egg on the

Malta was the most bombed place on earth.

In Valetta Queen Victoria sits untouched among the ruins.

blistering steel roof of his tank in order to prove something that everyone knew well enough—that the metal was too hot to touch.

It had been argued that these were no conditions in which to fight a campaign; that white troops could not endure the strain of fighting in such weather and that the atmosphere inside the tanks would be unendurable. There was the question of water, too—men and machines would require much more water in summer, more water than could be supplied.

It needed only one short trip into the desert to prove that all this was nonsense. Both sides were preparing for offensive on a scale that had never been seen in the desert before. They were amassing such numbers of tanks as had never been used up to now on any sector of the Russian front. Both Germans and British were standing up to the heat without any great difficulty. As the summer advanced the men became leaner and harder and browner, but they ate and slept just as well and moved and thought just as quickly.

In the long desperate race to pile up arms and men on the front line, it was hard to say which side was winning. Certainly the Germans and the Italians had all the advantages. Whereas they could bring a tank into the desert within one month of leaving its workshop in Europe, it took the British three months or more to get the same vehicle across from England or America. In two days Rommel could summon aircraft from Germany and Italy.

Ever since February this race to reinforce had been going on, and the history of what was to come was being written along the supply lines from Naples to Tripoli and from Liverpool to Suez. And the greatest of the battles for supply fell upon the island of Malta. This was turned now into a hell. Malta was a base for British submarines and aircraft preying on the Axis lines of supply to Libya. In the spring of 1942 the Axis decided to obliterate that base and they wanted to starve it as well. Right through the spring they turned such a blitz upon Malta as no other island or city had seen in the war. It was a siege of annihilation. One after another all the other great sieges were eclipsed—England and Odessa, Sebastopol and Tobruk. Malta became the most bombed place on earth.

Then one day a few Spitfires put down in the island. More followed. They had been flown in from aircraft carriers, notably the American *Wasp*. A few hours later the German raiders began coming over on their usual run. Suddenly they found the sky filled with the deadliest fighters in the Allied air armament. There was a ferocious burst of fighting in the sky. The Maltese and the British garrison, grateful beyond measure, saw some thirty Axis machines crash into the sea in the ensuing twenty-four hours. The *Wasp* sailed up the Mediterranean again and flew off more Spitfires piloted by men who had met the Germans over England, and Churchill wirelessed the American commander jubilantly, 'Who says a wasp can't sting twice?'

For the time being it was the turning-point in the air war over Malta. From that day until these Spitfires were themselves demolished, the enemy attack on the island weakened.

But sieges are negative. The object of Rommel's Malta blitz was to prevent the British operating out of there to raid the supply fleets going to Tripoli. It is certainly probable that he intended to invade the island as well, had he been able further to reduce it from the air, but the main thing was to get his guns and men across to North Africa. The blitz enabled him to do that.

On their side the Allies were making an even greater effort in the race for supply. They had a twelve-thousand-mile journey with their reinforcements around the Cape of Good Hope from England and America. They had to cope with a bottleneck at Suez where the bulk of the labour was native and the docking and railroad facilities inadequate. Then there was the long route out to the desert.

A procession of camouflaged trucks three hundred miles long was again strung out down the coast road from the delta to the front line. It was a remarkable thing to see. Penetrating a little inland one day I came on the advance guard of the water

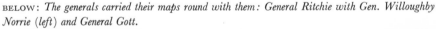

BELOW: *The generals carried their maps round with them: General Ritchie with Gen. Willoughby Norrie (left) and General Gott.*

pipe-line and railroad builders. Indians and South Africans were doing their jobs. They were pushing the railroad ahead at the rate of over a mile a day. Trucks dragged the rails over the sand to the head of the track. There was little or no bridge or embankment building. The ground was simply levelled off by the Indians and the rails fitted together. Every so often a whistle would blow and the men ran and flung themselves on the sand as enemy bombers came over. The railhead especially was under fire. Soon the line had breasted the escarpment, had cut through the frontier fence into Libya near Capuzzo, and had reached the outskirts of Tobruk itself. Every day long lines of tanks on flat cars went chugging up to the front. Soon, too, we had fresh Nile water in Tobruk. Steamers and destroyers were still making that hellish run from Alexandria to the desert front line with explosives, food and men. By the middle of May we were actually in a better condition to get local supplies than the enemy, since Cairo was only half the distance to the front that Tripoli was, and Tobruk, our forward base, was much nearer the front than Benghazi. Such convenience had its dangers too.

There was no doubt whatever in Cairo now that a battle was coming. Officers who usually drifted around the Turf Club and the sporting club on Gezira Island began to disappear. There were fewer and fewer troops in the crowded streets of the city. In the desert the rawest private was convinced that the lull would not last —heat or no heat. A curious air of expectancy and excitement hung over the front line. Discipline of its own accord became much better as it usually does when men are near danger.

On a featureless stretch of tussocky plain called Gambut, Lieutenant-General Neil Ritchie, the British commander, pitched his camp. So many cars laden with generals and liaison officers kept driving into the camp that soon its tracks were knee-deep in fine dust. The main British fighter base lay just across the main road and all day aircraft were overhead bringing in new supplies. At night an occasional

Luftwaffe squadron went hedge-hopping over the camp and everyone jumped for their slit trenches.

Ritchie had under him two lieutenant-generals, each commanding an army corps: Gott and Willoughby Norrie. With Auchinleck in Cairo, these three, all physically big men, all in their early middle age, all regular soldiers, hatched a new scheme of defence between them. Gott and Norrie, covered with dust, would drive up in their jeeps and disappear inside a yellow wooden caravan with Ritchie, and there they would confer for hours on end. Except for their scarlet tabs and capbands, the generals wore the same uniform as everyone else in the army—boots, knee-length socks, khaki shorts and "bush jackets", which are open-necked, belted shirts worn outside the shorts like a tunic. They carried large boards on which maps were spread and covered with sheets of talc. Most staff officers went about armed with these maps and bundles of coloured pencils with which to mark the disposition of the armies. Most officers for some psychological reason preferred to mark in the German forces with black and the British with red.

Looking back now I see how much those little red and black marks entered into our consciousness. How vital they were. How many hundreds of times did we drive up to a headquarters in the desert and cluster round the intelligence officer and his map. One glance told you roughly how things were going. You got to know the important spots in the line. If you saw the black marks on the map had moved eastward, you knew things were going badly. Sometimes with a leap of interest in the mind, we saw a new red mark far out in the desert behind the enemy lines—and knew that we had made a sudden unexpected push. Sometimes we stood round while the radio reports came in from the different sectors of the line and we watched tensely while the intelligence officer marked up his map accordingly. We took compass bearings on those little map marks. We altered our journeys according to how those marks went back and forth. And, as with everyone else, our lives often depended on those marks being accurate.

As we entered the third week in May, the conferences of the generals became more frequent and the red marks on their maps assumed a more and more definite form—the Gazala Line.

Somehow, without being dreary, I must describe the idea and the structure of the Gazala Line, because its design had an influence on a good deal of the open fighting in the war. Allied officers from other fronts were sent to study it on the spot.

Up to this date neither side had ever established a line in the desert which was defensible. The trouble was that while you could always base a line securely on the sea at its northern end, inevitably the southern end finished in the empty desert. Always the enemy could drive around the southern end of the line and attack the defenders from the rear as well as the front. General Wavell had taught the Axis that. And it was Wavell who had said to me in New Delhi only a few weeks before this 'Yes, I think that Gazala is just about the natural balance in the desert'. It was roughly in the centre of Cyrenaica, and whatever army crossed this point was looking for trouble.

Ritchie and his two lieutenant-generals decided to drop the idea of having a continuous chain of defences at Gazala. They decided to define their position with a solid minefield stretching about thirty-five miles from the sea southward into the desert but they did not man the minefield. Instead they sealed up their troops in or behind the minefield in a series of isolated forts or 'boxes'. These boxes faced four-

128

General Messervy, bearded.

square, ready to meet attack from any direction. It was the old idea of the British square at Waterloo, adapted to modern fast armoured fighting. Each box was completely surrounded with a ring of landmines and barbed wire. Guns faced outwards in all directions. The boxes were only a mile or two square at the most, and were provided with water, food and ammunition to withstand a siege. Narrow lanes led in through the mines and wire so that the garrison could be supplied.

The underlying idea was this—the Nazi tanks were at liberty to by-pass or surround these sealed-up boxes and seize all the rest of the Gazala area if they so desired—it was just empty desert anyway. But they could not proceed far lest the British should sally out of their boxes and take them in the exposed rear or flank. Moreover, the British tanks were kept fluid outside these boxes and were in a position not only to attack the enemy in the open whenever they wanted, but also to go to the assistance of any box that was hardly pressed.

There were half a dozen or more of these boxes manned by as wide a collection of Allied troops as ever entered the desert. The main boxes were at Gazala on the sea (South Africans); at a point a few miles just south of them (northern Englishmen from the Tees and the Tyne rivers); at Knightsbridge, in the centre (English guardsmen); at Bir Hacheim, in the extreme south (French); at El Adem, in the rear centre (Indians); and there was the big box of Tobruk itself (South Africans and English base troops).

Roaming about between these positions were three large new British tank brigades and attendant guns, all under the command of Major-General Messervy, who had taken over when Major-General Jock Campbell was killed. Messervy had done well as an infantry divisional commander in the winter campaign, but he had yet to prove himself with armour.

There were two great secrets about the British armour. One was the American Grant tank. The other was the British six-pounder anti-tank gun. The Germans suspected that we had something new, but they did not know exactly what or how much. The important thing about the Grant was that it was the first Allied tank to appear in the desert with as big a gun as the German tanks had—75-millimetre. The important thing about the six-pounder anti-tank weapon was that it could shoot faster and better than any anti-tank guns we had had previously. Elaborate camouflage and deception were used to get these weapons off the ships at Suez and into the desert without detection. The only trouble was that we did not have enough of them. The majority of our tanks were still British Valentines, Crusaders and American Honeys, mounting a two-pounder gun, and most of the anti-tank guns were the ordinary two-pounder.

As for the men on the British side, they were an odd mixture. The South Africans up in the north were led by Major-General Dan Pienaar, a lean grey wolf of a man who had come through many battles in the last war. He used to sit in his iron-roofed dugout high on Gazala cliffs above the sea and look sourly across the strip of desert where the Germans and Italians were hiding. From his headquarters one day I saw clearly a line of Axis trucks going along toward the coast. No one fired. It was one of those days when a strange lull came to the front, when no shot was fired, when the tens of thousands of men simply lay on the desert and waited—idly and un-questioningly and with patience since they knew they would have action soon enough.

Now and then the most forward boxes exchanged a shot or two with the enemy. For half an hour perhaps the shells would come over with that rhythmic and rising whine and erupt violently in the sand. Once or twice in the course of a morning Stuka dive-bombers stood high in the clear sky, then dipped their noses for the long singing slant toward earth that always ends with the graceful lift upward at the last moment and the shattering crash of the bomb below. Always somewhere out in the minefields at night there would be the distant shots of a patrol in search of prisoners and information—shots that sounded faintly and were soon over and meant nothing to the thousands of waiting men who were not directly concerned.

But the tension was there. It could be sensed right along the line. The men always knew when something was about to happen. You could tell of the tension perhaps from the way some boy from the veldt fingered his sticky bomb in a slit trench: from the marks on the map: from the rich and fruity voice of some English north countryman saying, 'Reckon it won't be long now': from the tanks that were steaming everywhere like battle fleets on the move across the horizon and the hurrying trucks raising lines of dust like the smoke-screen of a destroyer at sea: from some chance remark—or some silence—of an intelligence officer: from the calculated casualness of the guards officers' conversation as they sat round their vehicles taking a nip of whisky before getting to bed. Everywhere in many thous-ands the men lay in their boxes waiting for the battle.

Most of the activity was along the lines of supply and on the airfields. The British had decided to tighten up the co-operation between the army and the air force—a thing at which the Germans had excelled since the invasion of France when tanks were directed from aircraft and had their way paved by dive-bombing. Air Marshal Coningham, who lived at Gambut with General Ritchie, had given orders to his pilots that they were to avoid independent aerial combat if possible and concentrate upon giving support to the ground forces. Thus if a flight of British Hurricanes on a sweep saw a group of Stukas dive-bombing our men they were to concentrate on the Stukas and try to avoid the Axis fighter screen overhead. Whole squadrons and fighters were to be held ready to go to the assistance of any hard-pressed sector of the line.

As yet Coningham had no Spitfires to speak of, but he was soundly reinforced in light bombers, especially the American Bostons, and he still had his Kittyhawks,

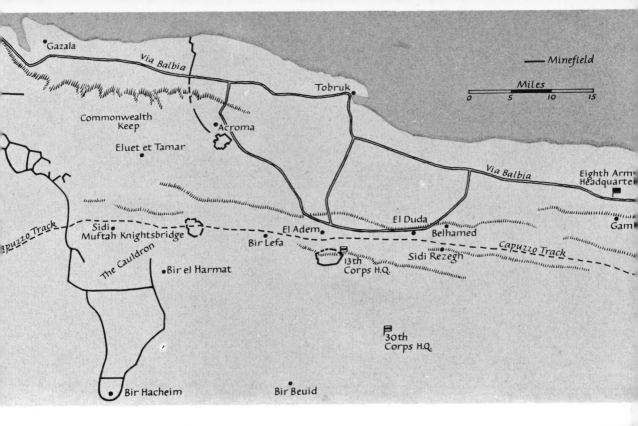

THE GAZALA LINE—MAY 1942

Beaufighters, Blenheims, Marylands, Wellingtons and the rest. A few Hurricanes had been equipped as dive-bombers. We were probably outnumbered in the air, but not by much.

Looking at it generally then, we had a few new cards to play and a sound position to start from. Coming out of one of his conferences Gott said, 'There are two places where I would like to meet the German tanks—either on the minefields or here'— and he indicated a spot on the map near Knightsbridge. He was confident. Right through the army the morale was good.

Over on the Axis side there was tremendous activity. Every day our patrols brought in reports of some new troop movement, of some great convoy of hundreds vehicles driving down to the front-line bases from the coast. There was also news that the Germans were training parachute and commando troops at Bomba. A general order went out through the British Army instructing all men to be on the look-out for parachute troops and special guards were to patrol all camps through the night. No one liked the idea of suddenly being taken in the rear.

But Rommel had much bigger fish to fry than parachutists. He had brought a great host with him into the desert. There were elements of eight Italian divisions— the Sabrata, Brescia, Pavia, Trieste, Bologna, Trento, Littorio and Ariete. The last two were armoured. There were the three German divisions of the Afrika Korps— the 90th Light Infantry and the 15th and 21st Armoured Panzer Divisions.

Most of these units had been brought up to strength since the winter campaign. Unlike the British, there was nothing especially new about the Axis equipment. Again they had their Mark III tank with the 50-millimetre gun (the Mark IV had a 75-millimetre); and there were Italian tanks like the L6 and MB. The most import-

131

ant thing was that large numbers of the mobile 88-millimetre all-purpose gun, both those made in Italy and Germany, had been brought in. This was the gun that was to dominate the battle.

In the air the enemy had the Messerschmitt 109F, still the fastest fighter in the desert, and the usual Stukas and Junkers bombers and troop-carriers. The Italians had the three-motored Savoia bomber and a considerable increase in the numbers of their fast Macchi fighters. Rommel, now a Marshal, was again in command and his immediate juniors were Generals Nehring and Cruewell. Marshal Kesselring was in charge of the Luftwaffe. Colonel Marx was also coming into prominence as a leader of the 90th Light.

In all then, you might estimate that each side had about ten divisions comprising roughly 130,000 men and 500 effective tanks, and their guns and air forces were fairly evenly matched in quantity. The surprising thing was that two great powers should have so nicely balanced themselves at this remote end of the long front line that now stretched from Murmansk in Russia to Gazala in Egypt.

As with us Rommel was keeping his tanks fluid somewhere about the north centre of his line until March 26th when he swung them south, leaving behind their camouflage to trick us (as it did). The Italians mostly were used as positional troops; the Germans as a striking force. The area over which the two armies were about to fight was about as large as the home counties of England, but it was nothing more than a wide, almost featureless, strip of land and rock. There was an occasional low ridge pitted with camel thorn, an occasional cairn of stones casually thrown up by passing Bedouin pilgrims, and for the rest it was arid, limitless desert as empty as the sea—and as dangerous. Gazala had just one dilapidated Italian roadhouse— and no other building.

Travelling westwards along the coast road you recognized Gazala at once, because there was a deserted airfield on your left, with broken aircraft lying about, and beyond that the sea swept into a narrow bay. At the end of the bay the road led across a flat scrub-covered plain, and after that you were in the cliffs of Gazala itself. They came so close to the seashore the road had barely room to squeeze past. A crazy and dangerous side track led up to the top of the cliffs, where there was a superb view along the sweep of coast back to Tobruk.

As a fighting arena the desert is superb. You get there as close to a straight out trial of strength as you will on any battle-front on earth. Gazala and all the thousands of miles of desert around it were not of the slightest value to either the British or the Germans. They simply chanced to meet on that spot as haphazardly as a hunter will meet his quarry in a forest. Neither side came into the desert for conquest or loot, but simply for battle. It would have mattered nothing to the British if the Germans had suddenly decided to seize a thousand square miles of desert to the south; or even if they had occupied the whole of North Africa. Provided that the British Eighth Army was still in existence at Gazala, the Germans could not hope to hold this territory. But once the Eighth Army was defeated, or even just the tanks of the Eighth Army were demolished, then not only Tobruk but the Nile Delta as well was laid open to the Germans.

It was a battle staged and announced with all the technique of an opera season and the approaching zero hour had all the studied drama of an opening night. On this tiny spot on the African map the future of the whole continent was being decided. As the month moved into its final week it was clear to everyone that the

The German mobile all-purpose gun dominated the battle.

time was running out. An overture was already sounding in a sudden burst of heavy bombing. A bright full moon came up and through its clear fresh light the German raiders went rushing over the tents of the British camps. They pelted the roadways with machine-gun fire. They dived on to the airfields where the British aircraft lay dispersed about the sand. No one could sleep very well.

Early on the morning of May 26th a British tank commander saw through his glasses an unusual pillar of dust going up from the south of Bir Hacheim. Straining his eyes through the early morning haze he saw the dust cloud deepen and expand. Little black dots were spaced along the bottom of the cloud. 'Looks like a brigade of Jerry tanks coming,' he reported over his telephone to his headquarters. He looked again and added sharply, 'It's more than a brigade. It's the whole bloody Afrika Korps.' The battle had begun.

Just a handful of British tanks under this commander took the first German rush. The British tanks outside Bir Hacheim were too weak to fight a delaying action. They were too late to get clear away. So they went forward over the uneven rock and sand to accept their destruction and all the desert from one end of the Gazala Line to the other erupted into an earthquake of shelling, bombing, flame and dust. One after another the British boxes reported they were engaged. From a hundred concealed crannies in the rocks the Italians unloosed their artillery on the South Africans and the British in the north. Stukas rode over the barrage, bombing and fighting. On the ground Italian infantrymen picked their way through the mine-fields and rushed the British outposts on the western rim of the box. The South African machine-gunners began the killing they had awaited for months. All through the morning while the artillery came in to swell the uproar, they went on killing men. It was the same at Bir Hacheim. The French slammed the doors of their box and opened up with every gun into the pall of dust that kept swirling around them.

For an hour or two there was much confusion. Many little pockets of British troops and unarmed convoys travelling through the open desert were swept up by the German host. No one knew exactly where the enemy was attacking or with what force. One after another the British boxes sealed themselves up and simply gave battle at anything they could see. The British tanks meanwhile went rushing south-wards toward Knightsbridge and the Capuzzo track where the main German thrust seemed to be developing. But there was no point of the battle zone that did not rock with gunfire or lie at times under the wrenching explosion of bombs.

By midday it was obvious that the Axis was sending its main force round the open desert south of Bir Hacheim and directing it north-eastwards into the midst of the region of British boxes. At least four hundred tanks and guns had come charging round behind our positions. All that afternoon and far into the moonlit night one small British tank force accepted the full tide of the enemy armour. Yard by yard it was forced to give ground, leaving behind the burning wrecks of its tanks and many of its men in death and imprisonment.

All that night and again next morning the main bulk of the British armour raced to get into position while still the enemy drove on. By the second evening the battle began to take shape. Rommel had done a bold thing. He had flung his men broad-cast into the heart of the British positions in an attempt to take Tobruk itself by storm—and at once. It was learned from prisoners and documents that he planned to have Tobruk not later than May 30th—five days from the opening of the campaign. His four or five columns had spread out like the fingers of a man's hand. The hand reached upwards clutching at Tobruk from the south. One small Nazi tank force on the extreme left had travelled right up inside the Gazala Line and reached the coast where a group of light coastal vessels coming from Derna had arrived to supply them on the beaches. Another column on the extreme right had gone off, more as a stunt than anything, to El Gobi, the scene of the previous winter's battle. A third column under Marx was more enterprising still. Striking north-east straight past El Adem it had arrived on the high ground to the east of Tobruk perimeter and occupied the vitally important ground at El Duda and Sidi Rezegh. The main part of the Axis forces—the armoured Panzer divisions and their two Italian tank satellites—had stayed in the centre near Knightsbridge in order to meet and destroy the British armour there before advancing on Tobruk. The enemy seemed to be swarming everywhere. They drove through the night shooting out Very lights, banging their guns off to make as much uproar as possible and give the impression of great strength. Even at Gambut Ritchie's headquarters were threatened. Tobruk and El Adem were forced to lock themselves in. The firing sounded from every direction in the desert and by night Axis aircraft were all over the clear sky. The fingers of the hand were beginning to tighten their grip. It was a brilliant opening.

The battle of the tanks: the new British anti-tank guns score direct hits.

It was as though a gang of thugs had invaded a house and were prowling through the passageways, while the inmates had locked themselves in their rooms. And as the intruders pummelled at the doors and the windows, it was a moment of high nervous strain for the householder and his family.

Then the British armour gave battle. The American Grants flung off their camouflage and went into action for the first time. The anti-tank guns came out of hiding. About Knightsbridge and the Capuzzo track the Nazi Panzer Divisions waited to receive them. The Germans knew the British tank tactics well enough— the headlong charge to get into range, the flanking movements. They waited confidently behind their big guns, ready to break up the first onset by picking off the British vehicles one by one. But the charge never came. Instead the British tanks deployed—one group to either flank, one to the centre. Then they settled into positions, hull down on the horizon. There was a moment of puzzling silence. Then a volcanic burst of armour-piercing shell ripped through the leading Nazi tanks. Then another burst and another—big 75-millimetre shells with instantaneous fuses kept falling from a distance that was almost beyond the Germans own range. The British anti-tank guns, the new guns, opened up with an aching, sickening barrage. All this was something quite new. It staggered the Germans for a while. The fluid fast-moving tank movement of the winter had been turned into an artillery duel. The Polka had become a Minuet.

Frantic appeals went back over the Nazi radio for reinforcements in 88-millimetre guns. Because they had no choice, the Nazis rushed their tanks into hull-down positions and settled into a steady answering fire. It was anti-tank guns and tanks firing together now from fixed positions. The 88-millimetre and the Mark IV against the American Grant and the six-pounder. It was almost static battle. The opponents at two thousand yards' distance or more could just see one another as

135

dark dots on the horizon, and all the intervening space was filled with the crash of shells and dust and the rising flames and smoke of the vehicles that had been hit. Both sides sent in their bombers to augment the wreckage and confusion. Soon there were broken tanks and guns on every side. Some tanks were merely put out of action by a broken track or a jammed gun. Some blew up. Some were grotesquely upended by the force of the shell that struck them. Ambulance men rushed blindly into the chaos and the burning, and were themselves hit as they tried to get the wounded away. Recovery vehicles came forward to rescue the stranded guns and vehicles and were smashed, even before they could get their cranes working.

The battle broke into parts and spread north and south of Capuzzo track. It rolled uncontrollably across the sand and wherever they could the lighter British tanks nipped in among the fire of the leviathans and cast out their two-pounder shell at close range.

Since the Germans were attacking and their most forward infantry troops were every hour in more urgent need of support, they had to go forward. They could not afford at this stage to fight it out shot for shot with the British in a slow-moving artillery duel. Again and again Rommel sent his men forward on to the British steel. It was the Germans who were charging now and the cost to both sides was appalling. One by one the Grants were knocked out but more and more Valentines and Honeys came in with artillery support to take up the fight against an enemy who was tiring.

Nor was the news any better for the Germans from the other sectors. The tanks that had crept up behind Gazala on the coast had been driven out. The supply barges had either been sunk off the shore or forced to turn back. The Knightsbridge box, the hub of the whole battle, was withstanding every infantry attack. Up on El Duda, Colonel Marx was exposed and alone and British forces were hurrying to deal with him. It was essential for the German armour to push forward if he was going to survive.

While the tank duel still dragged on, Rommel ordered an all-out offensive against Knightsbridge. If Knightsbridge fell he could reasonably hope to hold his positions and make good the awful damage his tanks were receiving. The 90th Light combined with Italian infantrymen, tanks, artillery and dive-bombers fell upon the box in a series of massed attacks from all sides. An immense battle-cloud rolled across the Capuzzo track and the whole area was enveloped in continuous sandstorms. In this unreal gloom the men fought. The Stukas came back again and again. The enemy artillery got on to the box from several sides at once and there was hardly a yard in the target area that was not ripped and ravaged with high explosive. In regular waves the German and Italian infantry came on, right up to the minefields and there they broke, divided and fell back. It was Waterloo over again.

The English Guards with their strange and slightly automaton code of behaviour were peculiarly suited to this sort of action. It was something they understood. A position was given you to fortify and then you got the order to hold it to the last round and the last man. It was simply a matter of progressing to that final point, unless of course, the enemy got tired first. One simply had to remain there firing through the dust and something or other would come out of the muddle. Whether or not the ground was wisely chosen, whether or not victory or disaster emerged from the struggle was not the essential point. The essential thing was that the

Guards had been given this piece of ground to hold and the reputation of the regiment required that it should not be given up until the regiment was wiped out or got the order to retire.

So these odd gawky officers with their prickly moustachios, their little military affectations, their high-pitched voices and their little jokes from the world of Mayfair and Ascot kept bringing their men up to the enemy, and the men, because they were the picked soldiers of the regular army and native Englishmen and Scots, did exactly as they were told. Knightsbridge did not break because it could not break. It stood through this maelstrom as a rock will stand against the sea.

Rommel gave up. It was no good: he could not go on. His tanks were getting nowhere. There were horrible losses on each side, somewhat more on the British than the German. Left in an impossible position without support or supplies, Colonel Marx evacuated El Duda in the night. From either side of Tobruk the enemy fell back toward the centre. Their blitz had exhausted itself like a spent rocket. Even at this stage things could have been retrieved if Knightsbridge had fallen, but Knightsbridge did not fall. And all night and all day the R.A.F. kept bombing, bombing, bombing.

Rommel now ordered a general retirement. It was impossible for him to get his whole army round the long route past Bir Hacheim—the British were marauding down there anyway. Some shorter route had to be found. He ordered the retreat on to the centre part of the Gazala Line. He ordered his engineers to cut a passage through the British mines so that the Axis Army could escape westwards. Mile by mile the Germans fell back. They left Sidi Rezegh. They by-passed El Adem. They came back from the coast near Tobruk. The battle-weary defenders of the British boxes and the tired tank crews suddenly found themselves disengaged. They still waited doggedly at their positions for they had not yet guessed the extent of the enemy withdrawal and they expected renewed attacks. Nor did the British leaders realize how thoroughly they had cut down Rommel in his stride. In that confusion and high tension it was difficult for anyone to see ahead and understand that a victory had been won.

Disheartened, bewildered and partly disordered the Germans and Italians struggled back over the sand toward the rallying point in the centre and the 88-millimetre guns kept up a ferocious rearguard action. They ringed the retreating men with steel and managed to get most of them under cover. Wrecked German vehicles and guns were left in dozens on the battlefield. First one gap, then two were made in the minefields and the survivors began to straggle out to the west.

This was the position after the first five days when I arrived at the front. The British, though still badly shaken, were just beginning to realize that they had, in fact, a victory on their hands. The German claws had been laid round them and now the fingers were relaxing their grip and drawing away. A signal came from Auchinleck: 'Well done, Eighth Army.' There was an air of exhilaration and excitement in Gambut Camp.

My first concern was to get to Knightsbridge where the fighting was still swirling about uncertainly. No one seemed to know clearly what was going to happen, so we drove first to Gott's headquarters near El Adem. Indian soldiers were dug closely into the wadis about the cliff as we turned in through the one narrow entrance between the minefields.

A light screen of armoured cars and anti-tank guns was placed round the box and the men were standing ready for action, since there were still numbers of enemy about and Messerschmitts were constantly coming over. Three huge steel-plated vehicles were dispersed under camouflage nets in the wadis. They looked like those big trucks that ply the roads between London and the north of England through the night. In one was the operational staff—the men who actually plan and direct the tactics. In the second vehicle, the signallers were at work. In the third was the Intelligence staff and they were the people we wanted to see. The truck was fitted as an office. It was a maze of telephone lines and switchboards, of radios, maps, codes, typewriters, telephones and papers. A 'blower' in one corner kept broadcasting the voices of men tuning in with information from the forward units—information not secret enough or too urgent to be put into code and sent by dispatch rider. Jeeps were buzzing about outside carrying liaison officers to different parts of the front. They were easily the most successful staff cars either side used in the desert.

Colonel Desmond Young, commanding officer of the Indian Army Public Relations Unit, was standing outside the intelligence vehicle and from him I got my first indication that something was going wrong. He had come straight from the battle an hour before and like everyone else he was cheerful about what had been done. There was no doubt about it, the Nazis were on the run.

'But,' Desmond kept saying, 'I don't understand why we aren't following up. We will have to move quick or you can bet your life they will reform a line. I can't understand it. I am only afraid that it is already too late.'

He had raised the point that was going to make many a bitter argument in the days to come. Our armour was temporarily weakened but all the other positions held. Could not the South Africans and the English have come out of their positions in Gazala and burst along the coast? They would have outflanked the partly disorganized enemy in the centre, and cut him off from his supplies. They were eager to do it. The 50th Division were, in fact, to show later how well it could be done. But today they rested in their positions. The Indian division got no orders to close upon the Knightsbridge area in force. Only light skirmishes occurred on the battlefield. The Axis, meantime, regrouped.

We slept that night among the rocks of El Adem. We were a big party with three vehicles; each of us found a deep grave and spread out his bed on the bottom of it. There was no great danger of our being hit by bombs in the night, but we found we slept better when we knew we were secure. The drivers brewed one of our famous stews and with a mug of whisky and water apiece we sat around it for hours in the darkness talking. Such nights were an enduring pleasure. The endless space of the desert made men turn to one another for company, and the sense of danger brought warmth and raciness to their talk. Every so often our conversation would pause and we listened to the sound of bombers low overhead or saw in the distance sudden yellow flares go up on the horizon. Atmospherically these moments had the flavour of a boy's adventure yarn.

It was midnight when we crawled into our sleeping-bags among the yellow rocks. I woke at 2 a.m. to find our little valley bright with yellow light and the sky above full of the noise of Junker bombers. One of their flares drifted like a chandelier across the dark rim of the escarpment and hung gently above us. I saw the others leaning on their elbows and watching and waiting for the inevitable sequel. But the bombs, when they fell, landed far off on the airport and we drifted into sleep again.

Wreck of a German Mark IV tank.

In the morning we drove on down the Capuzzo track toward Knightsbridge. All through the first hour we passed through the recent battlefield and it looked good at first. Many Mark III and Mark IV tanks lay about, interspersed with the damaged hulks of our own Grants and Valentines, and upturned guns and trucks of both sides.

The thing that made Clifford and me enthusiastic was the recovery that was going on. Huge tank transporters, the largest vehicles in the desert, were bounding over the tracks. Gangs were hoisting the tanks, both German and British, on to the trailers. We stopped and talked to one of the tank crews that had just come out of battle with a jammed gun. They said that a number of defects were showing up in the Grant. The tracks were somewhat vulnerable. The precision instruments were not so good as the British, the big gun did not always eject the shell promptly and

Recovery vehicles came right into the middle of the battle to retrieve their tanks.

'Lord love you, what a job she is'. Shells had not been able to penetrate the armour of this Grant tank.

the vehicle's aeroplane engine was still a little weak for the weight of the tank on heavy sand. Those were some of the teething troubles. 'But, Lord love you, what a job she is,' said the driver, 'and that gun there is a wizard. There's nothing wrong with the armour either. Take a look at that (a couple of jagged scratches on the turret) and that (a dent like a hoof print on the front) and that (a line of shrapnel holes through the rubber treads of the port track). Everyone of them is a direct hit from a Jerry Mark IV.'

They were going back now to collect another tank and get into the battle again. The place where they got their new tank was a square half-mile of desert covered with vehicles that had been wrecked in the battle. I crawled over many of the damaged tanks and talked to the crews. They were all delighted with the Grants, delighted with the sweetness with which the big brutes crawled over the sand. For the first time they felt they had an instrument in their hands which was the equal of anything the Germans could bring against them. The pity was that there were not more of them.

Much that the Germans had taught us about recovery in the winter campaign had been learned and improved upon. Each British armoured brigade had its own recovery unit and mobile workshops. The transporters were going right into the battle to lug out the disabled vehicles. At this forward workshop those tanks which could be repaired within three days were handled and sent straight back into the fight again with their old crews. The others more badly damaged were sent back to a desert tank hospital or to the railhead near Tobruk and thence the trains carried them to the Nile Delta where practically any job could be undertaken. New tanks were coming up all the time from Cairo and being manned near the front. In this way a constant stream of damaged tanks was coming out of battle and new and repaired ones going in again. It was the blood-stream of the armour, the thing that could turn defeat into victory.

Firing was now sounding intermittently from the direction of Knightsbridge and we hurried on—on into the most painfully memorable sandstorm of my experience. I do not think I can improve on the description of this day as I find it in my notes written on the spot when the dust was still in my eyes and my mind full of hate for the desert and all its parts:

'It had to come. Everyone knew that. Millions of tank and tire treads have ground the thin crust on top of the sand into loose powder. When a hot strong wind blew from the south yesterday morning, everyone got ready. At midday the visibility was fifty yards with occasional clear patches. At 14.00 hours it was twenty yards; at 16.00 for a good part of the time it was nil.

'Except for a little shelling and one or two skirmishes the two armies lost contact with one another. Germans and Englishmen may have lain a hundred yards apart and never have known it. Tanks that could have blown one another to bits passed by within easy range since the crews were blinded and their hearing numbed. Occasionally, when the sand lifted for a minute or two, the machine-gunners blazed away at one another, but then the pall fell again and the bullets spent themselves uselessly in space.

'I drove out toward the central front from General Gott's headquarters hoping to see something of the battle west of Knightsbridge. For the first hour it was not bad . . . just a matter of coasting along through the foot-deep dust of Capuzzo track. Weird shapes came out of the dust that was now rising half a mile in the air. It was like moving at sea through a heavy fog, except that the shapes which lunged up at you suddenly were five-ton lorry convoys, twenty-five-pounder guns, and tank recovery vehicles.

'We threaded through last week's battlefield where mingled derelict British and German tanks lay in the positions where they had been blasted to a standstill. We fouled a slit trench. Then, reversing, we swerved madly at the last second to avoid an armoured car that towered out of the gloom.

'My conducting officer had his head poked through the roof of our truck all this time. He was on the look-out for the Stukas which had been blitzing this track for the past five days. They dive on you from behind and you have to keep watching. But no Stuka could live in this storm and the officer drew his head in. His face was like sandpaper, his eyes bloodshot, and his fine military moustache, soaked with sand, looked like a piece of wet flannel.

'Each one of us—every man in the desert in fact—looked like a clown with red-rimmed eyes peering through faces daubed with sand and with lines of sweat running down our cheeks.

'Toward Knightsbridge a line of smashed German tanks showed where British mines had been strewn. And here the storm touched its height. Vivid, lovely colours filled the air according to how the sand thickened or thinned under successive gusts of wind. Sometimes it was pink, sometimes bright orange, then greys and whitish greys strengthening again into orange.

'A towel wound round his face up to his goggled eyes, a military policeman guided us through the mines into Knightsbridge. At walking pace we felt our way toward the brigadier's dugout. This dugout was straight "Journey's End". Six officers crouched there just below ground level, and their equipment was a couple of field telephones and not much else. It was impossible to eat; at times even difficult to talk as the sand drove clean through the dugout. It coated the maps so thickly in dust that you had to brush your hand across the paper to read it. "We're shelling when we can, but God knows what we're hitting," they told us, and like noises off-stage in a stage play, the guns sounded to the left.

'From somewhere out in no-man's-land one of the company commanders was shouting through the telephone, "There's something ahead of us, but we don't know what it is."

'"How do you know it's there?" shouted the brigadier.

'"Because," answered the voice, "every time I shove my head out of this hole I get a burst of machine-gun fire."

'On the other telephone the brigade major was saying to another advanced platoon leader: "No. Tell them to stay out there and push on if they possibly can. It's no use their trying to come back here for lunch and tea and all the rest of it—we haven't got any anyway."

'These men were Guardsmen, members of the oldest families in England. The brigadier is one of the wealthiest men in the army out here. All of us sat there with just one overriding idea apart from the battle—what would it be like to have a glass of cool, sand-free water?

'These were the soldiers who took the first shock of the German offensive. They held Knightsbridge for days while it was isolated, and in the end Knightsbridge—it bears this name, but really it's only just another bit of empty desert—has become the linchpin of the whole battle. The fighting keeps swirling around it and always the Germans know that at any moment the Guardsmen may sally out through their minefields and take them in the rear. The best thing I know to say about these men is that they are no longer amateurs, no longer a group of civilians turned soldier. They are professionals.

'Out in the sandstorm again a Guardsman told us the way through the minefields to one of the British armoured brigades we had been trying to catch for the past two days. The brigade was temporarily held down by the storm only a mile or two away and we set off. I walked in front of the vehicles as it was impossible now to see anything through the windscreens. The sand stung one's bare knees as though they were plunged suddenly in very hot water. We followed a pipe-line and skirted a minefield, keeping just two yards off from the tripwire. Other travellers called to us through the storm asking directions—Indians, South Africans, Tommies—but we could not help. Sometimes, unable to see anything or even think very clearly, I was forced to stop and stand for ten minutes. After a mile or two we gave it up. I am no desert expert, but I defy anyone to find anything in such a storm when even an oil compass plays tricks. I crawled back into the leading car gasping for breath—as all the others were.

'Even though our second vehicle kept three yards behind us and we made only three miles an hour, we lost it on the long return journey. It's no joke losing anyone in this area which can be overrun by the enemy at an hour's notice.

'It was not until nearly 21.00 hours when the sun, coloured pale ice-blue by the sand, was setting that the storm began to die down. One by one the things around us took shape and as visibility extended from a hundred to five hundred yards the desert began to take on its normal contours again. The whole landscape looked worn out and utterly desolate after this hateful day. In a few hours the wrecks of many vehicles have been half buried in the sand and new dunes and ridges have appeared. On the battlefield all the broken relics of the fighting have been covered over.

'Both sides suppose that the storm has been of advantage to themselves. Certainly

General Cruewell, sad prisoner in Cairo.

it has helped in giving cover to troops going to new positions. But I doubt if either side really benefits. The war simply has been made tougher and more of a trial of endurance than it was. If victory comes it will have been earned as much against the weather and the desert as against the Germans.'

It was Chester Morrison and his driver who were in the lost vehicle, and we were additionally worried about them because a scare had been raised at El Adem. We were told that the entrance had to be mined and closed immediately. The enemy were reported three miles away. Any vehicles that were going in had to do so immediately. What to do? Go inside and get locked up there for days possibly, while the enemy milled around? Stay where we were? It was out of the question to go looking for the other vehicle at night.

Chester solved it all by turning up at dusk and we ran down to the sea to eat and sleep and wash the dirt out of our ears. At headquarters next day there was still an astonishing absence of news. The situation was tense. It *felt* as though we were on the edge of a considerable victory. Yet there was no real news. We drove back then into the battle area and this time there was a real scare. In the late afternoon the firing sounded clearly about ten miles away—it was another of these indeterminate skirmishes that seemed to go on and on without getting anywhere. We decided to bed down for the night. The trucks were unpacked, the beds set up beside slit trenches and a stew put on to boil. Meanwhile the sound of firing was increasing. A few bursts of shellfire leaped up on the western horizon. This was between El Adem and Knightsbridge and we had judged ourselves reasonably secure for the night. But here were all the old ominous signs again—trucks racing through our camp, the increasing sound of shellfire. The vehicles broke over the horizon first

143

in pairs, then in dozens, then in scores. We had been long enough in the desert to understand.

We packed up swiftly, bolted down the stew and set off for the coast. Half-way there it grew dark and there were extraordinary sights in the desert. The coloured Very lights of the enemy kept bursting up from the east and, nearer at hand, the retreating British lorries were running on to minefields. Soon half a dozen lorries were blazing around us and we ourselves were not at all too sure of our direction.

Suddenly in the darkness I heard wood splintering under the wheels of my truck and caught a glimpse of a wire fence. I expect we all had the same sickening feeling at once—'mines'. We stopped and peered out. We were in the middle of a front-line cemetery. Broken white crosses lay under the wheels and farther back we could hear the other truck blundering into other graves. Feeling guilty and confused, we got out somehow and reached the road leading down to Tobruk.

Tobruk was in an uproar. Axis bombers were coming over dropping flares and from all the perimeter the tracer bullets were arching upwards in cascades of red light. In thousands the little red balls crawled lazily upwards or got lost in a confusion of explosive bursts. On the ground the gun flashes and the gun noise mingled with the light and the explosion of the falling bombs. It was a heavy raid and it went on for hours. To the west the artillery kept up a barrage through the night.

There was no peace anywhere around Tobruk. We camped one night six miles away by the sea; the enemy planes kept passing only a few hundred feet over our heads. A wall of ack-ack was going up from the port. One enemy pilot lost either his direction or his nerve or both, and dropped his flares directly over our tiny camp. It was as though one had suddenly been stripped naked. Every morsel of sand seemed to stand out in the blinding light. Then a stray bomber came and while we flung ourselves from our beds to the ground, we heard the whistle of the bombs leaving the bomb racks. They erupted mountainously five hundred yards away, and the earth wrenched and shuddered all around us.

Frank Gervasi, of *Collier's Magazine*, had now joined our party with another vehicle and with him we toured back and forth along the line trying to clarify the battle in our heads. Little by little, we began to realize what had happened. The chance of annihilating the Axis army on the minefields—if the chance ever existed —had gone. Whether through the lack of foresight, the poorness of communications or the insufficiency, or the combination of these things, our troops had failed to press on the heels of the enemy. He had halted his movement westwards. He had destroyed the minefields in the centre of the Gazala Line and the gaps, which he had made for his retreat, were now being used to bring in supplies. The Axis troops lay wedged in a solid block in the centre of the minefields and it seemed we were powerless to shift them. Attacks were sent in from the north, south and east separately, in stages, and at once. It made no difference. In these few vital days Rommel had had time to build a line and behind a ring of steel he was regrouping.

Someone, without much originality, had called this central area 'The Devil's Cauldron' and the name stuck. The R.A.F. Bostons pounded the Cauldron right through the daylight hours. The British artillery got on to it. The infantry charged its flanks at night. There was some bloody and desperate fighting. One of our best tank commanders was lost and many of his tanks with him. Now it was the British who were trying to attack, and again and again they ran upon those deadly 88-millimetre guns which Rommel had posted right round his precarious position.

It was about this stage that General Cruewell, hastening to the front in a Storch communication plane, was forced down into the minefields and brought in. His dead pilot's blood was still splashed on his boots when I saw him at Gambut. But the capture of a senior genior general was not going to make much difference either way at this moment. The two armies had got themselves inextricably mixed up and every day that went by was to the advantage of the Germans. Soon they had transformed a very precarious position into a fortress. Our mobile patrols acting on the lines of communication to the west could not do much. It was a deadlock. Tobruk for the time being was saved. It was useless to lament that we had not pushed our victory home when we had the chance. The thing now was to devise a new offensive before the Germans were strong enough to launch one.

From now on it was almost entirely a matter of reorganization and speed in everything. It was not a question of some general devising a brilliant scheme. On neither side had any real originality been shown. The tactics Rommel used were simply those employed by Wavell eighteen months earlier when we went round one enemy position after another. All that Rommel planned to do had been anticipated by the British and they had defeated him—or at least thwarted him. And now the British were quite powerless to initiate any new plan to shake the enemy from his positions. It was a matter of discipline, of the sticking power of the ordinary soldier, of the quality and number of weapons; or, in other words, of the whole system and construction of the armies. The army that was best trained and equipped was the one which was going to break this deadlock to its advantage. The situation required not so much a brilliant general as a large number of soundly trained young officers and N.C.O.s. Provided that he did nothing glaringly stupid, a very average general could have led the best trained army successfully out of this mess. Conversely, a very brilliant general could not have got a victory out of the army which was the more poorly equipped and officered. So now that the surprise elements were gone, the possible tactics exhausted, the morale about evenly

The Fighting French; there was a touch of Verdun about Bir Hacheim.

matched and both sides clutched at one another like tired wrestlers in a close
embrace, it remained to be seen which was the better army.

16

GENERAL KOENIG, a dark sallow-faced man wearing his blue and red kepi and the
cross of Lorraine, got word in the first days of June that the name of his Frenchmen
was to be changed. There were no longer the Free French. They were to be called
the Fighting French . . . La France Combattante.

His French, indeed, had need of all their fighting now. They had come down
here to this box at Bir Hacheim in the early spring and they were a very mixed
collection. Some, like Koenig himself, had been named by the Vichy Government
and declared traitors. All of them had been outlawed by France and dispossessed
of their property, their titles and their citizen rights. They were rebels and could be
shot if captured.

They had come together from the strangest places. Some had drifted in from
French Indo-China in the wake of General Catroux. Some had escaped in boats
from France, sailing northwards to England and southwards to Algiers and
Morocco. Some had come up from the Congo jungles in the south, or enlisted in
Syria and Egypt, some had got away from the Balkans or crossed from America.
There were regular soldiers and diplomats, Spahis and sapiers-pompiers, business
men and Foreign Legionaires, sailors and farmers, black and white. For the past
two years there had always been a couple of companies of Free French somewhere
near the fighting in the Middle East, but they were never in enough numbers to be
of much consequence and somehow they fitted oddly into the picture—strangers in
an Empire war.

But now in Bir Hacheim there was a full brigade of Fighting Frenchmen equipped like any other British brigade with anti-tank guns and twenty-five-pounders,
Bren guns and Bofors and good supplies of water, food and ammunition. They were
in the most exposed and isolated sector of the front. And, looking out from the bare
hot ridge where his troops were lying, Koenig saw that his position was no longer
only dangerous—it was critical. Rommel once more was going to attack.

The plans of the enemy were all too obvious. They were wedged solidly now in
the centre of the Gazala Line, cutting Bir Hacheim off from the British positions to
the north. They had repaired a great number of their tanks and guns and brought
up new ones. Their infantry was rested. Since the British had failed to dislodge
them and they had turned a difficult defensive position into a striking base, there
was no reason why they should not return to their original plans for the quick conquest of Tobruk. And the first step in that direction was the obliteration of the
Fighting French at Bir Hacheim. Once Bir Hacheim fell, Rommel could claim all
the desert south of Tobruk, he could speed his communications and remove the
threat to his right flank. He could make the whole Gazala Line untenable.

In the first week of June Rommel flung the full weight of his striking force on to
Bir Hacheim. It was apple-pie for the Stukas. They came over in batches of thirty
146

and forty from the first daylight hour and shattered the ridge from one end to the other. Koenig called for the R.A.F. He added that the enemy were creeping round him to the east and that he would soon be cut off unless something was done. The Hurricanes and Kittyhawks went out in force, for there is nothing in the sky so helpless as a Stuka once the fighters are around. The R.A.F. caught one batch just as they were about to bomb. There was havoc over Bir Hacheim. Frenchmen, lifting their grinning faces up from the slit trenches, counted ten, fifteen, twenty, twenty-two machines with the black German cross go spinning into the sand and burst. Right round the garrison black plumes of smoke stood up. Koenig radioed delightedly, 'Merci pour la R.A.F.,' and the R.A.F., equally pleased, signalled him in reply, 'Merci à vous pour le sport.' From that moment the R.A.F. took the Frenchmen under their wing. There was always a bomber or a fighter squadron somewhere over Bir Hacheim. But it was not enough. The German infantry crept closer and closer up to the French outposts—little groups of machine-gunners dug into the sand in the outer minefields. The Nazi 88-millimetre guns got the range and the ridge came under a bombardment that continued through the night, and grew heavier every day as more and more guns came up to strengthen the enemy infantry. Repeatedly Ritchie enquired from his Gambut headquarters, "Are you all right? How are you getting on now?" From the battle Koenig answered, 'All right. All right for the time being. But we shall need more supplies.' All his guns were in operation. The gunners were reporting they had only a few days' supplies left.

Ritchie sent down a convoy with twenty thousand rounds of Bofors ammunition. It got through. The next day the Germans attacked again. They were putting in staggered attacks that came at first from the south, then the north, then the west. Again Ritchie sent out a convoy and gave it a tank screen. There was bitter skirmishing on the route, but some of the heavily laden lorries got in. After that it was hopeless. Rommel shifted his armour right round Bir Hacheim. The garrison was cut off. The enemy now was intent on two things—to starve the defenders and keep them continually awake with a non-stop bombardment. Lack of food and sleep were the things that broke men's morale.

There were two women in the garrison. They had gone down to drive staff cars and act as secretaries. Now they became nurses and stretcher bearers, and they were all day and night among the mounting wounded. They cooked and served meals to release extra men for the front. Soon both food and medical supplies began to run out. There were no more such delicacies as coffee and that soup they used to prepare from the desert snails. It was biscuits, bully-beef and sometimes tea. The men in the outposts went for whole days without anything at all.

The R.A.F. made one more effort. Back near the Egyptian border the ground crews worked all night stowing supplies into Bombay troop carriers. Again and again the Bombays ran across Bir Hacheim in the darkness and parachuted down drugs and bandages, spare parts and petrol, bullets and grenades. But you cannot supply a brigade with a handful of Bombays. A good deal of the stuff was smashed or lost in landing. At the end of ten days the garrison was in a desperate position. Burning vehicles studded the ridge. There was no part of that ground that had not been pitted with shell and bomb holes. All night the bombardment went on and the enemy ring closed tighter and tighter. The rest of Ritchie's men hacking and thrusting at other sectors of the line to relieve the pressure on the garrison could still make no headway.

In this crisis there was revived spontaneously in the desert all the spirit of the French soldier in the last war. In its small way there was a touch of Verdun about Bir Hacheim. As the Guards had fought with stubborn discipline at Knightsbridge, so now the French fought with art and desperate comradeship and were gallant in their own way. All the bitter accusations against the French soldier after the fall of France were being denied and proved false under this little tricolour that kept hanging in dusty folds on the ridge of Bir Hacheim. Wherever you went in the desert, you found the rest of the men of the Eighth Army full of glowing pride for the French.

Twice the Germans swarmed over the outer garrison defences in the north-west. Twice the French swept them out with the hand-grenade and the machine-gun. But there were ten Germans to every Frenchman and the same defenders could not go on forever meeting fresh men and fresh guns. They wanted sleep, some pause. They never got a pause.

All this time the South Africans were held practically idle in Gazala. At no time apparently did Ritchie feel strong enough to risk getting them out of their fortified positions and sending them into attack on the enemy flank. In the end this may have been the deciding point and by June 11th it was all over. Koenig, without stores, without reinforcements, without much hope, reported he could not do more and he was ordered to come out.

This was Rommel's third demand to General Koenig to surrender Bir Hacheim.

At least three times through the battle the Germans had sent in officers with white flags to demand Koenig's surrender and had been contemptuously refused. They had even resorted to such tricks as sending out false instructions on the radio ordering him to capitulate. Even now Koenig would not surrender. On the night of June 11th, he began firing his remaining dumps and stores, and gathering his men into a closer ring. They hung on somehow through the 12th, and that night they boarded their trucks and set course north-eastwards to fight their way out. A rearguard was left behind on the ridge with the most badly wounded. They wrecked the remaining arms and covered the retreat.

Through the night there was bitter skirmishing. But the French now put forth their final effort. It was each man for himself and, with all the hate and desperation of soldiers in battle against odds, they ran upon the Germans in the darkness. It was a matter of the bayonet and the rifle now. And since the French were prepared to accept immediate death to get through and commit any risk, the enemy gave way in confusion before them. Koenig came out at the head of his Fighting Frenchmen and the next day was safe inside the British lines. It was a tired and shaken group of Axis soldiers who went in to occupy the barren waste on the ridge.

Bir Hacheim had been an epic struggle and the results of this defeat were great. The Gazala Line was cut in half. The British defensive position in front of Tobruk now resembled a big quadrilateral with Tobruk, Gazala, Knightsbridge and El Adem at the corners—and not a very good position at that. Still there remained the British armour. So long as that was in being, Rommel could not get through. Against this armour Rommel now sent every tank he could summon into battle.

The Germans drove forward in a great wedge eastwards along the Capuzzo track. They were taking no chances this time. Their tanks were kept bunched together and along either flank of the advancing wedge great quantities of 88-millimetre guns were spaced. These guns, in fact, formed a protective layer right round the Axis forces and there were more of them than had ever been seen in the desert before. It was not known that Rommel had so many guns or that he had rushed them forward so rapidly with his tanks. All the British scouts could see on June 12th was the approaching dust cloud under its screen of aircraft.

Again the British tanks raced to concentrate. We had to give battle now whether we liked it or not, for if the Axis forces kept going they would reach Tobruk.

The British tanks had been reduced from three to little more than one brigade, which was somewhat less than the German total. This discrepancy might not have mattered so much had we had the same proportion of Grants as before. But the Grants had taken heavy losses in the May battle and only a squadron or two was left. This meant that we were flung back on the Valentines and Honeys which were going to be outgunned from the start by the Mark IIIs and IVs. It was going to be a matter of destroyers and light cruisers against battleships.

This was one of the two vital things that governed this battle which has since been treated as such a mystery. The other thing needs a little longer explanation.

Rommel (as I know from a private source) had said to a British brigadier whom he had captured in the winter campaign: 'I don't care how many tanks you British have so long as you keep splitting them up the way you do. I shall just continue to destroy them piecemeal.'

The British commanders were well aware of the dangers of splitting their forces. But to keep tanks together in battle is not so simple as it sounds. On the evening of

Big brother: the huge German Mark III tank.

June 12th Ritchie had half a dozen isolated infantry groups calling for armoured assistance. The situation was extremely fluid, the direction of the Germans not yet defined and there was the possibility that Rommel might attack any one of several places—he might turn on Knightsbridge, or Gazala, or El Adem, or remain in the centre. What to do? If all the British tanks were sent in one direction the enemy might mop up a number of isolated infantry positions in their absence. If Ritchie withheld his tanks altogether he faced the possibility of the same result, plus the danger of the enemy getting right on to the Tobruk perimeter. Actually, on June 12th, the British tanks were scattered round the Capuzzo track and from that time forward it was the enemy which compelled their movements—not the general. As soon as the British outposts reported contact, events went forward so swiftly and fatally that there was no time for any effective single control.

It was usually like this in tank battles. No one on either side saw this action clearly and fully, neither the man in the tank, nor the brigade commander, nor the airman, nor the intelligence officer, nor the general. It was too complicated, too quick, too obscured by flying sand. Each man saw or heard of only a few restricted and dramatic incidents and the whole picture was not worked out on a map until after the battle was over. And just as one man saw only a limited sector, so the battle itself was divided into a series of fast-moving incidents which were a law unto themselves.

Through this action, as through so many others, there was very little the general could do once the action was joined. The information he got was extremely meagre and quite likely to be wrong. Ritchie knew that even if he issued orders based on this information they were not likely to reach all the men for whom they were intended, and in any case the situation would almost certainly have changed before the orders could be put into effect. Even the brigadiers in charge of the British forces, who had their headquarters in fighting tanks, quickly lost sight of the whole picture. So the real responsibility fell upon the individual commanders of the tanks. Isolated in their own vehicles they had to fight with their own wits and with not much direction from outside. It was the equipment and training that counted.

Through the night of June 12th, Rommel continued his drive eastwards and before dawn of the following day he realized that he had had the great good luck to get between the two British brigades. Saturday, June 13th—the nineteenth continuous day of battle—broke warm and clear. With the first light the two armies were engaged. Almost at once the battlefield was covered over with rolling sand and the smoke of burning oil. Confused orders and messages were flying over the radio on both sides. The front line British tanks called for assistance, and launched an attack from the north to cut through the base of Rommel's wedge. They ran at once on the 88-millimetre guns that had been concealed in the night. Simultaneously, the tip of the enemy wedge threatened the British armoured headquarters which were forced to decamp hurriedly eastwards. During this move the headquarters lost contact with a great part of the tanks joined in battle. And the battle was ferocious.

In an attempt to get within range the British charged headlong upon the German positions. In a few minutes it was a massacre for both sides. From dozens of concealed positions the 88s opened up a tremendous belt of fire. Those British tanks which had somehow escaped the opening salvoes and got right up to the enemy found themselves exposed and deserted by their comrades who had fallen by the way. Those who were only slightly hit at first and turned to get away were caught by the second and third barrages of gunfire. Those who came in as reinforcements found themselves in a confusion of blown sand, burning vehicles and deadly shell-fire that raked the plain again and again. When at last the British sighted the German tanks and went forward at them they were led on to other guns and demolished. Then and not until then, the German tanks came out and ran upon the British forces that had been largely cut up by anti-tank guns.

To a great extent it was the repetition of the oldest tactic on earth. Little brother goes down the road and the footpad springs out at him. Little brother runs back to the spot where big brother is waiting with a cudgel behind the corner. Big brother springs out and knocks the footpad down.

Both sides had many times lured or tried to lure enemy tanks on to concealed anti-tank guns. The Germans succeeded here not because it was a new tactic, but because the British were bound to attack to stop the march on Tobruk, and to attack they had to run into the 88 barrage in order to get their own guns within range.

One after another the British squadrons reported that they were taking heavy losses and needed immediate support. It was the Germans who were charging now, charging past the burning hulks, and they forced the depleted defenders to give battle. In this tremendous follow-up the British became isolated from one another and were forced to fight in small groups. These groups in turn got separated from their own anti-tank guns and their supply vehicles. Many tanks ran out of petrol and had to be abandoned. All the confusion which had overtaken the Germans in their earlier retreat was redoubled here in the British lines and at a time when we had no reserves, when only a few counters were left on the board, and so each counter was vital. This was the position that Rommel had reached in his big retreat from Sidi Rezegh in the winter except that it was we this time who had no more reserves. The great battle for the annihilation of the tanks—the only sort of battle that counted most in the desert—was nearing its end.

The bad news began to come in to British headquarters toward evening. Little haggard groups of men began filtering back out of the chaos and each with a story of overwhelming German forces that had crushed them first with the gun and then the tank. The story that we lost some 200 tanks on this day was, of course, nonsense. Actually the total was nearer 100. But we had no adequate reserves.

That night, while red fires shone through the dust and still the artillery sounded from the Capuzzo track, it was seen that the British armour was gone. There was not sufficient force left to meet Rommel any longer in the open desert. Only the experts realized the full grim horror of that position. The hard armoured coating round the British infantry was gone and the experts knew all too well that once that happens the victor claims the desert. The infantry becomes a liability instead of an asset. It is largely at the mercy of the enemy tanks even in a defended position.

Ritchie had only one order to give and he gave that quickly. 'Abandon the Gazala Line. Get out, and get out before it is too late.' The most now he could hope to do was to hold Tobruk. He resolved that, if possible, he would try to keep a land-ward route open into the garrison from the east since it was not worth while for the Navy to supply it by the sea this time. That was Plan Number One. If the land-ward route was cut and Tobruk surrounded then Plan Number Two would go into action. Tobruk would seal itself up and try to hold out for perhaps a month until the British could re-form on the Egyptian frontier and counter-attack for the relief of the garrison. But everything had to be done quickly even if only Number Two Plan was to go into effect. In the midst of the confusion, the sickening sense of defeat and doubt, the breaking of communications and the spectacle of the incoming wounded, the British commanders got to work. It was the blackest night they had faced in more than two years of fighting.

Tank tracks near Knightsbridge, 'that grim and horrible stretch of sand.'

On Gazala Pienaar and his South Africans and the British 50th Division to the south of them heard the news with black dismay. Immediate retreat. This was the dismal end to their high hopes, to all the weeks and months of planning and working and preparing. They had stood ready to advance, not retreat, to blast through westwards along the coast and take Derna. The men felt thwarted, restless and angry. They cursed as they dug out their guns and gathered their equipment. They cursed still more when they were ordered to blow up some of those priceless guns and demolish the dumps of fuel and food and ammunition which they had dragged with such effort to high crannies in the rocks. It seemed to them there was no sense in this waste. Why couldn't they fight?

But even angry moods were a luxury in this crisis. Hurrying from trench to trench in the darkness and shouting their orders the South African officers got their men into the trucks. Bumping and heaving, the vehicles lurched down through the rocks to the coast road, a long procession of disappointed angry men. Officers went up and down the line urging them to more and more speed. The whole South African division, ten thousand men, had to get into Tobruk before it was too late. Pienaar was being warned hourly that he had not much time left. The Germans were already swarming up inside the line toward the coast. Once they got on to the cliffs above the sea and dominated the road with their tanks and artillery, then Pienaar's position would be critical. A rough line of minefields had been hastily flung along the clifftops from Gazala to Acroma, just outside Tobruk, in order to keep the coast road open. Ritchie was rushing men there, but he advised the South Africans he could not hope to hold longer than forty-eight hours. Already, as the first South African brigade was hurrying down the coast toward the safety of Tobruk, Acroma was engaged. British gunners turned back the first wave of German tanks but one or two of the neighbouring ridges were changing hands almost hourly.

The retreat went on all through the 14th and the 15th. As the South African rearguard came to leave its positions on Gazala, the enemy finally burst through and there was a running engagement down the rocks. The coast road came under heavy fire and every vehicle was forced to take its chance of missing the shells that pelted down from over the lip of the escarpment and fell in uproar beside the sea. Drivers simply hung tight to their steering wheels and drove flat out. Some were caught in traffic jams and hit. Others were cut off. Like wolves in some Russian snow-sled melodrama the Germans kept closing in in increasing numbers from behind. In the end most of the South Africans got through.

Far down in the centre something of the same sort was happening to the Guards at Knightsbridge. With the same discipline, they smashed the guns which had done them great honour through the previous few weeks and began filing out of that grim and horrible stretch of sand for which they had been willing to give their lives the night before. Everywhere across the desert vehicles were streaming back to the east. Ambulances laden with wounded plunged through the dust and jostled for position on the tracks with armoured cars and tanks, jeeps and travelling workshops. All the men from Knightsbridge's satellite boxes, all the Indians on the Capuzzo track were now on the move. They tried to keep a decent dispersal for their own safety through the daylight hours, but at night the trucks closed in, bonnet to tailboard, and without lights of any kind, felt their way eastward through the gloom. It was a moment of such wide confusion, such complex movement, that no one, neither the German commanders nor our own, could say exactly what was happening. British and Germans passed one another within a few hundred yards in the night. And one by one each box was emptied, its heavier equipment destroyed, and the men got away.

There remained only the English 50th Division south of Gazala. It was too late now for them to follow the South Africans eastwards down the coast road; the Germans were already swarming there. They had three alternatives—they could surrender, they could try to find their way through the desert to the east, or they could go west. They chose the last. It was the one stroke of leadership and imagination that lightened the whole of this stage of the campaign—a forced march straight into the heart of the enemy. By going west they were turning their backs on Tobruk and the British lines: they were taking a chance of one in a hundred that they would be able to burst clean through the Axis line and then wheel south and east through the open desert right round Bir Hacheim and so on back to the Egyptian border.

This plan had something in it that stirred the men. With the feeling of high adventure they got to work. The whole division was split into small groups of a few vehicles each. Each group was composed as a commando and told to fight like one— silently, swiftly, and to kill and get away. Rations were carefully measured out— water was the main thing. All lights, all smoking, was forbidden. Even talking was stopped. Then they sallied out into the darkness against the Italians, each man for himself.

An indescribable confusion broke out in the enemy lines at the British threaded or blundered their way through the minefields. An attack westward was the last thing that the enemy had expected at this moment. The attackers seemed to be coming at them from half a dozen directions at once. Italian commanders who sent reinforcements to a threatened area suddenly found themselves under fire and with what strength and with what objective they did not know. Italian prisoners were taken as they lay sleeping on the ground. Convoys of enemy supply vehicles were ambushed and overwhelmed. Guns were put out of action before they could open fire. Dumps of food and petrol were pilfered before the guards could understand what was happening.

The 50th burst clean through the enemy defences leaving a trail of burning vehicles, panic-stricken men, bemused commanders and confusion everywhere. Had they been on an organized and supported offensive they might have scattered the enemy in this sector in a single night and cleared the road to Bomba and Derna. As it was, they were alone and with many extraordinary adventures they came around Bir Hacheim and reached the British lines almost intact.

It was now June 16th and nearly all the British positions west of Tobruk had either fallen or were about to fall. The line was broken. Rommel was triumphant along its whole length. Acroma held out fitfully for a day or two longer, then that collapsed. Only El Adem, south of Tobruk, remained and without wasting an hour Rommel flung upon it a succession of armoured attacks. The Indians fought from their high ground for several days and they were under almost continuous bombardment and bombing. Then they, too, could do no more and they came out first into Sidi Rezegh and then down into the Tobruk perimeter. Tobruk slammed its gates. The siege was on.

All through this chaotic period the R.A.F. was rising to a climax of endeavour. It was the one arm that was on the offensive throughout. While the enemy crept closer and closer Air Marshal Coningham still refused to abandon his forward air-fields about Gambut. The ground crews and the fighters kept going until the Nazi tanks were actually within ten miles of their fields, an unprecedented thing. They worked in a frenzy of energy, day and night. As the Germans closed in the British bombers made shorter and shorter runs until they were only fifteen or twenty minutes in the air at a time. The pilots would land, 'bomb-up', take off, attack the enemy vanguard and return, and this was repeated again and again through the day. Under shaded lights the mechanics worked all night getting the night bombers away. They packed their tents on to trucks and kept everything ready for instant departure and while waiting for the arrival of the enemy tanks, they still kept 'bombing-up' the machines, re-threading the belts of fighter ammunition, filling the tanks and getting the pilots into the air.

In the end they got word that the Germans would be upon them within the hour. Pilots and crews flung their bedding into their machines and took off. They dropped their last bombs and then hastened to other airfields which had been prepared farther back. The ground crews meanwhile jumped into their trucks and drove off a few minutes before their camps were overrun. They slept as they drove back to the rear fields, and then they set to work again. It was a tremendous burst of concentrated effort. These men, half dead with lack of sleep, delayed Rommel for several days.

Those days were vital. They enabled Ritchie to make at least a start on his plans for the defence of Tobruk and to regroup the main bulk of his army on the Egyptian frontier. Tobruk itself was swarming with men. As Pienaar's ten thousand came through he dropped off a battalion from each of his three brigades and this new composite brigade was left behind to strengthen the garrison while the rest of his South Africans hurried on to the border. There was great congestion on the roads.

On June 18th the picture became darker still. The Germans sent out a screen of armoured cars and these rushed Sidi Rezegh and El Duda. Soon they were plunging forward to the cliffs overlooking the sea. A few last British vehicles, through ignorance or courage or desperation, made a bolt down the coast road from Tobruk and some got through and some were caught. Ritchie and all his headquarters were cleared out of Gambut and the Germans quickly had Gambut too. There was no hope of holding a supply route open now. Tobruk was cut off. Those inside the perimeter were forced to stay there and get ready for what was to come. Those outside hurried on to the border throwing up road blocks behind them, blowing bridges, laying mines. Plan Number One was out of the question. Plan Number Two had to go into action.

Even now it was not certain that Rommel would attack Tobruk at once. All through June 18th his forward elements harried the British toward the frontier. Nazi tanks were seen even as far down the border fence as Sidi Omar. It seemed possible that Rommel might ignore Tobruk for the time being and make straight for Egypt in order to keep the Eighth Army on the run. And bit by bit the Eighth Army was falling back on Bardia, Sollum and Halfaya. Ritchie's headquarters were set up anew at Sidi Barrani in Egypt, some sixty miles from the Libyan border. Everyone was ready to move again at a moment's notice.

Then suddenly the Axis thrust toward Egypt turned back. The Nazi tanks and armoured cars wheeled round. They left Gambut and headed due west. If a clear

sign was needed that Tobruk was going to be assaulted, it was here. Egypt for the time being was saved. Tobruk was in deadly peril.

Just before this I made my last journey through the town. Driving from Gazala we came first to the tall concrete monument which the Italians built to commemorate the building of the Axen Strasse. The Axen Strasse was the road which the enemy built to by-pass Tobruk during the long siege of the year before. It split off the main road at the monument and, running in a great semicircle right round the thirty-five-mile perimeter, it rejoined the main road on the east of the garrison. The road itself was thinly metalled and part of the way it wound up the steep escarpments to the south of the town. Between the Axen Strasse and the perimeter lay the British minefields, and here and there a little dugout walled with rocks—the watching post of some sentry who had been smuggled out in the darkness.

We did not take the Axen Strasse on this day as we wanted to collect rations in Tobruk and so we drove straight down the coast road until a sentry stopped us on the perimeter. They were dynamiting parts of the road and all vehicles were being carefully checked. The perimeter itself was a series of small slit trenches and sangers —square piles of loose rock that from the distance looked like the crenellated battlements of a medieval castle. Behind this the guns and troops lay pressed to the ground. All these defence works were extremely primitive and flat. There was no built-up wall, no really good system of anti-tank trenches or upright steel spikes, and very few concrete pill boxes. Indeed, as you went across this flat neutral-coloured ground, you saw very little difference from the ordinary desert. But if you stirred the dust with your toe you would be certain to uncover a spent bullet, a piece of shrapnel or a newly broken bit of rock. For many months the defenders had lived in this waste and their life had been so crude and hard they had left practically no traces behind them. More minefields lay inside the perimeter and then the flat ground broken here and there by dried-up watercourses swept in a gentle slope to the cliffs above the town.

In the narrow sea plain between the coast and the cliffs, thousands of sand-coloured vehicles were dispersed about. We were in the midst of an immense car park. Crudely painted notices were posted along the road at every side-track. These led to ammunition and food dumps, petrol and water points, engineers' and tank stores, hospitals, unit headquarters, ack-ack batteries and rest camps. We stopped to fill up with petrol and take our pick of the first-class rations—tinned tomatoes, peas and potatoes, tinned American bacon and Argentine beef, South African biscuits and the mixture known as 'M and V'—meat and vegetables. We collected sacks of tea and sugar, big tins of cheese, jam and fish. We even got fresh onions and dates. There were enough of all these stores to have maintained twenty or thirty

156

thousand men for three months. There was no shortage of water. The petrol lay around in the flimsy square tins—millions of gallons.

That night we camped at Wadi Auda, the one part in this ugly worn-out place where palms and green things flourished by the sea. It was a remote and quiet valley protected by immense yellow cliffs and at its end it opened out on to a white beach perfect for swimming. The beach was heavily mined like all the rest of the Tobruk coast, but there was a spot near a sunken British invasion barge where we peeled off our sandmatted clothes and plunged naked into the transparent water.

All the rest of Tobruk was hideous. We seldom went into the town if we could avoid it, but on this last visit we needed water. Another red-capped sentry stopped us at the entry and then we drove in a slow procession of vehicles on to the rocky promontory where the white houses clustered row on row. Not one house had escaped damage. I saw hundreds that were simply marked 'Out of Bounds' and one look at the sagging roofs and crumbling walls told you why.

Every night the town was raided and although each time another ruin crashed into dust it seemed to make no difference to the general aspect of the place. Tobruk had been bombed into insensibility. There was little now that anyone could do to increase the wreckage and decay in the centre of the town. Yet still some troops were quartered there. Close to the church the Y.M.C.A. was serving meals, and there was scrawled on the white wall outside—'Hi, Cads, don't park here.' Parked cars attracted bombers.

The mosque was scarred only by blast and a notice warned the troops to keep it inviolate. Most of the Fascist signs and monuments had been defaced or replaced with such ironic descriptions as 'The Red Lion. Free Beer Tomorrow'—the to-morrow that never came. One mauled wreck of a building bore a large notice 'Score—100 not out.' At least a hundred bombs must have touched it. Nearly all the original Italian furnishings in the houses had long since been destroyed or burnt out, and in the empty shells I saw such things as makeshift decontamination centres (lice were getting bad), first-aid posts and a few dumps for spare parts and machinery. I walked down to a cliff above the port and standing there on a ruined tennis court the whole prospect of the wrecked harbour was spread out below. At the wharves immediately beneath, a direct hit had cut a freighter asunder and it spilled its twisted steel entrails.

All around and right across to the other side of the harbour lay the wrecks of good ships with their decks, funnels and masts showing above water. Even these rusty relics were pitted and twisted by high explosive. After they had been beached and sunk, still they had no rest from bombing, and some of the hulks now were becoming unrecognizable as ships. A red half-sunken Italian monoplane that had been shot down nearly two years ago still perched on a shoal close to that end of the bay the Italians euphemistically called 'The Lido'. There was still a passage through these wrecks and a steamer was unloading on to a pontoon wharf constructed of barrels lashed together. A destroyer was creeping out past the boom at the narrow entrance to the bay.

We left the town and crossed the plain to the high yellow cliffs where the road winds up on to the escarpment. On either side of the dusty, dirty and dispirited land many more lorries and ack-ack guns stood about half embedded in trenches. The soldiers had rigged up nets and were playing soccer close to a cemetery now filled with hundreds of white crosses and surmounted at one end by a concrete monument. A slight sandstorm was blowing and the sand was dirty. A strange sort of atmosphere prevailed over all this ground—a kind of apathy and ugliness one could not describe, but felt very strongly. The very earth looked exhausted.

It was difficult to see any tradition in this squalor, or feel the sense of history and heroic deeds. The depressing, degrading, levelling influence of war had made this place accursed.

That night the searchlights arched over the town again and bursting colour filled the sky. The ground shook with the weight of bombs. Somehow then Tobruk seemed to be more like its great name in the world, a place of action and excitement. Even the flares could not reveal the full horror of the worn-out earth. This was the war in action—noisy and exhilarating. Only the morning light revealed again the desolation and the hopeless aftermath of war.

Tobruk itself was not the business end of the garrison. These guns and mines and men scattered across the plain above were the town's defences and most of the garrison was stationed up here on the escarpment. Most of the telegraph poles had been cut off as they acted as ranging points for enemy artillery, and so again there was nothing much to see on this eastern half of the perimeter. The cross-roads where the vehicles turned off to El Adem airport was still busy when I passed. We were checked by the sentries at the eastern exit on the coast road and drove on smartly toward Gambut. It was always a relief to get out of Tobruk. I think we knew then that the place was doomed.

In command of the garrison was a South African, H. B. Klopper. He had proved himself an able Chief of Staff to Major-General de Villiers, and a few weeks before the battle of Tobruk he was promoted to Major-General and given this all-important post. Throughout the campaign he had under his command two full South African brigades with their artillery. At no time were they employed in the fighting and now on June 19th these fresh troops were disposed mainly on the western and south-western sectors of the perimeter. To them was added the composite brigade which Pienaar dropped off in his passage through the perimeter, various units of the Guards, including the Coldstreams, and about a brigade of Indians who had retired into the south-eastern sector of the perimeter after taking part in the fighting outside. In tanks the garrison was weak. About fifty of all classes were collected out of the workshops and put together as a scratch force. There were in addition the administrative personnel, non-combatants who were employed in the workshops, storage dumps and in the port. In all it was reckoned that Klopper had under his command more than twenty thousand men of whom at least half were fresh. In fire power and actual numbers they were slightly less than the garrison which had held Tobruk through the past year.

There was some doubt in the mind of the High Command whether the garrison should be held once again at all costs. For days beforehand I heard doubts expressed among the troops. Everyone wanted to know 'If the Gazala Line falls are we going to try and hold Tobruk.' It was the major question in the desert and as one disaster succeeded another the men felt they were being left in the dark. Few of them would have gladly chosen to go into Tobruk in these circumstances.

In the old days there had been no doubt in the minds of the men defending Tobruk. They had turned the earth with their own hands, had dug the original trenches, embedded the guns, seen their friends killed and wounded in sorties and raids, had faced impending disaster several times, and at the last moment driven it

158

off. They had the habit of defence. They were organized and keyed to it. Tobruk meant a great deal to them. They believed that they were defending London and their own homes across its scarred sulphur-coloured plains and the perimeter was as real to them as the cliffs of Dover.

Now it was altogether different. The new defenders had come as tenants into a strange house and, moreover, a house that had fallen somewhat into disrepair. Thousands of them had bundled pell-mell into the fortress at the last moment and they were tired and hungry and embittered from their setbacks in the past five days. Many came in without their equipment and their guns had been scuttled in the retreat from the line. Communications got into an appalling state and units were badly mixed up. A brigade would find its signallers or its engineers missing. Valuable hours were lost while men waited idly for orders. Ambulances got themselves in the wrong place and the roads were jammed with traffic. Things had gone so badly and so quickly. One defeat had followed another with bewildering rapidity and as is usual in such cases rumours far outstripped the actual facts. The anxiety in men's minds was expressed and passed on from mouth to mouth until it was quoted as a fact. Meanwhile the real urgent business of digging in and getting organized was badly delayed. And it was hours, not days, that counted now.

Moreover, it can scarcely have contributed to the morale of the defenders to see hundreds of lorries filled with troops passing straight through the garrison and on to the east. Inevitably, as these men passed through, they spoke of the enemy on their heels. Just as inevitably it suggested to the defenders that they were being left in the lurch, that they were being used as a rearguard in an action that was already doomed. And one must remember that all around them was the confusion of men seeking orders, of convoys not knowing where to go, of intense congestion round the petrol and water points, of mounting rumours helped on by the actual air raids on the garrison.

One other thing should be mentioned here and this was a broadcast by the B.B.C. When the battle was actually joined, an announcement came over the air from London suggesting that Tobruk was not after all vital and might be lost. How this disastrous and insane broadcast came to go on the air is still unexplained. The encouragement it offered to the Germans and the depression it spread among the isolated British defenders can be imagined. I do not suppose many of the men in Tobruk heard the broadcast at first-hand. But Klopper and his staff heard it and almost the last message that was received from Klopper said, 'I cannot carry on if the B.B.C. is allowed to make these statements.' By then it was too late.

The whole of this campaign had shown that we had in the radio a weapon of war which we underestimated and misunderstood. The B.B.C. was listened to intently every day in the desert because it was usually the only contact the men had with the outside world. The troops formed their opinions from the broadcasts. They listened avidly to everything that was said.

At the moment it was the Tobruk broadcast that counted. Presumably it was thought more important 'to prepare the public for a defeat' than try to hold Tobruk itself. Something of the same sort had been done to Czechoslovakia years before, when the London *Times* published a leader suggesting that the Czechs should try to find some compromise with Germany. To the non-combatants in the Middle East it seemed a pity to apply the same treatment to our own men. To the defenders in Tobruk it seemed an outrage.

The British High Command was all through this last day making frantic efforts to get the garrison ready. Before the perimeter was sealed General Gott had conferred with Klopper and issued a rousing order of the day. Ritchie could still communicate by radio with Klopper from the outside and he sent across a number of instructions. Auchinleck had visited the front and when he returned to Cairo he sent an urgent order to Ritchie that he was to expect immediate attack on Tobruk, and that it would most likely come from El Duda in the south-east. El Duda was the permanent weak spot in the perimeter. In 1941 the Australians had taken Tobruk from the Italians by attacking through El Duda. Rommel had planned to assault the garrison from that point in the previous winter. And it was to that point the defenders had sallied out in November. Tobruk, like Bardia, had originally fallen to us in a day. All the recent history of the desert showed that these tight-skinned perimeter fortresses fell very quickly once they were penetrated. Klopper, however, maintained his fresh South Africans on the west and south-west (possibly he had no time to move them), and the defence of the vital south-east fell to tired troops who had fought fairly steadily through the previous week, who were partly disorganized and who had lost quantities of their equipment.

Ritchie also was urged to collect and send out the meagre remnants of our armour from Egypt so that they could create a diversion on Sidi Rezegh and soften the blow on Tobruk when it came. The R.A.F. meanwhile had been forced right out of Libya and for the moment found themselves out of range. Given a few more days to organize landing-fields, something could have been done to get a fighter screen over Tobruk, but there was no question now of there being a few more days. Tobruk was going to its fate much in the same way as Crete did—without air protection.

Rommel meanwhile was not losing a minute. Now was his time to strike, while the British were still reeling from their series of reverses in the open desert. In thousands, Italian and German troops poured up the coast road. As they swung right along the Axen Strasse they debouched from their lorries and seized every good niche of high ground round the perimeter. The field guns followed. Soon the Italians were entrenched right round to El Adem and their guns were opening fire on the South Africans. The main part of the Axis striking force—the steel wedge that was going to be driven into the south-eastern perimeter—was rushed farther round to Sidi Rezegh and El Duda. It was a masterpiece of organization that the enemy could have mounted and adjusted their forces so rapidly.

The Axis assault troops comprised what was left of the Ariete, 21st and 15th Panzer Divisions, all armoured, the motorized Trieste Division and the 90th Light German Infantry. Naturally they expected that the British tanks outside Tobruk would attempt to take them in the rear so anti-tank guns were set toward the east and south and one of the panzer divisions detailed to stand by. The Stukas were rushed forward to the former British landing fields at Gazala.

All the German genius for method, order and speed, which had temporarily deserted them in retreat, returned to them now that they were in attack.

It began on the morning of Saturday, June 20th. While yet the sun showed red through the ground mist, German and Italian bombers in numbers unknown before swept on to the fortress. They came over in twenties and thirties, tracing and retracing a pattern of bombs across the wadis, and the sand flats and the entrenchments. And through this tumult of bombs and their great curtains of black smoke the Axis shells began to rake the perimeter from one end to the other. They forced the defenders to the ground, they delayed all movement or stopped it entirely. They painted the clearest of all possible warnings across the Tobruk sky—'This is the zero hour. This is the moment of attack.'

Then something new in the desert happened—whether by design or accident is not known. The Stukas came up. They hung briefly above the barrage and then dived, not on the defenders, but on the minefields in the south-east. Many of the bombs missed entirely and simply made craters in the bare sand. Others went up with a double explosion and whole strings of mines erupted together. Sappers of the German infantry crept forward to drag out with their hands the mines that had not gone up and soon a pathway was opened. Across the skyline of El Duda a line of fast-moving enemy tanks appeared and, wreathed in their own dust, made straight toward the pathway. Guns firing, they ran forward into the gap and halted. Then came the wave of German infantry. Carrying mortars and machine-guns as well as their rifles and hand-grenades, they crept up to the tanks and passed them. Some among them carried smoke machines and these spouted grey clouds among the running men so that they were obscured and the British shells and bullets had to be flung haphazardly into the battle arena. And all this time the Axis artillery was laying down a box barrage. It made a wall of explosion and blast and black smoke in front of the advancing men as they hacked through the barbed wire, overwhelmed the British outposts and tore up the remaining mines in the centre of the perimeter.

Then the infantry stopped, their first objective won. They had pierced the perimeter, they had forced and made secure a gap. Now the tanks came on again to exploit it. They ran past the infantry again, bringing their guns with them in this strange and terrible game of leap-frog. The little scratch force of British tanks was waiting for them in open formation, hull down, the last real barrier between the Germans and the sea. In one cataclysmic rush the full weight of the German armour burst upon them. The British artillery now was giving back shot for shot. The British infantry on either side of the gap was pouring small-arms fire and mortar shells into the ranks of the Germans as they rushed through. Reinforcements were coming up from the centre of Tobruk to swing their guns hastily into

The fall of Tobruk: third round to the Germans. British supplies captured in Tobruk in July 1942.

action. And ceaselessly the Luftwaffe kept dive-bombing, ground-straffing and bombing again.

Outside, near Sidi Rezegh, the remnants of the British armour had attempted their diversionary attack. They had run full tilt into the Panzer Division that had been set to lay in wait and soon they were driven off with heavy losses. That was the last attempt to help Tobruk from the outside.

Klopper had his headquarters well inside the perimeter against the cliffs. But at the very earliest moment of the attack he was bombed out and forced to go to another place. Then again the Stukas got on to him. Through these critical hours he was hounded from one place to another, and inevitably his communication broke down. It was not yet midday and his messages to the outside world became fewer and fewer. Back in Egypt Ritchie could do nothing more. As in the Crete action the senior generals had simply to sit and wait for news, and were unable to act upon it when they got it.

At midday the battle touched its crisis. The door was splintered; the enemy was rushing into the fortress. Most of the British tanks lay about burning in their tracks. On either side of the gap the British infantry was brushed aside and large numbers of exhausted prisoners were falling into German hands. And still more and more Germans were pitchforked into the El Duda funnel. Once through they began to fan out, principally to the west. Nothing then could have saved Tobruk. Rommel had a masterly position. All this time the fresh South African troops on the south, south-west and west sectors had not been engaged at all except for shelling and bombing. They had simply heard the distant noises of the battle in the east. Now suddenly fighting began to sound behind them. It was the 90th Light Infantry coming up inside the perimeter, forcing the South Africans to face two fronts at the same time. Through the hundreds of stationary vehicles, machine-gun bullets began to rip back and forth. Soon many lorries were ablaze and little knots of men were running from one place to another seeking cover as the grey-green wave of Germans came on.

162

In his extremity Klopper radioed Ritchie that the position was hopeless. He said, 'I will try to fight my way out to the west.' Ritchie had no choice but to accept this advice and he agreed. There was a long silence on the radio. Tensely and helplessly, the rest of the Eighth Army waited for the news—news that could only now be bad. Then Klopper's last message came in saying tersely, 'It is too late. Most of my vehicles have been destroyed and it is no longer possible to move. I will continue resistance only long enough to carry out essential demolition.'

This was the last word out of Tobruk that day. As when a ship sinks at sea and the radio splutters and falls silent so now the town plunged into its disaster and was isolated from all the outside world at the end.

Under its rolling battle-cloud Tobruk was submerged into an utter chaos of fire and explosion. Those millions of pounds worth of stores which had been carted to Tobruk at such a painful cost of ships and men were set upon by the demolition squads. Down on the wharves the navy personnel flung themselves into the job with such haste and reckless daring that some of their own men were killed. Waterpoints were blown in. Thousands of gallons of petrol, ignited by electricity or even by hand-grenades, leaped burning into the sky and rolled immense black volumes of smoke across the town. Dumps of shells and mines, bullets and hand-grenades went up in sheeted flame and with such an unbelievable crack that it sounded above the continuous thunder of the artillery barrage. Now Tobruk had been gashed open, it was being destroyed by its own internal combustion. Yet still all this destruction could not do away with the huge quantities of food and oil and ammunition which lay about the cliffs and beaches.

Four or five small freighters in the harbour were ordered to clear for sea at once. No troops were put aboard—it was simply a matter of saving the ships. It was at this moment that the German tanks and armoured cars reached the El Adem crossroads. Some split off along the track below the cliffs to the west where many hundreds of lorries stood about helplessly. The others made straight for the cliffs overlooking the harbour.

At once the tanks opened fire on the moving ships in the harbour. They flung their shells especially on the little boats and lighters which were trying to reach the larger vessels, already under steam and beginning to slide out through the eastern reaches to the open sea. The wounded and the dead in the upturned boats simply went to the bottom, others struck out and managed to get picked up, some returned to the shore and waited there, wet and helpless, for the moment of their surrender. Four of the larger ships got away.

All this time the bulk of the South African troops in the west and south-west had not been seriously drawn into the battle. They were now astonished and bewildered to receive from Klopper the order 'surrender'. Bitter and confused dispute broke out. The officers who brought the orders were surrounded by angry men saying, 'It's a lie. You've got it wrong. What the hell is happening?' Some declared they would not obey, others urged delay, others again said they had to obey orders. All this time the Germans were creeping closer.

There was little or no difference in the colour of the vehicles of both sides—indeed the Germans by now were using many of our trucks. And so the enemy traffic mingled with the British traffic on the roads and tracks leading into the town, and westwards toward Klopper's headquarters. Men who were riding back to the dumps for supplies heard horns blowing behind them. They waved the approaching

General Staff of the 3rd Grade; drawing by Edward Ardizzone.

vehicles on and as these passed, the British drivers looked up and saw they were full of Germans. By now the enemy was more desirous of infiltrating right through the fortress, of stabbing it in its heart, than taking prisoners. British and German vehicles rode down the roads together and by-passed one another without opening fire. All over the plain and among the wadis, the British were coming out holding up their hands. Klopper himself surrendered, though two soldiers on his staff later escaped in his car. Others held out through the afternoon and night in the remote wadis and were still fighting on the following day.

In defiance of orders, or in their absence, these soldiers simply went on shooting at anything they could see, because they felt there was nothing else to do. When British officers were sent to them by the Germans to demand their surrender a few refused and shot it out to the last. There were many bitter skirmishes.

Some lucky few, including the Coldstreams, took matters into their own hands and under the cover of night fought their way out and escaped to the east. A few more came out in dribbles of fours and fives for days afterwards. But these totalled only a few hundreds. All the rest of that garrison of twenty-seven thousand were killed or captured. It was defeat as complete as may be. In equipment alone the enemy had won the richest treasure the desert had ever yielded. Rommel had here enough British vehicles, enough tanks and guns, enough petrol and fuel and enough ammunition to re-equip at once and drive straight on to Egypt. The road lay open before him. He left four Italian battalions behind to handle the prisoners and reopen the port. Then he set out. The smashing of Tobruk had taken just one day.

164

The Stukas came over.

17

ROMMEL'S forces were roughly equal to ours when he began the campaign. Now with the fall of Tobruk he was twice as strong. He still had about eight divisions, the best part of a hundred thousand men. As far as one could judge from the disordered state of the Eighth Army, we had about four divisions (Indians, British, South Africans, and composite forces). Rommel still had over a hundred tanks and he was adding to them from captures and his own workshops at the rate of at least a dozen a day. We had practically no tanks at all. Of our losses roughly 45 per cent. were South Africans and 55 per cent. were British, Indians and others.

The tables turned : British prisoners in Tobruk.

It was no longer a question of whether we could hold the Egyptian border but of whether we could hold the old fortress of Mersa Matruh, 130 miles farther back. So Bardia, Sollum, Halfaya and the Omars fell without a fight, and in less than a week from the fall of Tobruk, Rommel presented himself before the approaches to Matruh, an astonishing performance.

In a statement issued to his senior officers Rommel had made an estimate of the relative quality of the Allied troops fighting in the Middle East. At the head of the list was the New Zealand Division, which had all this time been quartered in Syria. It was this division, hardened in Greece, Crete and the desert, and by common consent the finest infantry formation in the Middle East, that was flung into Matruh at the last moment to peg the Axis tide.

On June 26th, when the British were still far from being ready, a fluid and bloody battle was fought on the cliffs about Matruh mainly between the New Zealanders and the 90th Light German Infantry and the Axis tanks. Freyberg, a man of incredible personal courage, had trained his New Zealanders in the gospel of the bayonet charge. Up to date, both in Crete and in the desert, no troops had been found on the Axis side who were willing to stand up and fight when the Maoris came over the top at the run, yelling their war cries, and lunging out with their bayonets. The Germans were no exceptions. But bayonets could not break tanks. The New Zealanders were forced back in the wake of all the other British forces. The Axis troops rushed into Matruh and within a day or two they had successively entered Bagush, Fuka and Daba, which meant the loss of all our forward landing-grounds, of more men, of many more trucks, guns and stores, especially at Daba. Daba always used to be our first halt on the way down to the desert. And still the German drive went on. Only one barrier lay between them and the Delta—the Alamein Line, 150 miles from Cairo, 60 miles from Alexandria. The vanguard of the enemy arrived on the Line on the last day of June.

Only now was the full extent of the danger realized. Churchill was in Washington when Tobruk fell, conferring with Roosevelt, and together they heard the shocking news that the whole British position in the Middle East was in danger of immediate collapse. It promised to be the greatest disaster since the fall of France. Into the Middle East for three years the British Empire had poured every man, gun and tank it could spare. Here alone the British had a front against the enemy. The loss of Egypt would precipitate a chain of misfortunes almost too disastrous to contemplate. It would force England back to the dark days of the Battle of Britain.

With Egypt would fall Malta and all British control of the Mediterranean. The Suez Canal would be lost and with it the stores and equipment worth fifty Tobruks. Suez, Port Said, Alexandria, Beirut and Syrian Tripoli might go. Palestine and Syria could not then hope to stand and once in Jerusalem and Damascus, the Germans would be in sight of the oil wells and Turkey all but surrounded. The Red Sea would become an Axis lake and once in the Indian Ocean the Italian fleet could prey upon all the routes to Africa, India and Australia. India would be approached from both sides by the enemy. Finally, Russia's left flank would be hopelessly exposed.

All this was possible as the Germans came up to the Alamein Line on July 1st. And on that day, and the day following and the day after that the Alamein Line was in no condition to resist any sort of really determined attack whatever. It was ready to crumple. Such troops as we had left would fight—yes. But if the Germans

Soldiers in the Museum at Leptis Magna; drawing by Edward Ardizzone.

Soldiers in the ruins at Cirene; drawing by William Wessel, Rommel's war artist.

came on the way they did at Tobruk there was no question but that the Line would break. Behind Alamein the road lay fair and straight into Alexandria, a two hours' drive. There was nothing much to stop the enemy on that road. In the desert itself, beyond Alamein there was nothing much to stop their cutting the Cairo road and driving straight to Cairo.

The British Fleet had left Alexandria. The demolition gangs stood ready. The town was emptied of most of its troops and those that remained were put under a curfew. Orders went out every hour for all officers to drop whatever they were doing and rejoin their units immediately.

In Cairo there was another curfew. The streets were jammed with cars that had evacuated from Alexandria and the country districts and military traffic that had come from the front. The British consulate was besieged with people seeking visas to Palestine. The east-bound Palestine trains were jammed. A thin mist of smoke hung over the British Embassy by the Nile and over the sprawling blocks of G.H.Q.—huge quantities of secret documents were being burnt. All day a group of privates shovelled piles of maps, lists of figures, reports, estimates, codes and messages into four blazing bonfires in a vacant square of land between the G.H.Q. buildings. Some of the R.A.F. papers being bundled down a chute on to another fire blew over the fence and fluttered down into the crowded street outside. I went into one office and the floor was covered in ashes and the smell of burning rag hung over the whole building.

Long convoys were setting out for Palestine. Every unit that did not have essential business in the fighting was being ordered to get out at once. Part of the United States military headquarters set off in the dead of night for Khartoum and Asmara in Italian Somaliland. The South African women volunteers were hurried on to a south-bound train and elements of the South African Army base troops were dispatched after them. The wives and families of British soldiers were warned to get ready for immediate evacuation—some were to be sent to Palestine, the rest put on to ships at Suez.

The British Embassy headed by Sir Miles Lampson, was going to stay. King Farouk had decided he was not going to be a Nazi puppet ruler and was prepared to leave. Auchinleck had in the previous week removed Ritchie from his command and had at last gone down to the desert himself to take charge. Lieutenant-General Corbett was left in command in Cairo, where the new Minister of State, Richard Casey, had just arrived.

There was a great deal of tension and anxiety behind these moves, but no outward panic. The astonishing thing was that the people at large took the crisis so calmly. Beyond the heavy traffic and the queues waiting round the banks there was nothing to show that the enemy might in a day or two be in the town. The Egyptians especially behaved with fatalism and patience. All that side of the Arab and the near-Arab which bids him say, 'It is the will of Allah' came to the surface at the crucial moment. Many like Nahas Pasha the Premier were compromised with the British, and yet they remained in their homes and went about their work.

On the whole, the Egyptians had much reason to take the situation calmly. Their immediate concern was to avoid being bombed and shelled in their homes and this was not likely to happen. For the rest, there was a definite swing toward the British. Many began to see that they were most unlikely to enjoy such prosperity and opportunities for making money under Axis rule. If the Germans were willing to

168

pay the prices and allow the native a certain amount of leeway, the Italians certainly were not. Then, too, the British in Egypt had become a habit. The Egyptian Government had achieved its freedom and there was nothing specific it could hope to get out of the Axis, especially in wartime. By now the German planes were dropping pamphlets. One of these was a facsimile of a Bank of England note on one side. On the other was printed in Arabic something to the effect that once this note had been valuable; now it was not worth a beggar's time to pick one up. Good pamphlets. But they made no great impression.

Domestically then things were not bad; the British did not have to cope with riots as well as the enemy. And all their emergency precautions went forward calmly and briskly because it was judged by the High Command that the situation had reached a stage of extreme seriousness. The fall of Alexandria and Cairo had to be envisaged and preparations made to carry on the war from another place.

It was not the intention of the High Command to abandon Egypt outright. Even if Alexandria were lost the fight would go on among myriad canals and green fields of the Delta, on the Nile itself, on the desert between the Nile and the Canal, on the banks of the Canal, in Palestine and in the last resort on some sort of a line through Iraq reaching from Basra through Baghdad to Mosul.

But all these were last-ditch alternatives, and could only delay the overrunning of the Middle East. Egypt was the key to the situation and for the moment the most important place in the world. During this anxious first week of July people simply could not bring themselves to believe that the country could fall. And yet there had been France, the rest of Europe, the Far East.

Driving out of Cairo we had scarcely passed Mena House and the Pyramids, when we came on a sight that bore the marks of a full-scale retreat. Guns of all sorts, R.A.F. wagons, recovery vehicles, armoured cars and countless lorries crammed with exhausted and sleeping men, were pouring up the desert road into

169

Cairo. When we reached the half-way resthouse, which was about a hundred kilo-metres from Alexandria and less than two hundred from the front, the procession thickened instead of slackening. The vehicles were pressed bonnet to tailboard, all coming back from the front, all full of desperately weary men who slept piled on one another oblivious of the discomfort and the jolting. The traffic crawled east-ward slowly, an immense lizard over a hundred miles in length, a fantastically easy target for enemy aircraft. Yet no enemy machine appeared. Yard by yard the procession edged its way toward Cairo. We asked ourselves, 'Is the whole army in retreat?'

It was nerve-racking to see them go by. There seemed to be no end to the hundreds and thousands who kept pouring back in such haste that they were making no attempt to obey the order that at least a hundred yards should be kept between each vehicle on the road. Some in their anxiety to get through turned off the macadam surface and tried to get by over the loose sand beside the road. But most of them stuck and as the men dug their vehicles out we stopped to ask, 'What is happening? Why are you coming back?' No one could answer us. No one had any news.

The road on our side—the side that carried vehicles up to the front—was clear, and that too, was ominous. We turned off it now and came across a sand track into Auchinleck's headquarters. The General himself was farther forward and we picked up what information we could from the intelligence officers. A good deal of the traffic going back, it transpired, had been ordered into the Delta to prepare defences there. The battle went on meanwhile at Alamein. The South Africans were in the line in the north and the other sectors were being held by the New Zealanders, the Indians and the British. The 9th Australian Division was being flung into the line. This last was good news. It was the 9th that had held Tobruk. Their reputation was second only to that of the New Zealanders and a very close second at that. They were fresh. They had all their equipment. The only question was whether they would arrive in time.

We felt a little more cheerful about the situation. After all, the line was not turned or pierced yet. There was a tremendous flurry of British bombers and fighters over our heads. At least the R.A.F. was in full action. As we debated, other war correspondents and officers began coming in from the front. One reported that a small group of German tanks had broken through in the south and was headed straight for the Alexandria–Cairo road. A second said that firing had begun on the line and that in the opinion of one of the senior generals there it could be held only another twelve hours. A third said that two Axis thrusts were being made—one in the centre of the line, another in the north. The enemy tanks were coming round the south to isolate all the troops in the line itself.

We decided to drive on to see for ourselves. Back on the road it was the same story again—the endless chain of vehicles on the move eastward. A sandstorm was blowing up now in the later afternoon to make matters worse. At the junction where one road forks into the desert and the other into Alexandria the going became impossible. Salt marshes lie on either side of the road near this point and now the trucks had packed themselves on the highway, two and sometimes three, abreast. It was impossible to get past, impossible to turn off on to the salt flats where a vehicle would be irretrievably bogged. It was now growing dusk. We decided to give up the attempt to reach Alamein and turn instead into Alexandria.

Foot by foot we edged down the road. Sometimes we were forced to stop altogether. Then gradually the traffic thinned out and abruptly died away altogether. I had never seen the approach to Alexandria so empty, so ominous. All those entrenchments, those salt flats that had once swarmed with soldiers were now barren of human life. Even the Bedouin seemed to have fled. Occasionally a military truck or a staff car packed with soldiers would burst round the corner and disappear in the direction of Cairo. But the old camp where the Poles had trained, the compounds filled with newly arrived equipment and vehicles—all these were strangely empty. I caught one glimpse of a company of Indians drawn up to listen to an officer. They looked very like a rearguard or a demolition squad. A little farther on another company of Indians was marching down to a line of trucks. Each man carried his bedding roll.

Then Alexandria itself; overnight the life had gone out of it. The silver barrage balloons still rode above the town but nearly all the ships had gone, many shops were shut and the streets, which normally were bursting with people at this evening hour, were now half empty.

We pulled up at the Cecil Hotel on the waterfront. It had always been our headquarters in Alexandria and was a gay place filled with naval officers and crowds of women. Now it was changed. We got rooms easily. The bar was half empty and those who were there mostly sat around in groups discussing the news—or lack of news. Two military police came in and ordered us to leave at once to rejoin our unit. We told them we knew of no place where we could report except army headquarters, and it was impossible to return there now through the traffic block. It was agreed then that like all the other officers staying in the hotel, we were not to go outside again until the morning.

It seemed clear to me now that the battle had touched its crisis. Once the line went Alexandria could not be held. The Germans would not attempt to cross the anti-tank ditches and narrow defiles before the town; they would simply run round the town to the south and cut it off from Cairo. The bulk of the British Army would be forced to retreat on Cairo itself. Clearly too, the next few hours were going to decide the matter one way or the other. There was no point in being cut off in Alexandria. The state of the roads made rapid communication with the front impossible. The place to be was in Cairo where the news could be gathered and sent off and from there we could set off for the front again—if there was a front to go to.

Lorry overturned after collision; drivers were so tired they fell asleep.

Soon after dawn next morning we set off up the Delta Road toward Cairo, hoping to find it clearer than the desert route. Except for one long convoy of army trucks the route was almost empty. Apparently in the general confusion this delta road had been forgotten. We had only one vehicle now and we perched on the roof of the truck like three strange birds on a housetop. It was a fresh and cool morning and the way lay through groves of trees and bright fields, and over many canals where the cotton barges were still floating peacefully by. Even in the remote villages the people had guessed that something dramatic was happening in the war. For one thing the Germans had been broadcasting in Arabic that they would be in Alexandria the following day. They even had the poor taste to suggest that 'the ladies of Alexandria should get out their party dresses'. And now these people came to the roadside and cheered us as we went by. I suppose villagers will automatically cheer or shout at any sort of an unusual procession through their streets, but still these people were definitely friendly. The children gave the thumbs-up sign and we gave it back to them.

Back in Cairo we realized that already the crisis was passing. Like most great dramatic moments of the war, it was not seen for what it was at the time and all the finesse, the luck and dangers of this gamble were only realized when the game was done. Alexandria, perhaps the whole of the Nile Delta, had lain in Rommel's hand for a moment. He stood on the threshold of the greatest victory of the year. Now, suddenly, and in a few hours, the prize dissipated like a mirage and he was left not among the trees and cities of the Nile but in the arid desert. And all this came about not because Rommel made a mistake or because Auchinleck achieved an eleventh-hour miracle, but because the German Army was exhausted. It could do no more. The German soldiers were wearied to the point where they had no more reserves either of body or of will-power, where all the goading and enticement could make no difference, where they were compelled to stop and sleep. It was part of the gamble of the war that they should have reached this extremity when they had endured all the worst hardships and needed only to continue for a couple of days.

The 90th Light German Infantry especially had been tired out. For three weeks they had been in continuous action, fighting, patrolling, travelling. They had fought a dozen separate engagements including the attack on Tobruk. They had come three hundred miles and for a good part of the journey they had had to fight their way through. Always as the shock troops they had been kept in the van, given the toughest jobs. Recently they had come up against the New Zealand division. For three weeks they had run short of sleep and rest.

Now suddenly it was too much. The drivers of the lorries fell asleep and turned their vehicles over beside the track. The men flung out on the sand lay there too tired to move of their own volition. When they got the order to get up and move on again they did so mechanically and numbly without being very clear about what they were doing or why. They were unkempt and physically dirty. Rommel's officers kept telling them, 'Just a little more. You will be in Alexandria tomorrow. Just one more effort.' And so on tomorrow and the next day until the men slept as they stood and walked dazedly to the guns beyond caring what happened. They had reached the limit of physical despair.

All the mechanical difficulties of supply and maintenance multiplied the farther they advanced. Tank tracks broke. There were no tools at hand to make repairs. Petrol failed to arrive. The British trucks they were using were strange to handle

Although the Qattara Depression was considered impassable, no chance was taken with the left flank. A continual watch was kept.

and when they went wrong no one knew how to fix them quickly. The food was late in being prepared and sometimes did not arrive at all. The men were living mostly on hot coffee and cigarettes.

On the British side the reverse influences were gradually taking effect. The Australians were getting into the line and they were fresh and even eager for a fight. All the British forces were right back on their base now and it was the matter of barely half a day to send into Alexandria for a spare part or more rations and petrol. Behind the Germans there was a week's forced march back to Benghazi. Tobruk had not been opened up as a supply port yet.

Because the soldiers in this war were human and no soldier enjoys a defeat, the morale of the Germans and Italians was undoubtedly higher than the British. But now that exhaustion had become a major factor of the battle other matters came into play. The Germans were led on by the hope of reward and the pride of achievement. The British, on the other hand, knew that their last chance had come, that if they failed here then everything would be lost. So they fought with that touch of desperation that had brought wonderful strength to Moscow in the previous summer and to England in the winter before that.

Feeble, half-hearted assaults were made by the enemy at several places along the line. The tanks that had attempted to run through in the south returned to the German lines. An Indian position was overrun in the centre, but the Indians counter-attacked. The R.A.F. was working at a rhythm and a speed that eclipsed all their earlier efforts. While the Luftwaffe was still toiling up the coast to man new airfields, the R.A.F. sat on their home bases and ran riot over Alamein and Daba, over Fuka and Matruh, over the whole of that long weary procession of enemy who were moving slowly and still more slowly up to the Alamein Line.

On July 4th the British position was intact. On the 5th it was still intact and getting a little stronger. At the end of the week the situation was definitely better. The muddle on the roads behind the lines was being straightened out, communications were getting better. By the opening of the second week in July, the British were set to give battle on the line.

Auchinleck had not done badly since he had taken over. His presence in the desert had spread confidence among the troops and the direction of the battle. After the fall of Tobruk, Auchinleck had simply accepted the situation as he found it. The overriding will of the Axis Army was to come forward; of the British Army to fall back. Auchinleck, because he had no other choice beyond making a suicidal stand, decided to let these forces have play. He let the Axis Army come through. He sought to impede them only at Matruh and when that went wrong he brought his men back again well ahead of the enemy. His whole object was to keep the Eighth Army in being. He believed that for the time being the Eighth Army was more important than all the desert, more important even than Alexandria and the Delta. He was prepared to withdraw even as far as the Suez Canal so long as he kept the army together as a fighting force capable of reinforcement for a counter-attack. The proposition was—'If I lose the Delta I have always the hope of winning it back again. If I lose the Eighth Army then I lose everything.' So the General allowed the Germans to come on, hoping that they would wear themselves out. He tried to keep his troops from battle so that they would live to fight another day when they were stronger and the enemy weaker.

There were also excellent tactical reasons for falling back on the Alamein Line. The line was unique in the desert; no other line had a top and a bottom. Every other line, British or Axis, had been turned because its southern end lay in the open desert. The Alamein Line was based at its northern end on salt lakes by the sea and at its southern end on the Qattara quicksands. It was only forty miles in length. The Qattara Depression is a geological freak in the desert. It is a long, lozenge-shaped hollow, some of it below sea-level. The desert here breaks up into steep cliffs and little plateaux and the flats below will not support armoured vehicles. By laying wire netting on the ground, it is possible to get vehicles across, but not a great many in a great hurry. To run round the Depression and make the long trek across the open desert to the south was out of the question for Rommel at this stage. He was simply not equipped for it and would have been exposed to the R.A.F. and raiding columns every mile of the way.

So the enemy was forced to come along the coast. The next important thing about

One of the peaks of the Qattara Depression seen through the windscreen of a patrolling vehicle.

174

Australian humour on the Alamein road.

Australians, rough, tough, the finest shock troops of the desert.

the Qattara Depression is that it approaches the coast as one draws near to Alexandria, and Alamein is its narrowest point. It is, in fact, a bottle-neck and therefore excellent for defence. Months before, its importance had been realized. Alamein, which is on a ridge, had been formed into a box with a number of concrete underground dugouts and earthworks surrounded by barbed wire and minefields. A number of other positions had been prepared inland.

Let us take a closer look at this line as it was when I arrived on it in the second week of July.

Clifford and I took the train down to Alexandria. It made us both remember the Spanish War when people were able to take trains up to the front at Lerida. At the Cecil Hotel we picked up a conducting officer and a couple of battered-looking trucks and set off. Coming out of Alexandria we ran first through fig plantations now in full green leaf and a soothing splash of colour in the glaring sand. Then we ran on to the ridge we used to call 'The Ripples'. It always was an appalling bit of road. It ran for thirty miles along a crest of yellow rocks, the gleaming green-blue sea on the right, the railway down below on the left. Since the surface had been built in a slap-dash way, even for Egypt, it was an interminable succession of bumps and now these were exaggerated and increased by the heavy traffic. But there was order and method in this traffic now and most of it was going forward. At the end of the Ripples we ran into Alamein Box. It already had a formidable edging of coiled barbed wire and more was being put down. Gangs were nonchalantly digging mines into the ground.

Australians swarmed everywhere and they looked magnificent. None of us had seen such troops before. They had adopted a new uniform during the long months when they were fattening and working in the sun behind the lines. It consisted of a pair of boots, short woollen socks, a pair of khaki drill pants, a piece of string holding two identification discs round the neck, and a wide-brimmed hat turned down all the way round. Their bare backs and shoulders fascinated me. They were burnt brownish-black by the sun. Under the shining skin the muscles bulged like tennis balls.

175

The long siege of Tobruk had hardened and trained this 9th Division, and given them a pride in fighting. They were the Rats of Tobruk. Their long hibernation behind the line had relaxed them, filled them with good food and fresh air. They had grown tired of garrison life. They wanted to fight. They were delighted to be in the desert.

In these two years another subtler change had taken place in these Australians. To Europeans at first they had seemed boastful and quick to take offence, lax in their discipline in the field, and quarrelsome on leave. The usual thing you heard was that the Australians had an inferiority complex, and adopted a truculent noisy manner to hide it. As an Australian living abroad, I had had many arguments about them. I had tried (quite unsuccessfully) to explain to Englishmen that the Australians' manner was the sign of their independence and the freedom of their way of life and that some of their physical vigour might not come amiss in England. To the Australians I tried (even more unsuccessfully) to point out that the Englishman's voice and reserve did not indicate animosity or contempt or weakness, and that some of the Englishman's quiet mental tenacity might not come amiss in Australia. Underneath, I knew the Australians were deeply attached to England. I believed, too, that the English had an affection for Australians that took deep root in the last war. It was usually the officers of both armies who rubbed one another up the wrong way. The men got together as soon as they began to understand one another.

But this 9th Division that came so willingly into the Alamein Line was altogether different from the other Australians I had seen in the Middle East. They spoke much more softly. They were much more sure of themselves and they no longer attempted to impress themselves on a stranger—they knew what they were and who they were. Tobruk had discovered the Australians to themselves. Rest had given them leisure to explore their discovery. Their discipline was far smoother than I had ever seen in Australians before and it was the smooth, definite discipline not of the parade ground but the front line. They worked like blacks and with a new efficiency. They were not two hours in the new positions before Major-General Morshead had them building new fortifications. And with all this they remained among the finest shock troops of the Empire.

These, then, were the men holding the north of the line, and, as we drove on to the centre of the Box where the artillery was firing, we came among thousands of South Africans, the men who had held the Gazala Line and now at last were being given a chance to fight. The Australians held the western perimeter of the Box, the South Africans the southern sector and a stretch of the line reaching southward outside. We arrived at the moment when the Australians were putting in an attack on the Tel el Eisa ridge to the west of Alamein. The object was to make a 'blister' in the enemy position on the coast so that we should be able to sweep in behind them if they started to drive in on the central sectors of the line.

It was an extraordinary scene in Alamein on that bright morning. The colours ran in vivid parallel lines. First there was the green-blue sparkling sea itself, then the snow-white beach and the sand dunes, then inside the dunes the grey salt flats that were pitted with shell holes and bomb craters and looked as the surface of the moon might be. Then came the ultramarine salt lakes edged with floating reeds, then the yellow hogsback of the ridge with the black road on the top, then finally out beyond that the yellow desert.

176

Flies.

Flies: drawing by Edward Ardizzone.

All this area was under fire—fire both going and coming. Choosing a slack moment we crossed a narrow causeway across the lakes to the sea and saw from there the battle clouds roll across the Tel el Eisa ridge. The ridge had fallen to us the night before and now the Germans were coming in with tanks. They had got a new tactic against infantry. Each tank fitted one of its tracks into the Australian slit trenches and tried to crush the men below to death.

'I just held my breath,' one of the wounded told me as he came out of the fight. 'I pressed my face down on the bottom of the trench as hard as I could, but the track touched my back and it was like a series of knives being driven into you. But they didn't get any of us with the first tank or the second. Then when the third one came over we were ready. We pelted the back of it with sticky bombs. One of the boys chased it for a hundred yards to make sure of it. Then it blew up.'

I talked to the Germans coming in, wounded and prisoners. Some had bayonet injuries. There had been a series of charges underneath this roof of shells that still kept arching over our heads as we talked. Gun flashes quickly smothered with smoke and dust were flickering right along the ridge ahead of us.

As we turned back across the causeway the battle suddenly veered in our direction. It started in a second and was all over in ten minutes, a bad ten minutes. Thirty Stukas dived in relays and we just flung ourselves headlong where we were. Between the explosions we crawled into ditches and tank ruts. Then the German shelling started. It was sporadic stuff—evidently they were ranging for a new target and our spot was the target. Like heavy hail the shrapnel kept dropping round us. Each time we tried to move another one came over. The Germans were using anti-personnel shells which burst in a black cloud about a hundred feet above the ground and sprayed downward, a damnable weapon. It penetrated to the bottom of slit trenches with red-hot metal. A dud landed a few yards away from me with a dull 'oomph'. I watched it. It did nothing. I ran.

War correspondents: Clifford of the Daily Mail and the author prepare to move off after spending a night in the desert.

All this time the British gunners alongside us kept firing with their four-point fives and they stood up to the incoming shells as though they were nothing. I know one feels twice as good under fire when one has a job to do, but this performance was a thing to see to be believed.

The firing quieted presently and we started up the truck again. Through the days ahead our conducting officer, who stood watching on the top of the truck, was to say many times 'Scram' and we would scram. Driver and all, we would leap straight from the truck on to the ground and then wait for it to heave under the incoming explosions.

Standing on Alamein Ridge and looking south you could clearly see Ruweisat Ridge. This was a second razor-back which rose out of the desert parallel with the coast and the scene of the armoured fighting. Soft sand lay between the Alamein Ridge and Ruweisat so you had to double back along the coast road for a bit and then turn inland over a track that was being bound with wire netting.

The Indians held Ruweisat and kept attacking westward along it. South of Ruweisat there was another flattish plain covered with pink rocks and this was held by the New Zealanders and British motorized units. Beyond that again was the Depression. The British armour roved up and down ready to rush in and plug a weak spot in the line. Practically its whole length was covered with minefields.

The rival armies having been equal at the beginning of the campaign, and two to one in favour of Rommel after Tobruk, began to approach equality again. Rommel still had his four armoured formations, but they were much reduced and could hardly muster a hundred tanks in all. Additionally he still had his 90th Light and elements of all the Italian divisions. They had been rested but were somewhat thinned out partly through losses, partly because they had to man the supply lines and leave garrisons in places like Tobruk, Sollum and Matruh. A second-class German division which had been acting as gaoler in Crete was being flown and shipped across. In all, you might estimate that the enemy had about seven divisions and between fifty and sixty thousand men. On our side the tank strength was gradually getting back to normal with the arrival of reinforcements from America and England. At times we even outnumbered the enemy two to one. In men we had between sixty and seventy thousand in or near the line. In guns both sides seemed about equal since the Germans were using so many of ours they had captured *en route*.

178

The quality of the enemy troops was good but very uneven. The Italian Sabrata division seemed to be the one that was always getting into hot water. They were garrison troops anyhow, and it was hardly fair to put them in the front line. It was the Sabrata that had given way before the Australians on Tel el Eisa. They surrendered in hundreds. Down in the centre another group of Italians, who had surrendered, said to an Indian Army intelligence officer, 'We are the Brescia Division. You think we're poor troops, don't you? Well, you should see the Sabrata.'

Most of the Sabrata were withdrawn after this and the actual front line was given to the Germans to hold while the Italians dug positions behind them. That was the first good sign that the tide was turning. The enemy presumably would not have dug in and spread minefields if they planned to drive into Alexandria.

The Alamein Line, of course, was a reporter's paradise. It was so short and compact that you could visit the whole front in the course of a day and, whereas in Libya we had taken as much as a full day to call on Corps Headquarters, this was now only one of our journeys. If an engagement flared up anywhere we heard about it within a few hours and were able to get to the spot at once.

The correspondents had a wonderful camping spot by the sea about fifteen miles east of the Alamein Line. Each morning the first hot baleful shaft of sunshine used to wake me about six o'clock. Then the first baleful fly. The flies were terrible. This first one would peck at my face, buzz away to call the others, and then sneak up on me again. I would try to escape by shoving my head inside the sleeping-bag and it was too hot. Immediately my head came out again the fly would pounce, and this time he would have a squadron of twenty or more at his back. I would decide to get up.

Every morning in the desert was a beautiful morning full of gold light on the sand dunes and birds stirring in the clean air. And there were usually shells in the clean air as well, since the morning barrage over Alamein opened about this hour. From this distance, however, it sounded very remote, at any rate not loud enough to wake the others in my party. They slept in a row on camp beds beside the truck and the dew like heavy rain lay on every bed. Reluctantly I peeled off the sleeping-bag and standing at the rear of the truck in my pyjamas I lit the petrol stove and put the kettle on. We shaved every day, and I remember that I was forced

War correspondents eating.

to use the rear-vision mirror of the truck as I could never keep a mirror longer than two days in the desert.

For once there was plenty of water for everybody—it was carried in cans looted from the Germans—and by splashing about noisily I knew I could get the driver, Commerford, out of bed. Commerford was a famed cook in the desert. He would go straight to the stove and fix the tea and eggs we had bought from the Bedouin on our way out from Alexandria. Presently I would hear him say, 'My word!' This was his ultimate expression of irritation, the phrase he used in a sort of contempt for the usual swearing and cursing that went on monotonously in the Army. It might mean that he was cursing the flies or the enemy barrage or the fact that the stove had gone out or that every other egg was rotten. When he said it for the third time we guessed breakfast was ready, and Clifford and the others climbed out of bed.

As we sat around on boxes eating, the first argument of the day would begin. Clifford would have a hunch that something was doing in the extreme southern sector. Legge, of the *Daily Telegraph*, would have a theory that the enemy was bound to attack along the central ridge. I would want to go up the coast to Alamein because I thought that the barrage might be the beginning of something bigger. We would all produce snippets of information to back up our theories. Mundy, the conducting officer, would stand by saying nothing, but the expression on his face was all too plain, 'For the love of heaven, make up your minds.'

At 7.30 a.m., in the midst of all this, the first dispatch rider came bouncing across the rocks, his greatcoat buttoned up to his chin, and he brought with him the mail tied up in a red cloth bag. The arrival of the mail was a great moment and we grabbed at it eagerly, for it contained cables from our offices in London and New York, letters from home and news from headquarters. I have known correspondents on opening their cables to announce that they had to go to Peru or Moscow, and half an hour later disappear out of the desert for ever. Others might glower at some rebuke because they had missed a story or again, with heavy modesty, reveal that they had a word of congratulation or a raise.

We handed over our messages to the dispatch rider each morning and he carried them off to an airfield where they were flown to Cairo to be censored, and then cabled and radioed abroad. After that came the business of bundling up the bedding and clothes and stowing the truck. All this time the argument about our day's destination would continue and in the end some sort of compromise would be reached.

It was only a short run down to the Alamein Box, but sometimes the Nazi 105-millimetre guns were shelling the road. One felt a slight constriction in the throat as one rumbled slowly across the target area. The road at this time was full of vehicles and it gave one confidence to see so many others passing back and forth, apparently unconcerned.

At forward headquarters an intelligence officer would come out of his concrete dugout, map in hand, and explain the previous night's operations: a small enemy attack put in without tank support on Tel el Eisa: the German forward platoons gone aground under our artillery barrage; nothing more expected for the rest of the day. That meant the end of my theory. We would set off for the central ridge to explode theory number two. Several times we would have to jump down from the truck and push it through heavy sand before we got on the ridge. Once there

Into action 1 : Armoured cars come under heavy shell fire.

the going was solid but the dust appalling. It made the midday heat seem twice as
bad. Often we got lost and wandered for an hour or two among batteries of twenty-
five-pounders, petrol dumps, passing jeeps, and ambulances and tank workshops.
Every turning would turn out to be the wrong one. It did not take long for everyone
to feel hot, thirsty, and irritable, especially if there were enemy planes about.
There would be one or two casual dog-fights in the distance and always the noise
of guns, but still we would have no story and no clear idea of what was happening.
The man who favoured going to the southern front would point out that we had
lost two valuable hours by going first to Alamein.

Lunch came about 2.30 p.m.—a tin of peaches, biscuits, cheese and a mouthful
of warm water taken without getting out of the truck. By this time we were fairly
covered in dust and bored with the war. And that would be the moment when
something happened.

A new track would take us to an armoured divisional headquarters and there they
would be full of news of a tank and gun skirmish earlier in the day. There would
be prisoners to see, freshly come from the fighting. Then, sure enough, a German
counter-attack would develop in the evening when the setting sun was shining in
the eyes of our men. Skirting past the British batteries going at full blast, we would
always find a spot from which to see where the shells were falling, and the lines
of dust going up about the infantry pressing forward into the enemy barrage.
For an hour, while the light lasted, the desert would be full of the noise and
movement of battle, and everywhere one turned one gathered a new fact fresh
from the fighting.

Coming to the rear as the battle died down, we would check the day's events
at brigade, divisional and corps headquarters and gradually a complete picture
would form in one's mind.

Reaching our camp by the sea before dusk, there was always that unfailingly
pleasant moment which was the reward for all the irritation and strain of the day—
when we stripped naked and dived straight off the world's most perfect beach

into the world's most perfect sea. In a second the sand was washed out of our eyes and ears and hair, and it was exhilarating just to be cool. A stew of bully-beef, peas, potatoes, tomatoes and onions would be bubbling as we came back from the swim and while it cooked we sat about on the rocks or on the sand typewriting our messages. At this hour the evening barrage over Alamein would start again. Overhead, the first flights of the British night bombers, tightly packed in a Vee, would go by. Someone would fill half a dozen mugs with whisky and sandy water and at twilight we would eat.

Then, in the rising moonlight, we would knock the dust out of our blankets and rig our beds beside the trucks. We would sit for a while in the warm darkness turning over the day's events, arguing about the war, guessing what was going to happen on the morrow.

At ten o'clock the talk would veer round to books, shop talk, home—anything. Continually it was interrupted by some distant noise of war. Propped on one's elbow in bed, one could sometimes see where the gun-flashes were stabbing in an uneven ring round the high ground to the west. We could hear, too, the convoys of unlighted vehicles making up the coast road to the front. Then, by some chemistry, all of us would get tired together, the talk would snuff out into solid sleep. The next thing would be the same damn fly again.

It was not a bad life, better for us, of course, than for most people in the desert, but still nearly everyone you saw looked healthy and reasonably cheerful.

And so the hot July days went by one after another and every day something was happening. Each side now had adopted the policy of offensive defence—that is, by making limited attacks they meant to break up the immediate opposition and prepare the way for later offensive. Neither army was geared to fighting a static war nor equipped for breaking a line—and neither side would admit it. Six heavy Axis attacks were put in at different points. Six times they were driven off, and at least six times the British tried to roll the Axis back to Matruh.

Every day each side got stronger. The Germans could not shift the Australians from Tel el Eisa. We could not get forward in the centre. Standing on Alamein Ridge one evening we watched the heaviest of all the German assaults come in along the dusty plain between Ruweisat and the sea. It started with a series of low bombing raids and here and there across the plain trucks burst into flame and the ack-ack shells hummed and spluttered in the evening air.

The artillery followed, and after the artillery, tanks. At one moment the plain was dotted with British vehicles and guns. The next all disappeared under a rolling cloud of smoke and dust and through this dry fog the shells were bursting as lightning will burst through a thunderstorm. Just for a minute the fog would lift and you would marvel to see that the British vehicles on the plain had survived the tumult and were apparently intact. Twenty shells would be in the air together over our heads, you could hear them whining on their course, both toward you and away from you, and sometimes half a dozen of them would come down together.

The German infantry reached the edge of the Alamein Box that night and began tearing up the mines. At that moment the combined British artillery got on to them and that was the end of the first big Axis attempt to break the Alamein Line.

Two days later, we made our big effort to break the Germans. It began with the heaviest artillery barrage ever seen in the desert. Clifford and I and the others were standing on the top of our truck on Ruweisat Ridge at zero hour. We knew the general plan of the coming battle. After the barrage the South Africans would attack in the north, the Indians in the centre and the New Zealanders in the south. They were all to go forward about five thousand yards on to a series of low ridges and they were to hold their positions through the night. In the morning the British tanks would attack in the centre.

A sunset made unusally beautiful by the dust delayed the darkness a little that night, and its orange light was still slanting across the sand when the guns opened fire. They came in, gun by gun, and battery by battery, until at dusk there was one continuous uproar, a jagged band of violent explosion. The night bombers passed low above our heads and over the German lines we could see long filaments of smoke reaching up to them and shell-bursts like new stars in the sky. All this time the infantry were going forward under the cover of the barrage and close behind us we heard the rumbling and creaking of many tanks. All day they had been coming up the ridge, a vast procession of vehicles. The armour had to be ready to go in at dawn to meet the inevitable German counter-attack.

By now the artillery was firing for twenty miles along the horizon and the gun flashes made a dancing series of lights in the darkness like the lanterns of some garden carnival swaying in the wind. Just before midnight we saw the sign we were waiting for—coloured Very lights and star-shells mounting from the German lines and tracer bullets, mostly red, skidding right and left a few yards above the ground. That meant that the British infantry had engaged. The patter of machine-gun fire came faintly to our ears. At midnight the barrage died away. Somewhere out in the darkness ahead the grim business of 'mopping up' was going on. Hand-grenades were being flung into trenches, prisoners were grabbed at the point of the bayonet, men were crawling forward through the rifle fire, others were struggling up the rocks with ammunition. This was the first of our night infantry attacks, and the whole front now was isolated into a number of dark little pockets where the troops fought for their lives, each man for himself, each man entirely alone in the world. There was nothing for us in the rear to do but sleep and wait for news and the morning.

In the morning another batch of infantry went in and we drove forward to the assembly point to see them go. The firing was very heavy out in front now. Clearly the enemy counter-attack was developing.

I wonder how many people who are in this war know what it is like waiting to go over the top. As a spectator I can only guess. To me it is always the most highly charged moment of any battle—that infinity of time between the moment when the men are told they will attack and when the actual attack starts. These men were Indian soldiers mixed with some British troops and officers. They sat in their lorries, twenty men to a lorry. They had on their full marching kit and they smoked cigarettes. They sat in rows not talking much, but their eyes were always going from one place to another and they gave the impression that they were listening, listening intently. Each man gripped something with his hands, a rifle, the tailboard of the truck, a cigarette—their hands never lay relaxed and open at their sides. They did not glance at their watches. They knew the time—each passing second of it. At each new explosion on the ridge before us—the ridge that presently they were going to charge—they did not move or show in any way that they had heard. Only their eyes kept travelling in the direction of the noise.

There was a shouted order. They got down quietly from the trucks and stood waiting. They knew what was coming. Another order. They spread out and began to go over the hill, using that strange crouching walk of men going into fire. It was very undemonstrative, a routine manœuvre and a small one; yet still I felt this tense constriction in my lungs just watching them go. It was always easier, the men said, when they actually started to use their rifles. As the Cockney put it, 'Yer git yer blood oop.'

With the infantry the British tanks went in . . . and this was another of those heart-breaking mistakes and misunderstandings that kept occurring in the midst of the British attacks—the little things that you could have sworn would never happen, but yet did happen and made the difference between victory and stalemate.

It was a brand new brigade of tanks from England. The crews had trained and trained thoroughly but they were new to the desert. Only three weeks before they had come ashore at Suez with their Valentines. One wondered if it was a good thing to send troops into action immediately they arrived in the desert. The guns will shoot just the same, of course, but it was not quite like Salisbury Plain. It was not like manœuvres. If petrol ran out it was not just a matter of running back two miles down the road and taking the first left where there is a filling station. Maybe the petrol-supply vehicles did not arrive in the desert . . . Maybe you had to take a compass bearing to find the nearest petrol dump, which is just a spot on the map. Maybe you were not too good at reading a compass and you missed the way. Maybe the dump had moved when you got to it.

There was no workshop close at hand if a track broke or a gun stuck. It was hot and the heat played tricks with the eyesight. Then again everything disappeared under dust and smoke once the action was joined, and the best eyesight in the world wasn't much good to you half the time.

Anyway these tanks arrived. The Indian sappers cleared a track for them through the enemy minefields during the night—that was the idea of sending the infantry in first. So in they went at dawn, these freshfaced boys from England, and they were full of confidence and courage for this, their first real action. Someone gave them the wrong direction. They missed the track entirely and ran instead on to the mines and there the German gunners caught them in a cross-fire. Of the eighty-odd tanks that went out, only a score came back. Two years of training, months of building, a voyage half-way round the world—then everything gone in a minute. Because they were given the wrong direction. And one little Cockney among the survivors shoved his head out of his tank and said to me, 'We couldn't understand what had gone wrong. We never had a chance to fire the gun. We couldn't see anything hardly. Shells kept hitting the tank on both sides and throwing us off our course, but we couldn't see who was firing them. We heard the other tanks blowing up all around us. Then one of the officers jumped on board and squeezed into the turret. He said his tank had been hit and just as he said that, a Jerry shell came clean through my turret on the port side and went round and round until it hit the officer on the back of the head and he fell forward on top of the gunner. There was blood all over the place. I was told to go five thousand yards, but when I looked at my speedometer I had done five thousand five hundred. So I turned round and came back again. I seemed to be the only tank that had got through on my sector so I thought I better come back.' And he added quite sincerely and simply, 'We'd like to have another crack at them, sir.'

The Germans made mistakes, too, many of them. But still that did not seem to

184

Into action 2: Among the shell bursts,
the infantry go over the top.

Into action 3: Supplies come up through the barrage.

make our own much better, especially as we had plenty of these little Cockneys who wanted, who really wanted, to fight.

In the north, the South Africans had won their objective—indeed, the Germans had withdrawn their front about six thousand yards the previous night. So we turned to see how the New Zealanders were faring. We knew that the previous week a battalion of theirs had gone forward to an exposed point and had offered to stay there until the morning, provided that they got support from the British armour. Something went wrong. The armour never arrived. Most of the battalion was wiped out.

And now when we reached the New Zealanders' headquarters in the pink southern desert, we found it had happened all over again. They had attacked the previous night. They had gone in with the bayonet. The Germans rallied and for the first time in desert history tried a bayonet charge of their own. They ran crying, 'Hitler, Hitler.' The New Zealanders cut them up and reported the position was won. They reported that a Nazi counter-attack with tanks was likely to come against them at dawn. Should they stay or retire at once? Stay, they were told. You will have the tanks to support you. Again it went wrong. As the grey light lifted over the desert, the New Zealanders looked back to their flanks and saw nothing but empty desert. Out in front thirty German tanks came over the hill. In a minute or two the tanks had split the New Zealanders in half. The defenders had a few anti-tank guns with them. The crews decided to stay and fight it out in order to give their comrades a chance of getting away. They accepted the full enemy charge. They did not budge. When the officer died, an N.C.O. took his place. When the gunlayer died, the man who fired the gun took his job as well as his own. They all died one by one. When the Germans came to occupy the position, they found the gunners lying dead across their guns. I had known some of these men for the past two years and they were really great soldiers, disciplined and firm and wonderfully collected under fire. It was an intense and personal grief to report that they were dead and one railed against the bad luck or the stupidity that had let the tanks go astray.

Coming back we ran through a German position the New Zealanders had overrun

185

a few days before. The sand was blackened with shell blast. Burnt-out troop-carriers and wagons stood about surrounded by ashes. Several 88-millimetre guns had been demolished. The nozzles of the barrels were splayed out like tulips. There were a few German graves with swastikas on them. Perhaps the New Zealand gunners did not die meaninglessly, the victims of an error. They had their share in this, too. It might be granted that they have a share in any other victory on any other sector of the war.

When we got back to Corps headquarters, we found the attack had fizzled out. It was a stalemate. A solitary German prisoner stood beside the intelligence car, smoking one cigarette after another, and carefully digging the butts into the sand with his toe. He was a deserter. He had had enough. It seemed, too, that for the time being both armies had had enough. They had tried, and tried bravely, to break one another. The fighting had been close and very bitter. There had been casualties of up to ten thousand on the line in these July battles and still neither side was able to get anywhere. As soon as one army made an attack the other drove in behind and the attacker was forced to withdraw. It was a system of stresses and balances. It was something new in the desert. For the first time since the desert war began, there was a front line. Both sides were laying down long entrenchments, hundreds of miles of barbed wire, thousands of mines. Dugouts were coming into fashion. The armour mostly stayed in the rear, while the infantry clashed with the bayonet, the tommy-gun and the grenade. There was even some trench warfare. It was now simply a matter of both sides holding their position until one or the other judged himself strong enough to attack. It had always happened like this in the desert—at Sidi Barrani, at Sollum, at Jedabya, at Gazala, and now here at Alamein. Two or three months' sharp fighting, then four or five months of getting in reinforcements. In the end, the side that got the most and best reinforcements most quickly was the one that was going to win. In the meantime as July drifted into August, the British could at least claim that they had emerged from their blackest hour. Egypt was safe at last.

18

WHAT was wrong? Why were the British armies constantly forced to retreat? Why had Norway, Dunkirk, Greece, Crete, Singapore, Burma and Egypt followed so closely upon one another? Was it the generals, the equipment, the men, the War Cabinet, the unpreparedness, the structure of the army, or just bad luck?

On the face of it Dunkirk happened because the French and Belgian armies collapsed; Norway, because the expedition was too late and too small; Greece, because we undertook an impossible job for political reasons; Crete, because we had no aircraft; Singapore and Burma, because we held the Far East on a bluff and not much else; and finally Egypt, because the necessary reinforcements were sent elsewhere.

But more and more the public was rejecting these obvious explanations. More and more they blamed the generals. So many had been 'bowler-hatted' or removed

British and German petrol cans. The Germans' tins (on the left) were superior in every way.

to secondary posts since the war began—Gort and Ironside, Dill and Wavell, Ritchie and Cunningham. And now, this August, Auchinleck himself was about to be replaced by General Alexander. In the R.A.F. also there had been many changes in the Air Marshals. The public drew the obvious inference that the generals were to blame.

I had been in the Middle East since the war started and as an observer had seen something of half a dozen campaigns in Western Asia and Eastern Africa as well as in the desert. I had met most of the senior generals and had seen their plans in operation. And now when I sat down this August to try and work out an explanation of our failures, I simply could not find the answer in these men. There were so many other factors. Look at just a few of them.

There was equipment. Oliver Lyttleton, the Minister of Production, put the matter very clearly in his speech to the Commons during the Tobruk debate. He said that England had had to choose between making a great number of inferior guns and tanks or a few of equal or better quality than the Germans. The times were pressing. England chose the great number; she had to get some sort of arms spread round her Empire rather than none at all. The factories simply could not change over to new patterns overnight.

Now see how this worked out on the battle-front in the desert. We had as many tanks as the Germans all right, hundreds of them. The only serious difference was that the Germans could shoot a thousand or fifteen hundred yards and we less than a thousand. They had a 75- and a 55-millimetre gun and we had the two-pounder. When the Grants came along with the American 75 they were able to stave off the enemy for a bit, but there were not enough Grants and at the time of Tobruk we were back on our two-pounder again.

We had a new six-pounder anti-tank gun carried on a fast truck and it was a good gun. Again, too few arrived too late. The Germans and Italians had their magnificent all-purpose 88-millimetres, a great many of them, and they had had a long time to train their crews. Our Bofors could not be compared with the 88 as a combined anti-tank and anti-aircraft weapon. Our twenty-five-pounder and our four-point-five were good guns, but they had other good Axis guns against them.

We had at the most half a dozen Spitfires in the desert. Neither the Hurricane nor the Tomahawk nor the Kittyhawk can catch a Messerschmitt 109F. Apart from a few improvised fighters we had no dive-bombers at all. It is useless for military strategists to argue, as they will and fiercely, that the Stuka is a failure and very vulnerable. Ask the troops in the field. Its effect on morale alone made it worth while in the Middle East so long as we had insufficient fighters. Anyway, we thought it good enough to attempt to evolve a dive-bomber of our own.

There were many other small items: the water and fuel containers, for instance. The Germans experimented and designed what appears to be the best container for the desert. It was a flat, solidly built can holding about five gallons, and so constructed that the last drop could be poured out. It could be used over and over again. By simply painting on each can a special marking—a white cross was employed for water—they were used for diesel oil, ordinary petrol, aviation spirit, kerosene and water. The great bulk of the British Army was forced to stick to the old flimsy four-gallon container. The majority of them were only used once. Thousands were smashed in transit and leaked entirely. Every day in the desert we would have the same trouble. We would put a couple of petrol cans in the back of a truck. Two hours of bumping over the desert rocks usually produced a suspicious smell. Opening the back of the truck there, sure enough, we would find one or both of our cans had leaked and we had to go off hunting for more. It was time as well as petrol we lost.

In general, then, the enemy had a clear advantage in equipment. Whenever the British Army took the field, it knew that it would have to face superior weapons, and that makes a certain effect on morale. There is just one other point here. The enemy could get all his replacements and reinforcements three times quicker than we could. Often he used aircraft to carry many of his supplies and reinforcements to the front. They arrived ten times quicker than by land and sea.

Now all this question of equipment had little to do with the general. He specified what he wanted, of course, but he had to take what he could get. No Middle East general would have taken Valentine tanks if he could have got Grants. But he couldn't get the Grants.

Then strategy and tactics. It was no longer the general in the field who decided when or where a campaign should be fought but the War Cabinet in London. In every one of our campaigns political consideration had carried very much importance and the diplomats had had almost as much a say in their conception as the generals. We had gone to war on a political and not a military issue. In every case a general had simply been selected and told to get on with the job. Even in the framing of tactics he did not have a free hand. The tactics were those which were recommended by a staff of experts or those which were forced upon the junior commanders at the front by the fortunes of the battle. Before all their Middle Eastern campaigns both Wavell and Auchinleck called upon many technicians to deliver their appreciations of the position. Estimates and reports were sought from the staffs of the engineers and the armourers, from the Royal Army Supply Corps, from both political and military intelligence, from the Ministries of Shipping and Production, from geographers and meteorologists, from the various branches of the R.A.F. and the Navy, from the operational staffs and the junior commanders, from the leaders of the Allied forces, from security, from the transport experts, from the Dominions and the American Lease-Lend administrators—to mention only a few. All these reports and estimates were collated and submitted to the central direction of the war in London. The chief duty of the Commander-in-Chief, Middle East, in this was to see that the best men were giving him these reports and that the facts they submitted were accurately tabulated and assessed. Once an offensive had been decided upon, the problems of how it should be fought rested not upon one man but fifty or more. The best the general could do would be to see that all went forward smoothly and energetically until the day of the attack, and then, like a coach who has sent a football team into play, he could do nothing more but sit back and watch how his men got on.

In actual fact neither the winter nor the summer campaign had produced any vital new tactics. It was the old business of making wide sweeps through the desert, of getting round behind the enemy, of striking him at his weakest point and following up fast. Rommel had revealed no genius in planning or timing. Living at the front he had certainly been in a position to take quick decisions, but if there had been any genius at all on the Axis side it had been the genius of the average German soldier for organization. In all its branches the German war machine appeared to have a better and tighter control than our army. Many believed that this was because the Germans had been so long in training for this war. One of the senior British generals said to the war correspondents after the fall of Tobruk, 'We are still amateurs. The Germans are professionals.' One saw this talent for organization in all directions. The Luftwaffe, for example, had a much closer liaison with the ground forces than we, though we made big improvements in this time and again, one would note the steady rhythm of a German attack—first the Stukas, then the artillery, then the infantry, then the tanks, then the Stukas following up again. Once the action was joined, the Germans tended to dispense with coded signals which wasted time at both ends. Rommel's own voice could be frequently heard on the air ordering his troops to do this, that, or the other thing. By the time the British could make use of this freely given information the action would be over.

It was in the control of tanks that the Germans revealed their greatest gifts. They were tank technicians pure and simple. They were the élite of the Afrika Korps, as compact, as neat and efficient as a team of acrobats. They had been trained to the nth degree and as a group, a group that could be controlled very nearly as easily as one tank. They were self-contained. Stukas, tanks, recovery vehicles, petrol wagons, anti-tank gunners, all went forward together and their senior officers were often in the van. Toward the end Rommel evolved a number of still smaller self-contained armoured groups. There were notably his own bodyguard and the Marx Group. They moved about very rapidly and very successfully. The co-operation between the tanks and the anti-tank gunners was their best achievement. The Germans no longer used tanks to attack equal enemy armoured forces. Let me repeat that—they did not attack with tanks. On the Alamein Line and outside Tobruk they avoided tank action unless they greatly outnumbered us. They preferred always to send out scouts by land and air to plot the positions of our anti-tank guns. Then they used aircraft and infantry to attack those guns.

They used artillery too. Then when the British guns were silenced or partially silenced, and the landmines lifted, they used their tanks to mop up the battlefield, and break through to the unprotected British infantry. In defence they used very nearly the same methods—that was how we took our vital losses on June 13th. They had another stunt too—using the tank as a scare weapon. As I remember on that night when we ran into the graveyard at El Adem there was only a handful of German armoured cars and tanks in the German thrust. But they got through to the British infantry and there they made a terrific hullaballoo—shooting off Very lights, firing all their guns, stirring up great columns of dust. They knew that the word would spread through the British lines that the German tanks had cut loose and they exploited the scare for all it was worth. It was effective.

We could not hope to marshal and drive our tanks as the Germans did. We were simply not trained to it and they had years of practice. It was not difficult for us to train the gunners and drivers. Theirs was a mechanical job, and many in the desert were equal or superior to their German opposites. But it takes much longer training and a higher kind of brain to command a tank. The man who can handle large groups of tanks is a much rarer bird still. Among other things he needs experience in actual warfare. About the time of the fall of Tobruk, we found ourselves seriously short of young tank officers, men who knew the desert, and knew their tanks through and through. A number of higher officers in command of the armour were weeded out there and then on the battlefield because of blunders, but no large-scale changes could suddenly be made among the junior ranks.

All these things—the system of the army, the training of the men or the lack of it, the type of discipline—were fundamentals that no general in the field had the time or the means seriously to alter. The system was in being. For better or worse, it had to be used as it was. It would not have helped the commanding general to complain that the army was based on the ideas of 1918, that its methods were redundant and slow, that the men were insufficiently trained and the equipment inferior. He had to accept the situation and make the best of a difficult job.

Morale was important too, but this depended on many factors beyond the general's control. The propaganda system in the Middle East was no better or worse than the rest of the army. It took its defeats in the same way. The Axis Army paid the closest attention to morale and the control of morale through propaganda. Where our men in the desert had not seen a newspaper for months, let alone any other reading to divert and encourage their minds, the Axis troops were abundantly supplied. Every one of their camps I saw was strewn with recent magazines and pamphlets.

Here again we were improving. The radio was putting on special programmes for the troops; four publications—*Parade*, *Crusader*, *Gen* and the *World's Press Review*—were being specially printed for them in Cairo. And airgraphs and airmail letter-cards were passing to and from the Middle East, sometimes taking less than a fortnight. But still it was not enough. The troops needed more cheering up, more music, more books, more radios. Their food was good.

Beyond this there was the deeper question I have written of before—the need, the really urgent need, to explain to the men the reasons why they were fighting. It should have been easy. If, for example, the four great allies, China, the U.S.A., Britain and Russia, were to have set out a social and political programme for the world and a plan for the peace it would have made a remarkable impression on

Many nationalities fought on the British side; here, left to right, a Pole, an Englishman, an Indian, an Australian and a Czech.

the minds of the men. Morale would have improved. I do not suggest that it was bad. But let us accept that the best morale comes through victory or the hope of victory, and if we could not have victory at once it might have been worth while raising a few planned hopes.

In the German Army I saw no signs of any breaking in morale. Why should there have been? They were winning. To encourage them they had their loot, the sight of conquered territory, promotion, decorations, all the apparatus of victory. They were solid—woodenly solid if you like. It must be conceded that their morale was higher than ours in the Middle East.

So then in all these things, in equipment, training, organization and morale, we had to accept a disadvantage through this year of war in the desert.

The further you go into this huge problem, the more factors and influences you discover. Consider the nationalities of the men. The Axis had Germans and Italians—that was all. Just two languages to cope with, two temperaments to consider. On our side there were at least seven different nationalities fighting, at least five different languages used. There were the men from the British Isles, Indians, French, Poles, Greeks, Australians, South Africans, New Zealanders—to mention only the main groups. Every one of these groups had its own way of doing things, its own domestic political problems, its pride—pride that counts for a great deal in war. Of course there were arguments and misunderstandings.

Here, then, was a major problem for the Allied side, a problem that ranks with any other aspect of the war. All these elements had to be composed and organized, the right nationality given the right job at the right moment, and always things had to be adjusted so that no one took offence. The friendly, but non-belligerent, Egyptians and Arabs were another little problem of their own.

Then again a major point of local strategy: always Syria and Palestine had to be guarded. There was no moment when Auchinleck could say (as Rommel could), 'Now we will throw all we have got into the Western Desert.' What about the landing-fields the Axis was preparing in the Greek islands? What about the training of parachutists on Crete? What about the massing of caiques and invasion boats in the Dodecanese Islands? Was the enemy going to strike now at Cyprus and Syria? Was he going to make a parachute landing on Palestine and the Canal? These were the questions that went before Auchinleck every day. He had to fight constantly looking over his shoulder.

Churchill, with sunshade, visits the Western Desert.

If really bad luck had impeded the British, it was as much among the dead as among the captured. There seemed to be a curse on the lives of British generals in the Middle East. At a most critical moment the Generals Gott, Briggs and Lumsden were talking together at the front one day when a Stuka charged them. Briggs and Lumsden were hit and put out of the battle. Only Gott, the man with the charmed life, escaped. Gatehouse took command of the armour. He was putting some of his own fire into it when he, too, was hit and taken back to Cairo. Freyberg was the next casualty—Freyberg who had stood unmoved through impossible risks in this war and survived the last with Heaven knew how many wounds. The enemy got him at last at Mersa Matruh. The old lion continued directing the battle until nightfall and then, so seriously hurt that they had to hold him down, they motored him straight through the enemy lines and got him to hospital.

Added to all these were the generals who had been removed because of errors and bad judgment, and the Eighth Army, you will see, was in a bad way over its commanders. Only Gott remained of the original men, and he stood out like a giant in this bitter, thankless fighting, the one great name left on the British side, the one man who had survived death, capture, or major error.

It was unfortunate, too, that Auchinleck should have chosen this moment to institute a scheme behind the lines which might have been an excellent one at another time. He began moving G.H.Q. out of the fleshpots of Cairo to a spot nearby in the desert. He wanted to get everyone under canvas, the way Allenby had done in the last war, so that the staff men should be less distracted by the baubles of Cairo, and able to devote more time to their jobs. He wanted to remove the criticism that the men at the base were living in ease while others fought their

192

Churchill with Field Marshal Smuts in the gardens of the British Embassy, Cairo. Summer 1942.

battles for them at the front. Auchinleck was the first to go out. He shut up his town house and moved into a tent. With ironic but good-humoured malice the army immediately dubbed the new G.H.Q. 'The Short Range Desert Group'. It wasn't a bad idea this move to the desert. The trouble was that, coming in the middle of a crisis, it badly disrupted things. At a time when things should have been going with special smoothness at G.H.Q. there was commotion and delay and much grumbling from the staff men who thought the idea crazy anyway.

Then there was this final point which is so obvious that it has been forgotten. This was Rommel's offensive, not ours. Presumably when you make an offensive you hope to get through with it; you hope to gain territory. If you don't, then it is a worse failure, as a rule, than if you never tried at all and merely stood your ground and gave way a bit. Rommel had planned this offensive as far back as nine months before and failed. Tobruk, too, had never before been submitted to an organized, full-scale attack since we held it. It is possible that it might have fallen had Rommel been allowed to attack it as he planned to do when we struck him first in November 1941.

These then were the conclusions I reached when I tried to make a summing up at the beginning of August in Cairo. The list is not exclusive and many of the men who fought in the campaign will disagree with them. But to me they were a full enough explanation. They dispelled in my mind any question of there being a mystery over the fall of Tobruk and our collapse into Egypt. There was no mystery. Everything moved forward step by step, logically and precisely as it was destined to do.

Just as the German Army had produced through long training and a passion for

war an abler junior officer and better organization and weapons to fight with, so at the top it had produced an abler general. It was simply a great pyramid in which every stone had to fit into place and at its apex the rightly shaped stone was set in position. This topmost stone was the one most people looked at because it stood alone at the top and first arrested the eye. But it was not more important than any other stone. Without those stones at the base the whole pyramid could not have existed. Each stone, whether it was at the base or in the middle or at the top, had to perform its function, and no function was more important than another. It was the solid collective mass that counted.

Looking back to 1940, I found it hard to believe the changes that had taken place with us, hard to realize that that little tinpot force of a couple of divisions had grown into the army that now sprawled across an area several times the size of Europe. In every separate department there had been a steady improvement and the rate of improvement was accelerating. There had been no such improvement on the German side. Slowly, and with many pains and disasters, we were overhauling the lead the Axis had held over us from the beginning of the war. This became blindingly apparent in this last summer's campaign. The Axis then produced no new piece of equipment whatever; they simply had overwhelming quantities of the same good material and much training. On our side we had the new Grant tank and there were even better tanks arriving; we had the new six-pounder gun and hundreds of them were beginning to flood into the Middle East. The new Spitfires were starting to come in at last. The Americans, headed by their air force, were taking their positions in the desert.

When I got back to Cairo the best energy and brains among the Allies was being put into the job of reorganization. We had had a bad shock. The old business of holding the Middle East on a shoe-string was going to cease. There was going to be no more bluffing. So Churchill flew in from London one morning to hold his conference in Cairo. He had with him Averill Harriman, the American Lease-Lend administrator; General Sir Alan Brooke, Chief of Imperial Staff; General Sir Ronald Adam, the Adjutant-General; and one or two others. Wavell came across from India. Smuts flew in from South Africa. All the generals, the senior Admirals and Air Marshals of the Middle East were gathered. It was a momentous conference, one that was going to change the course of the war. It meant that at least we acknowledged that we had a second front right here in the Middle East, a place where we were immediately in contact with the enemy and able to buttress Russia's left flank.

There was the usual purge of generals—Alexander, a dynamic little man who had done well at Dunkirk and as well as possible at the fall of Burma, took the place of Auchinleck. General Maitland Wilson was given a separate command in Syria and Palestine. More important still, a new and strange leader was given command in the desert—General Montgomery. Several other generals were replaced and reshuffled. This much was announced. But the changes went much further. At this conference a new army of the Middle East was given birth, an army that for the first time was going to include Americans as well as British. A tide of reinforcement such as the Middle East had never known before was going to come in, and from it a better army was going to be built.

An era of the war was over, a bad era, but one from which good was going to come.

At G.H.Q. we heard a shocking piece of news, news that somehow more than any other single thing made me feel in a moment that an era in the desert was done and that it was time I went away. Gott was dead. They had killed him in the air. He had talked that morning with Churchill and the others in the desert. Churchill had offered him the greatest opportunity any general in the British Army could hope for—command of the Eighth Army—and Gott had accepted. Then after some months of daily danger and unending work he had stepped into a Bombay aircraft to fly back to Cairo for a few days' leave. The enemy had been stopped; he was due for a holiday. Two Messerschmitts returning from a raid saw the slow and cumbersome troopcarrier. The British pilot almost got the Bombay down. As the wheels touched, the Germans fired incendiaries and the machine caught fire. Gott was dead when they got him out. His body rested on his chosen battlefield, the sand. He was the last of the old desert rats to go. He was a great man for England.

Gott's grave in the desert; 'a great man for England'.

WITHIN four months—from October 1942 to January 1943—the British Eighth Army did amazing things in the desert. It advanced fifteen hundred miles across some of the most inhospitable country in the world. It smashed the Italian Fascist Empire in Africa. It fought one major action at Alamein in Egypt and two minor ones at El Agheila and Zem-Zem in Tripolitania.

It captured 30,000 prisoners including a dozen important generals and killed and wounded something like 40,000 men. In their retreat the Axis lost perhaps 500 tanks, 1,000 aircraft, 1,500 vehicles and stores worth many millions of pounds. Three vital ports, Tobruk, Benghazi and Tripoli, were in our hands and in operation. We failed to catch Rommel, but the power of his Afrika Korps was at least halved. Incontestably the Eighth Army was the finest fighting machine in the Anglo-American forces and the name of its general stood higher than that of any other.

Bernard Montgomery, as we saw him when he first arrived in the desert, was a slightly built man with a thin nervous face, an ascetic who neither drank nor smoked. He was a military scholar who had cut away from himself most of the normal

New blood: General Sir Harold Alexander, the new C-in-C, with General Montgomery, the new Commander 8th Army.

Montgomery comes into the picture. In the Western Desert with Churchill and Alan Brooke, August 1942.

diversions of life, and this left him with a fund of restless energy, part of which he expended in a religious faith in himself and his God and part in a ruthless determination to make battle. Like most missionaries he was flamboyant, and there was in him an almost messianic desire to make converts and to prove his doctrines were the right ones. An unusual man, not an easy companion.

General Montgomery represented central control in the British Army as against the democratic ways of most of the other generals—Wavell and Alexander, for example. These last preferred to accept the army and its system as they found it. They tried nothing revolutionary but endeavoured to improve on the existing state of things. Now Montgomery was just the reverse. He believed in surgery, not homœopathy. If a thing was not going right or only partially right, then cut it out altogether. By the Montgomery method the whole art of war was reducible to a pattern and a series of numbers; it was all based on units of man-power and fire-power and so forth. He by no means rubbed out the human element; he simply believed that a correct system and good leadership would inspire the troops and draw out hitherto wasted resources of energy.

Paratroops on patrol duty in Tunisia.

Montgomery had this system and this faith, and he believed in them passionately. He was itching to put his ideas into practice. Suddenly Churchill gave him the chance.

When the General arrived in the Middle East in August 1942 he had the great good fortune to find a ready-made and experienced army waiting for him. Two years' fighting and training had made many of them wonderful troops and there were plenty of them. The three armoured divisions—the 1st, 7th and 10th—were English, and there were in addition two English foot divisions, the 50th and the 44th. The Empire had provided five more infantry divisions—two South African, one Indian, one New Zealand and one Australian. There was also the Highland Division. A total of eleven divisions, all ready to go into battle. Moreover, the equipment was pouring in at a rate never approached in the Middle East before— British guns, American tanks and aircraft from both countries.

'The dead seem to slump into the earth with such overwhelming unnatural tiredness.'

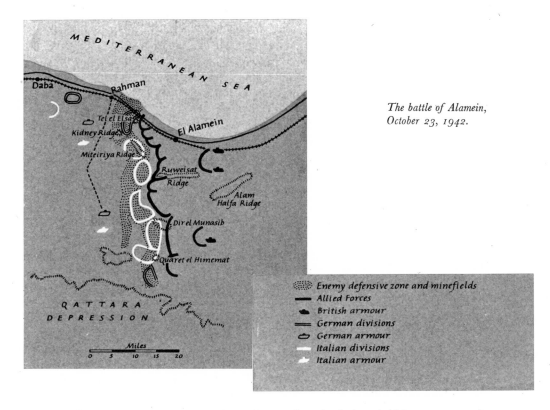

The battle of Alamein,
October 23, 1942.

Map legend:
- Enemy defensive zone and minefields
- Allied Forces
- British armour
- German divisions
- German armour
- Italian divisions
- Italian armour

In itself this huge instrument of nearly two hundred thousand men was ready for anything. But the things it lacked badly were a clearly defined purpose and a leader. They got both in Montgomery. 'Follow me,' he cried, 'and we will smash Rommel.' Since the General believed this himself, it was not long before the troops began to believe it too. Before their own eyes great squadrons of tanks and guns were pouring into the desert and naturally the new General was given the credit for it. From now on the subordinates took a very subordinate position indeed. Everything came straight from the General. Moreover, the new General was a man the troops could understand. He was very much one of the boys. He painted Monty on his tank and he went round wearing a most stimulating array of hats and badges. He harangued the army like a prophet. All this might seem like bad form to the officers of the old school, but the troops loved it. Monty had won them over before the battle started. His shrewdest move of all was to spread the idea that the Eighth Army was an independent striking force, taking its orders from no one. He was their General and he was going to lead them on their own private crusade across Africa. Behind all this there resided in the General a long and very solid military training. If his battles lacked genius at least they were fought brilliantly and with good sound logic.

Alamein will be studied in military academies for many years to come. The Eighth Army found itself in front of a short line, barely forty miles long, that could not be turned because the sea lay at one end and a marsh at the other end. Consequently it had to be attacked directly. The Australians had already made themselves a good big dent in the enemy positions along the coast; so clearly this had to be used. But we needed two lines of attack to prevent the enemy concentrating,

REINFORCEMENTS ARRIVE AT SUEZ:
RIGHT: *A tank is slung over the side.*
BELOW: *In good heart.*

and a point half-way down the line seemed to be the best second line of advance. The Germans on their side had mined their ground in great depth and covered it with artillery and smaller guns firing on fixed lines. Both sides held their armour in reserve, ready to rush to critical points once the battle was joined. The British outnumbered the enemy in everything except men by possibly as much as three to two, but still they needed this advantage since they were going to do the attacking.

The British had one other thing in their favour: Marshal Rommel, whose intelligence staff must have been terrible, was away in Germany, and his substitute, von Stumme, did a thing which Rommel would never have done—spaced his forces more or less equally along the whole line. Whereas the whole basis of his defence should have been to keep his best forces fluid until the battle took shape,

Monty's cap badges. The troops loved it.

he left them lying in static positions, from which they could not be quickly moved.

Montgomery attacked by night. He risked the danger of confusion in the darkness so that he should have the advantage of surprise and so that his striking units could get right up to the enemy without being seen. Before dawn each morning the British dug in furiously in order to meet the inevitable counter-attack at daylight. Then at night they attacked again. We struck not with tanks but with men, aircraft and guns. The tanks for the most part were kept out of it until the guns and aircraft—in this case mostly the twenty-five-pounder and the American medium bomber—had softened up the arena and the infantry had overwhelmed the minefields and anti-tank batteries. Then once a good solid hole was made in the enemy lines the tanks went roaring through. They fanned out behind the enemy infantry and panicked them, and they forced the enemy armour to do battle in the open ground beyond.

Rommel, who had come racing back from Berlin, took one look at this chaos and apparently decided there was very little he could do about it. Indeed, there was hardly a mistake his subordinates had not made. They had been bluffed by a dummy concentration of vehicles the British had erected behind Alamein. They had confused the position of the real British spearhead, and when they did find it, the situation was too late to be restored. After trying to peg the gaps at one or two places, Rommel wisely abandoned the Italian infantry and got clean out of Egypt and Cyrenaica with the remainder of his tanks and his best mobile units.

I personally was not at the battle of Alamein, but Lieutenant-Colonel J. O. Ewart, one of Montgomery's intelligence officers, supplied me with this compact and lucid account:

Direct hit.

'The twenty-third of October 1942 was a still and moonlight night in the desert. At 9.40 the roar of 800 guns broke the silence and marked the start of the battle of Alamein. Twenty minutes of flashing, deafening chaos, interrupted by a nervous silence while the barrage lifted from the enemy's forward positions to his gun line. For these twenty minutes the sky was lit by the winking flashes along the horizon, then a quiet, broken by the sound of tank tracks and the rattle of small arms. The Eighth Army was unleashed. Since Rommel had left his hopes of taking Egypt with forty blackened tanks south of Alem Halfa ridge late in August, the army had been waiting and building. There had been endless activity round the back areas and in the workshops of the Delta. More tanks, new tanks—the Shermans—more guns, new guns—the Priests—more and more six-pounders, more men had been pouring up the switchback road. Tracks had been constructed leading up to the assembly area, carefully camouflaged, and behind the lines there were as many dummy tanks as real ones, to mislead the enemy as to the point of our attack.

'The Germans, too, had been busy. Rommel had fenced himself in behind barriers of mines and wire, sandwiching Italian battalions between German battalions. It was the deepest defence that either side had constructed in Africa, and there was no possibility of outflanking it. In front of the main position, a strong line with great keeps, there was a forward line. It was not so strong, but was joined to the main line by a series of connecting walls, so that the whole system was like a ladder. The front parts of the line between the "rungs" were weaker,

Preparing to charge when the barrage ends.

so that our attackers would be canalized into a series of hollows and would lose direction. Into these "Devil's Gardens" as Rommel named them, a murderous defensive fire was to be laid down. In some areas there were as many as nine successive minefields to overcome.

'General Montgomery had decided to make a break-in in the north, using the 30th Corps which now included the 9th Australian Divisions (the Rats of Tobruk), the 1st South African Division, the 51st Highland Division (newly arrived in the Middle East) and the New Zealand Division. He chose the north because a break-through in the north threatened the coastal road, the enemy's life, and imperilled

A wounded creature at bay—in this case a German officer.

In the early morning the tanks wait to advance.

the security of all his forces on the southern part of the line. The 30th Corps was to make the gaps, mainly by grinding away at the German defences with infantry supported by some heavy tanks. Then the 10th Corps, consisting of the 1st and 10th Armoured Divisions, which had been reorganized and retained in the Wadi Natrun area half-way from Cairo to Alamein, was to go through the gaps into the open country beyond and there deal with the enemy's armour. On the southern part of the front the 13th Corps with the 7th Armoured Division was to attack to contain the enemy reserves opposite them.

'By first light on the 24th the greater part of the objectives had been gained, and we had bitten deep into the enemy's main defences. Gaps had been made in the minefields and the armour of the 10th Corps had started to move up. We had broken in, but not through. On the enemy side there was confusion. Rommel's deputy, Stumme, had been killed by a stray shot in the first moments of the battle. The Axis command was taken over by von Thoma, who was comparatively new to the desert. His handling of the situation was indecisive. He could not make up

204

ABOVE: *Prelude to the Battle; drawing by Edward Ardizzone.*
BELOW: *The Rifle Brigade had knocked out fifty tanks.*

his mind whether the main attack was in the north or in the south, or whether it was a seaborne lading west of Daba where light naval forces had been demonstrating. And so he failed to concentrate his reserves. He left the 21st Panzer and the Ariete Divisions in the south, and the 90th Light and Trieste along the coast near Daba, and tried to plug the gap in the line with only the 15th Panzer and the Littorio Divisions.

'The first phase of the battle continued until the 26th. While our infantry ground down the enemy defences slowly and steadily and beat off the counter-attacks of the 15th Panzer Division, the sappers were making corridors for the armour

The British 6-pounder anti-tank gun.

behind. The second phase began on the 27th. A purposefulness appeared in the enemy's movements. We guessed that Rommel was back. Subsequent evidence proved we were right. He took an immediate grip on the situation, and concentrated all his reserves in the north. Meantime Montgomery was building up a hitting reserve behind the "bulge" as it was now called. There were some desperate moments during these days, especially when a battalion of the Rifle Brigade in an advanced position we called Kidney Ridge was counter-attacked five times in a day by the 15th Panzer Division, but held out.

'Montgomery was making his plan for the break-through. The threat from the 7th Armoured Division in the south had paid its way, and the division was now brought north into reserve. Everyone moved up one, with the result that there was a spear formation, the 4th Indian Division in the bulge. The plan had the simplicity of genius. It was to persuade the Germans that we were going one way, and then to go the other. It worked perfectly. On the 29th the 9th Australian Division, after bitter fighting, advanced due north across the coast road almost cutting off an enemy force of about two regiments in a strong point known as

206

German tank crew surrender.

Thomson's post. On the map it looked just like a thumb stretched up toward the sea. The Australians were exposed in this precarious salient, but they were told to stay there. Rommel was drawn. All day on the 30th and the 31st the enemy dashed himself against the Thumb. Gradually the whole of the enemy reserve, including the 21st Panzer and the 90th Light, was concentrated astride the road, right in the north. It was tired and battle worn. The Australians had not yielded an inch.

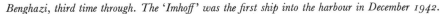

Benghazi, third time through. The 'Imhoff' was the first ship into the harbour in December 1942.

ABOVE: *General Ritter von Thoma steps into the bag.*
BELOW: *Montgomery counts up his gains.*

'It was the moment Montgomery was waiting for. After a night attack by the Highlanders and the New Zealanders, gaps were made farther south, and on November 2nd the whole weight of the Eighth Army's armour poured west straight out of the bulge. The Germans were caught off balance. Their attention was toward the north, and the Thumb had become an obsession to Rommel. Before he could re-concentrate to meet the threat from a new direction, the 1st and 10th Armoured Divisions were among him. A fierce battle was fought at El Aqqaqir, and it was here in this flat out, hammer-and-tongs fighting on murderously open and featureless ground that the final pressure was applied. By nightfall the enemy had cracked, and was starting to disengage.

'But Montgomery had another trump in hand. The 4th Indian Division broke south-west through the Trieste and Trento Divisions, now ripe for surrender, and through the gap poured the 7th Armoured Division. Meantime the armoured cars of the South Africans and the Royals were clean through. Like pirates back in their element after months of waiting they preyed on the enemy soft-skinned transport and caused pandemonium in his rear.

'Rommel's main stocks and dumps and workshops were at Daba, some twenty miles up the coast road. To cover their evacuation he tried to stand, but the old, old story had begun. There was no longer a line with two firm flanks. The southern desert flank was open and the 7th Armoured Division was round it before Rommel could call a halt. The Afrika Korps commander, von Thoma, was in the bag, and

Traffic diversion on the Derna road; this was the cross-roads of two armies.

the retreat for the moment became a rout. Tanks, guns, vehicles, stores were abandoned, burnt out and scattered along the roadside, while Rommel tried to break right away. Past Daba, where the tank workshops were left almost intact, and a train was still steaming in the station, past Fuka, the Axis remnants streamed, pounded ruthlessly by the R.A.F. Tanks were abandoned in panic when they ran out of fuel, aircraft abandoned intact on the Daba landing grounds.

'Nose to tail, two deep, the Eighth Army poured west, back past the old familiar places, tanks, guns without number, without an enemy aircraft disturbing them. In the other direction marched long columns of tattered, tired, dejected Germans and Italians, to join the four divisions Rommel had abandoned in the southern part of the line, and to continue their dreary march into captivity in Egypt, the land they had so nearly conquered. The Axis had suffered its first great defeat of war, and the tide had turned.'

After Alamein began the usual bi-annual cross-country race across Cyrenaica. It was an especially brisk affair this year, as the Eighth Army fetched up on the finishing line at El Agheila inside three weeks—a record. But there was just this difference from the other two British advances—Montgomery was given the means to plan his supply ahead so that he would be able to hold what he had already won and eventually push on to Tripoli. Nine-tenths of desert warfare is the battle of supply. Whoever first gets up most water, food, fuel, guns and men, wins the campaign.

This time the British had engineers waiting to repair the roads, railways, bridges and ports. This time the ships were waiting to put into Benghazi, and the port was open for them to unload three thousand tons a day. This time we had American Douglas aircraft to carry urgent supplies at speed with a rapid shuttle service between Cairo and El Agheila. Despite a violent three-day storm which wrecked the ships in Benghazi, despite the foul and bitter weather all over the desert, Montgomery won the battle of supply.

He was planning to attack again at El Agheila on December 14th. Rommel neatly anticipated the matter by slipping out two days beforehand. Nevertheless, Montgomery very nearly accomplished what he had set his heart on doing— capturing the Afrika Korps—and his plan is interesting because it shows the effect of the lessons learned at Alamein. At El Agheila he developed the tactics which were the distinguishing mark of all Montgomery's actions—a direct blow with the right and an encircling blow with the left. These tactics were more or less forced on the General since he always had the sea on his right and, except at Alamein and his one unsuccessful engagement at Enfidaville, the enemy line could always be outflanked in the empty desert to the south. Like nearly every other innovation in the desert, this tactic was first discovered by Wavell; but Montgomery gave the plan incisiveness and additional speed. Wavell's left-right blitz on the Sidi Barrani Line in 1940, his schemes for the reduction of desert strongholds, and his general plan of striking straight for Benghazi while his mobile forces cut across the desert behind the enemy have become classic desert lore now, and neither Rommel nor Montgomery were able to make any basic improvement on them; but they were supplied with much faster and better machines than Wavell and they controlled very much larger armies.

On this occasion, Montgomery sent the New Zealanders off on a staggering

Heavy German tank on fire.

march around and behind the enemy positions at El Agheila. The New Zealanders got into position on time and then found they had been asked to bite off far too big a mouthful. They spaced their infantry brigades around Rommel's rear as best they could and stood by to receive the shock of the full Afrika Korps. Rommel, months before on the Gazala Line, had failed to capture a full British division, the Fiftieth, which was caught in much the same position, so now the Germans, profiting by that lesson, escaped in just the same way. They split into small commandos, each led by tanks, and slipped through the New Zealanders in the dark.

There remained nothing for Montgomery to do but take up the weary chase, and the Eighth Army plunged ahead into regions the British had never entered before. Apart from supply, which dominated everything, the chase developed into a battle of wits between the German and British engineers. A great deal of the German mining technique, which later was a crucial thing in the battle for Tunis, was learned out here in the desert where this one black ribbon of road wound on interminably over the waste of sand. It was a cruel business, mining, a thing that gratified no one's instincts for combat, for it was a stab in the back and the stabber ran no risks himself.

The German S mine projected three prongs above the ground. When a man stepped on it there was a small explosion, a metal ball jumped waist-high into the

Man and tank smashed together.

air and then burst, ejecting small shot in every direction. Its mission was solely to wound and kill soldiers who were off their guard. The German Teller mine was a round metal tin, rather larger than a soup plate, which was buried just below the ground and it contained enough explosive to break a tank track or demolish a lorry. The Italians had a rectangular mine for the same purpose. There were variations of these mines, but all of them were either anti-personnel or anti-vehicle. In addition there were booby traps of half a dozen varieties mostly based on the idea that if a string were pulled unawares the pin was jerked out of a hand-grenade which thereupon exploded.

The Germans developed this mining to a science along the road to Tripoli. Everything likely or unlikely was mined or booby-trapped. To give you some idea of the complexity of this mining, here is what would happen when the retreating German sappers got to work on a bridge. First the bridge would be blown up. Then the fallen rubble would be S-mined. Then the approaches to the crater on either side would be mined with Tellers. Then the earthen tracks which wound round on either side of the fallen bridge would be Teller-mined by placing one mine above another so that when the British sappers came along and pulled up the first mine they would be blown up on the second. Then, presuming that the crew of a tank or truck would jump out immediately they struck one of these mines, the Germans spread S mines about at the point where they estimated the tommies would land. Then, in case they still escaped, trip-wires attached to booby traps would be strung between the bushes, or among discarded ammunition cases or in overturned vehicles. Often the road-mines would be varied so that they did not go up until several vehicles had passed over and the drivers believed the path to be clear.

The Germans were wonderful toy-makers. They made a wooden mine which could not be detected with our usual apparatus which is a flat metal plate on the end of a rod. The mine searcher wears earphones and the electric device in the instrument emits a high-pitched whine if the plate is placed over metal—but not over wood. Still another device of the Germans was to place the detonator for a mine at some distance in advance of the mine itself.

These savage inventions were the things that held up Montgomery on his long march until at last in January he found himself poised over Tripoli and the Germans once again massing in front of him. The enemy chose a three-pronged wadi called Zem-Zem and mounted their guns on the more westerly of the three ravines. Once more Montgomery struck with a right and a left—the Highland Division leading the frontal assault, the New Zealanders making another forced march through the desert to the south. This time the New Zealanders had to go through country so rough that even the desert veterans were left speechless. Tanks had to stand by all day dragging the vehicles up the worst bits.

The Germans were wonderful toy-makers. Their 'S' mines held 260 pieces of shrapnel.

*The 8th Army enters Tripoli,
January 1943. Pipers take
in the Gordon Highlanders.*

*At last, after thirty months
of warfare, the desert soldier
stood beside the playing
fountains of Tripoli.*

Meanwhile a third force was converging on Tripoli. General Le Clerc and a brigade of Fighting Frenchmen had made a fantastic forced march from Lake Chad in the centre of Africa, taking one oasis after another, and now they were ready to strike in from the south.

Once again Rommel, after a few sharp rearguard actions, withdrew his army and the Allies marched into the open town of Tripoli. The Highland pipers went piping into the main square; and at last, after thirty months of warfare, the ragged and dishevelled desert soldier stood with wonderment and emotion beside the playing fountains. If one excepts the entrance of the Germans into Paris, of the Japanese into Singapore and the return of the Russians to Stalingrad, there can have been no moment in the war to equal to this one.

In the swaying battle of the desert, Tripoli had for two and a half years appeared as a mirage that grew strong and now faded away again, and was for ever just beyond the Eighth Army's reach. So many had died or been withdrawn through wounds at a time when the struggle looked futile and endless. So many had recovered hope only to lose it again. So many had aged and grown sick and weak.

ADDRESS

Hymn

of our fathers, known of old.
rd of our far-flung battle-line,
ath whose awful Hand we
   hold
minion over palm and pine—
 God of Hosts, be with us yet,
 we forget—lest we forget.

tumult and the shouting dies;
e captains and the kings
  depart;
stands Thine ancient
  Sacrifice;
a humble and a contrite heart.
 God of Hosts, be with us yet,
 we forget—lest we forget.

Far-called, our navies melt
  away,
On dune and headland sinks
  the fire,
Lo, all our pomp of yesterday
  Is one with Nineveh and
   Tyre!
Judge of the Nations, spare us
  yet,
Lest we forget—lest we forget.

If drunk with sight of power,
  we loose
Wild tongues that have not
  Thee in awe,
Such boastings as the Gentiles
  use,
Or lesser breeds without the
  Law,
Lord God of Hosts, be with us
  yet,
Lest we forget—lest we forget.

For heathen heart that puts her
  trust
In reeking tube and iron shard,
All valiant dust that builds on
  dust,
And guarding, calls not Thee to
  guard,
For frantic boast and foolish
  word—
Thy Mercy on Thy People, Lord.
     Amen.

Solemn Remembrance of the Fallen

They shall not grow old as we that are left grow old.
Age shall not weary them nor the years condemn.
At the going down of the sun, and in the morning,
  We will remember them.

Answer. We will remember them.

PRAYER

Lord God of our fathers we pray that Thou wouldest accept the ser- and sacrifice of our comrades who have fallen in battle. Do thou grant them a place of refreshment and peace, where the light of Thy coun- ce shines for ever, and where all tears are wiped away. Through Jesus our Lord. Amen.

THE KING
THE BLESSING

30 CORPS ORDER OF SERVICE

OF

Thanksgiving and Remembrance

After the Capture of Tripoli

Sunday, 31st January, 1943

Hymn

God, our help in ages past,
Our hope for years to come,
Our shelter from the stormy
  blast,
And our eternal home.

Beneath the shadow of Thy
  Throne
Thy Saints have dwelt secure;
Sufficient is Thine Arm alone,
And our defence is sure.

Before the hills in order stood,
Or earth received her frame,
From everlasting Thou art God,
To endless years the same.

A thousand ages in Thy Sight
Are like an evening gone;
Short as the watch that ends
  the night
Before the rising sun.

Time, like an ever-rolling
  stream,
Bears all its sons away;
They fly forgotten as a dream
Dies at the opening day.

O God, our help in ages past,
Our hope for years to come,
Be Thou our guard while
  troubles last
And our eternal home. Amen.

SENTENCE

I Will lift up mine eyes unto the hills: from whence cometh my help. My help cometh even from the Lord who hath made heaven and earth.

Hymn sheet for the Thanksgiving Service held at Tripoli.

Churchill, Montgomery and Alan Brooke rejoice over Tripoli.

Only those who had suffered the test of the desert, and for a long time, will be able to understand the emotions of the victors at the end—the constricting excitement of the last few hours when the army was about to penetrate the green suburbs, the bursting elation of the actual entrance into the town and the inevitable sense of anti-climax which followed.

This sense of anti-climax came all the more sharply upon the army because it was suddenly made to realize that its job was not yet done. Tripoli had always been for them the conclusion of the African war, the ultimate reward for the men coming

Spahis, the most decorative troops in North Africa.

216

Confidences at Casablanca.

The Mark IV Special.

out of the desert. But now something more was asked of them. The majority of the army was not even allowed to go into the town—it was obliged to plunge once more into the wastes and pursue Rommel across the border of Tripolitania, into Tunisia.

*

In the last week of March the Eighth Army fell upon the Mareth Line. Again Montgomery attacked by night. Again he began with an intense artillery barrage. Again he struck first with a direct righthanded blow and then with a left-handed flanking move. And again the Air Force was very closely interlocked with the advancing troops.

Rommel had already surrendered Médenine and the outlying defences without much argument some weeks before. He had established his real defence on the Wadi Zigzaou, a formidable rift in the land with very steep sides and still treacherous with winter mud.

The battle did not go well. The British 50th Division crossed the wadi, but only with great difficulty—at places the men were clambering over one another's shoulders to reach the opposite side. A slender bridgehead was made, but when morning came the anti-tank guns had still not been got across. When the inevitable German counter-attack came in, the British infantry were hopelessly exposed, and Panzer tanks charged right in among their positions. In some confusion the division was withdrawn across the wadi again.

This left the left-hand flanking column in an unhappy position. It was again the New Zealanders who had gone round, with a brigade of tanks, toward their objective —El Hamma—behind the enemy main line. Rommel now wheeled his heavy units on to El Hamma, and General Montgomery was obliged to think very quickly indeed. Those who had grown to believe that the General was incapable of anything more than his standard right-left plan now saw something new put into effect and at speed and in a crisis.

A new sector was opened between the coast and the New Zealanders. At the same time all available armour and aircraft was flung into support of the New

218

Zealanders—possible the boldest thing Montgomery ever did. Rommel was forced then to withhold some of his strength from the New Zealanders and deal with the new threat in the centre. Immediately he saw the Germans splitting up, Montgomery ordered the New Zealanders and their armour into attack. Again the pressure was applied at the coast, and by March 27th it was all over. The Eighth Army rode into the hamlet of Gabes, taking many thousands of Italian infantry, who had again been left behind, while the Germans retired to their second position on the Wadi Akarit, a few miles farther north. It was a battle that had begun badly and might have bogged down indefinitely but for the quick change-over in the British plans half-way through.

Ten days later Montgomery went crashing in for his last great battle, in the south at Wadi Akarit. This time he charged head-on with his Highland Division, the Indians and the 50th. The Eighth Army was a wonderful machine when it was geared up to fight. It went forward with a terrible momentum and in a wonderfully adjusted rhythm—first the bombers, then the guns, then the infantry, then the tanks. Six gaps were blasted in the enemy line along the Wadi Akarit, and then the 1st Armoured Division and the New Zealanders poured through for the kill. Once again the German line broke under the stroke of the piston. For one hundred and fifty miles along the coast north of Akarit the German general von Arnim had no defensive position. It was every man for himself now in the enemy camp. If you were lucky enough to possess a truck, you jumped aboard with your pals and lit out for the north with all the speed you could make. The R.A.F. fell on that retreat, but it was too great to smash entirely. A vast crocodile of German vehicles filed northwards day and night. It ran into Sfax and out again. It streamed into Sousse and still flowed northwards.

20

Now the great moment was approaching: the link-up between the Eighth and First Armies. All this time, while Montgomery had been driving the Germans along the seaboard from Alamein to Tripoli and from Tripoli to Mareth, the First Army, which had landed in North Africa in November, had been fighting their

Americans in action in Tunisia. The gun is nicknamed a 'duckshooter'; in the background the ancient fort of Gafsa.

Seaforth Highlanders scale the side of Wadi Zigazou.

way from Algiers up to meet him. I was with them when they entered Kairouan, just about the same time as Montgomery was approaching Sousse. Beyond Kairouan the good hard road ran straight to Sousse on the sea. All my instincts now made me want to meet the Eighth Army again. I had left them eight months before at Alamein, and at a moment of indecision and defence. Now they rode on a great victory, and I was curious to see if my friends had changed. Sousse lay only eighty kilometres away from Kairouan, but the road was empty and no one yet had passed along it.

We picked our way past cautiously. The country here had burst into a wild fantasy of colour, and that overworked cliché 'a carpet of flowers' became a proven fact. It was just that, a rich deep Persian carpet woven of bluebells and poppies, of sweet-peas and tulips, of daisies and lilies; and these grew so thickly that for miles you could not see the ground or the grass, only flowers. They made patterns that swept over hill-tops, hilarious, shouting bands of colour.

We came on scattered villages where the people ran out and waved flags as we went by. Twice we ducked into a wood and hid from aircraft. The country began to break up a little into hills, and then at last we turned into the town of Msaken and saw the Eighth Army. We had come in off a side road and just for a moment it seemed that we had made a bad mistake. The vehicles running up the main road were all German or Italian. Then drawing closer I saw the British troops in the lorries. The British desert soldier looked like no other soldier in the world. He looked at first sight like a rather rakish and dishevelled boy scout, the effect, I suppose, of his bleached khaki shorts and shirt and the paraphernalia of blackened pots and pans and oddments he carried round in his vehicle which was his home. He practically never wore a helmet, and he had a careless loose-limbed way of walking which came from living on the open plains and which was altogether different from the hill troops weighed down by heavy battle-dress. The desert is a healthy place especially if you can camp by the sea. These youths were burnt incredibly by the sun and they had that quality of brimming health that made them shout and sing as they went along.

220

Very content to be among them again, I struck up conversations with the troops as we bumped along in the cavalcade. It seemed that they had taken over the enemy vehicles when their own had broken down. Montgomery's forces had split into two halves, one going directly into Sousse on the coast, the other splitting off northward here at Msaken because the main bridge was blown by the enemy.

For an hour or more we coasted along over a rough and filthy track, and after many months I felt almost pleasurably my lungs filling up with dust again. It was much warmer here on the coast and the palm trees still gave the flavour of the desert. The progress was very slow and sometimes we ran into traffic blocks, for ten minutes or more. The Eighth Army was swarming through the countryside and every side road was choked.

At last we cut around a field of cactus and joined the main road north of Sousse. With the main road we hit the New Zealand Division coming head on toward us— in the way the enemy would see it coming. They rolled by with their tanks and their guns and armoured cars, the finest troops of their kind in the world, the outflanking experts, the men who had fought the Germans in the desert for two years, the victors of half a dozen pitched battles. They were too gaunt and lean to be handsome, too hard and sinewy to be graceful, too youthful and physical to be complete. But if you ever wished to see the most resilient and practised fighter of the Anglo-Saxon armies this was he. This wonderful division took a good deal of its fighting morale from its English General, Freyberg, the V.C. who through two wars had probably been more critically wounded more often than any other living man.

Against this tremendous flood of vehicles, all painted a brilliant light desert yellow, we rode into the blasted town of Sousse. For months this place had been attacked by the R.A.F. and the United States Air Force; and now driving in through the target area along the docks it was a frightening sight, a vision of what we were one day going to see in the Ruhr, in Germany. It was not so much the general devastation, it was the violence with which everything had been done. A grand piano had been picked up from a basement and flung on to a house-top. The roof of one apartment building had been flung bodily on to the next building. The palm trees on the waterfront looked like those photographs one used to see after a hurricane had passed across Florida. The ships in the bay were set in a frame of blackened warehouses and they were in all stages of decomposition—the ships that had been merely hit and sunk, those that had been beached by a near miss and subsequently broken up by the waves, those that had been entirely disintegrated. Bits of cork, broken scraps of lifeboats and rope and spars were mingled with the tangled mess of the railway lines that ran down to the docks. The walled Arab section—the Kasbah—had been split open and the midday sun poured in over all its tawdry and shabby secrets; the labyrinthine brothels, the sweet-vendor's shops, the miserable fœtid courtyards where the Moorish women wasted their obscure and furtive lives.

Beyond this, away from the port, the modern city had been untouched, and now the civilians were in the excited high-tide of their relief that at last the hell of bombing was over. And so they made the soldiers welcome. A day or two later when Montgomery drove through the town in a jeep a great crowd saluted him, 'Vive Mong-goum-ree, vive Mong-goum-ree,' and an unusually attractive little French girl offered a bouquet and flung her arms round the General's neck. But today they were still a little stunned.

I hunted about through the ruined streets looking for my friend, Alexander Clifford. I was quite certain he would turn up. He had, of course, entered the town within an hour of its fall and we met in the main street.

And now I began to understand the differences between the First and the Eighth Armies. Already there was a good deal of superficial jealousy and fundamental misunderstandings. The soldiers who had been struggling all winter in the mountains and the mud of northern Tunisia regarded the desert soldiers as noisy and over-confident, an army that was sunning itself in publicity, and they looked forward with grim and unfriendly relish to the moment when the desert fighters struck the mountains.

In the same way the First Army men themselves were not understood. They appeared to the veteran soldiers in Montgomery's forces as a parade-ground army, beautifully equipped but not much good at fighting.

I do not say that these feelings went very deep, but the antagonism was there, and it continued until the troops went into action side by side. Then they began to know one another.

The fact was that the Eighth Army was not a European army any more. To a great extent it had become an overseas army, an army based not on London but on Cairo. For months and years it had been cut off from Europe, and in their isolation the troops had developed a complicated set of private habits, and even a slang language of their own. Anyone who did not fit into these habits, who had not shared their adventures, was an outsider. The Eighth Army had been encouraged for the past few months by Montgomery to regard itself as invincible, as an independent and private expeditionary force knowing no law except its own. It was irksome, therefore, for this vigorous and victorious force, to learn, following the Casablanca conference, that it had been placed under the command of Algiers. They felt a little aggressive about it and showed it.

Meanwhile the fascinating spectacle of the desert army entering the mountains was going on. The enemy had halted about thirty miles north of Sousse around the village of Enfidaville. It was an obvious place in which to make a stand, for at that point the mountains came down almost to the sea.

The white walls of the holy city of Kairouan.

The attack began long before dawn on April 19th. Feeling our way forward in the darkness to the New Zealand headquarters we heard enough to know that it was not going too well. Enfidaville itself fell quickly enough, but beyond that the enemy were dug into fearsome hills, hills that had to be assaulted directly. For an hour I watched them sending down concentrated mortar fire and the Eighth Army's guns bayed back in force until the hills were full of teeming smoke from the shell-bursts. The Indians, the New Zealanders and the Guards went in and soon found themselves obliged to swarm up sheer cliffs. The enemy above had merely to fire their guns straight down on the climbing men. The Gurkhas were in their own country here, and when they did get to grips with the Italians they did terrible things. They used the knife. There were even hand-to-hand struggles where men sought to throw one another from the heights.

For the rest of the men their first contact with the hills was not easy. Some confessed they even had that same feeling of claustrophobia I remembered on arriving in Tunisia, the feeling, too, that one was being constantly overlooked—as indeed one was.

It is doubtful if any army could have broken through that Enfidaville position without support from the left flank. Unit after unit was sent in. Some reached the caves where the enemy were in hiding, but there were always more caves higher up more mortars, more open slopes to cross against machine-gun fire. By the end of two bitter days of many casualties it was evident that the first attack was not going to break through.

Tanks could not operate in this congested space, and it was at this point—about April 21st—that Alexander diverted the First British Armoured Division away from Montgomery's army and attached it to Anderson's forces in the Goubellat Plain.

Again and again the desert fighters thrust forward, always making a little ground, but never forcing a decisive action.

There followed a number of rapid conferences among the generals. Clearly now we were in sight of victory. By this time Rommel had surrendered his command and left Africa for good. To General von Arnim fell the grisly and thankless task of making a Stalingrad on the Mediterranean. The enemy was compressed into the last tip of Tunisia. We dominated the air—it had been a wonderful sight seeing our machines flying out all day over Enfidaville. We out-gunned the enemy and we out-tanked him. But still he stood on the vital passes—Green and Bald Hills in the Sedjenane Sector, Longstop Hill in the Medjerda sector, Pont du Fahs farther south and then finally at Enfidaville.

It was no longer a matter of friendly rivalry—who should get into Tunis first, the Eighth or the First Army. It was a question of whether we were going to get in at all and of how to do it with the least loss of life and machines.

There were three known centres of interior enemy resistance which were capable of standing even when the outer passes had gone—Bizerta, Tunis and Cape Bon Peninsula. No one at that time exactly knew von Arnim's intentions, though it was fairly clear that Cape Bon was going to be used as an evacuation area.

Standing on the coast one day in the purple and white village of Hergla I looked across and saw the heights of the Cape Bon mountains, but that did not mean we could get there. Already by April 21st it was becoming pretty evident that we were never going to break through on the coast. The Medjerda Valley still appeared to be the best way in. But the Medjerda Valley was blocked so long as the Germans held Longstop Hill. On April 23rd Alexander attacked the hill.

21

WHAT a legend Longstop had become. We checked it on a dozen different maps. We explored the roads and tracks around the hill. We talked about it . . . 'Once we are on Longstop . . .' The veterans who had mounted the hill before we were thrown off in the early days declared that on a clear afternoon you could almost see Tunis from the heights.

For five months it had lain right in the front line, the fortress of the Medjerda Valley, the locked gate on the road to Tunis. We climbed the surrounding hills and looked down upon the hill and it always appeared darker than the surrounding country and more sinister, a great two-humped bulk that heaved itself out of the wheatfields like some fabulous whale beached on the edge of a green sea.

Beyond the last battery we crept around the crest of a steep hill until we were in view of the enemy in Heidous village across the valley and Longstop lay below us on the right.

From that height everything appeared to happen in miniature. The Churchill tanks climbing on Jebel Ang looked like toys. The infantry that crept across the uplands toward Heidous were tiny dark dots, and when the mortar shells fell among them it was like drops of rain on a muddy puddle. Toy donkeys toiled up the tracks toward the mountain crests, and the Germans, too, were like toys, little animated figures that occasionally got up and ran or bobbed up out of holes in the ground between the shell explosions.

Most of our shells were falling on the near slopes of Longstop. The barrage kept rushing over our heads and falling among the black gorse on the hill, and at

224

*American troops
land in
North Africa.*

times it was so heavy everything disappeared in grey-black smoke and the hill
became a cloud of fumes and dust.

On Longstop the Germans had dug trenches which had a horizontal shelf deep
below the surface. During a barrage such as this the Germans lay under this shelf
and waited in safety. Their guns were fired from below the surface so that it was
only in the very last stages of an assault that they had to put their heads out. They
had ample stores of food and water and ammunition. The Germans knew that the
British infantry would have to cross the minefields first and that they would have
to expose themselves as they climbed upward. It was no use our ignoring Longstop
by going round it. The Germans would still be able to shell the two roads running
into Tunis. They would break up our convoys. They would launch counter-
attacks from the hill. And so it was necessary now, even at great cost, for the 78th
Division to make a direct assault.

On the second morning of the battle, when the British guns had done all they
could, I went with my party down on to the plain before Longstop to see the
the infantry go in. The brigade in charge of this operation had taken over a farmhouse in a little grove of trees. The command vehicles were drawn up against a wall
close to a ruined tennis-court.

The enemy seemed to be aware that this was a headquarters because they kept
firing at the place, occasionally with 88-millimetre shells, occasionally with mortars
that sent up puffs of black or white dust according to whether they landed on rock
or soil. It was never quite clear until the last second whether shells would fall over
the farmhouse or short of it.

We could see the lower slopes of Longstop quite clearly from brigade headquarters, and even here, only half a mile off, the hill looked dark and uncouth.
Zero hour for the attack was 1.30 p.m., but the Germans above could see our infantry massing, and they were already firing very heavily upon them with mortars.

225

It was hot, and presently through the dust Bren-gun carriers came rattling down the track that led from the hill. The wounded were piled on the carriers just as they had been lifted there in the midst of the firing. They lay quite still on their backs, staring upwards, and the blood dripped down among the instruments inside the carriers.

The drivers sat fixedly in their seats and said nothing. They brought the vehicles to a standstill beside a line of ambulances sheltering under the cactus hedge, and the stretcher-bearers lifted the wounded on to stretchers and slid them into the ambulances. Then the Bren-gun carriers turned and went back through the dust into the battle again.

One of the officers who came back took his helmet off and let it drop on the ground. 'The men are very tired,' he said. 'It's not the opposition so much, it's sleep. They have been going for a long time now.'

'How long?'

'I don't know—a long time.' The officer himself was very tired. He had been in the line for a week, and during the previous night some of his men had just fallen on the ground and cried. They cried because they had no strength any more, not even the strength to stand up. They had continued without sleep for two days under the compulsion of their brains and beyond the point where the body will normally function. But now, when their minds would not work any more, they discovered that the strength had already gone out of their bodies and that, in fact, they had no control of anything any more, not even of tears. The tears came quite involuntarily and without any sense of relief because the body was incapable of feeling anything any more, and what became of the body now was of no consequence. And so they had lain about the hill for an hour or two in a stupor. The cold and the dew bit into them through the night and brought them back to consciousness. Then they had stumbled about in the darkness until they found their platoons. They ate a little cold bully without tasting it and took swigs from their water-bottles. By morning their brains were operating again, not their bodies, but their brains, and they were able to contemplate themselves and consider what still had to be done. Some of them slept in the sun through the morning and this brought back a little strength into their bodies—enough to co-operate with their minds and give obedience. At noon then, they had regrouped, and they mechanically registered the order that they had to attack again, and they assessed their strength against what was required by the order. These were the men who came back in the Bren-gun carriers.

The wounded were not yet in great pain because the shock of the bullets in their flesh was still taking effect. They were very dirty, and the dirt ran in lines in the sagging hollows of their faces. Their hands dropped over the edges of the stretchers, lumpish hands, coloured a greyish yellow colour that was inhuman. No one could look at them without protesting.

The German prisoners came next. Black jack-boots, green gabardine uniforms, wings on their chests, cloth caps with the red, white and black badge, the Afrika Korps. They marched stolidly in columns of three, the officers in front. They were not so tired as our men, since they had been lying in provisioned dugouts, and they marched mechanically, but well. One of the officers started to argue. He wanted to see a British officer. A Scots sergeant waved him on bleakly with the tip of his bayonet.

226

That night they took three-quarters of Longstop Hill. As soon as it was light in the morning I drove to brigade headquarters. A young signals officer was going up to the hill in his truck and he offered to take my party with him. We got only half a mile in the truck and then, leaving it under the cover of the high wheat, we began climbing on foot, keeping to the right-hand side of the hill.

Now we were on the hill, I saw that it was much more thickly covered with scrub than had appeared from the distance; and it did not consist of two big humps, but a whole series, seven in all, with many subsidiary ridges. As soon as we pulled ourselves to the top of one slope another appeared above us. Over all this ground the troops had fought the day before, and now the carriers were bringing up water-cans that had to be lugged the last half of the journey by hand.

On the lip of the third rise we came suddenly upon a scene so dramatic, so complete in itself that I recall it now, detail by detail, almost as I would remember a painting or a play in the theatre. It was a front-line trench. The Germans had dug it, but our men had occupied it the day before. It was a shallow trench and it made a zigzag suture through the blackened grass on the slope of the hill. On the piles of freshly turned yellow soil the men had thrown their battle-dress jackets, the tin mugs and plates from which they had been eating, the empty salmon and bully-beef tins.

227

Sappers lifting mines among the flowers . . . bluebells and poppies, sweet peas and tulips, daisies and lilies.

A Gurkha sharpens his knife before the battle.

A profusion of things lay about all the way up the trench—empty packets of cigarettes, both British and German, water-bottles and hand-grenades, half-used boxes of cartridges, German steel helmets, bits of notepaper, discarded packs and torn pieces of clothing. Through this mess the rifles and machine-guns were pointing out toward the next slope, but the men were not firing. The sun was shining strongly and they sat or leaned half in and half out of the trench. Some smoked. One man was mending a boot. Another was sewing on a button. But mostly they leaned loosely on the earth and rested. Every time an enemy gun sounded they cocked their heads mechanically and waited for the whine that would give the direction of the shot. It was only a slight movement and you did not notice them doing it at first. Sometimes the shells landed short, three or four hundred yards away, sometimes very near, perhaps only fifty yards down the slope, but anyway not on the trench. No one commented on the nearness of the shells. They had had much heavier shelling than this all night, and these spasmodic shots were only a nuisance that still had the power to hurt unless one watched.

It was useless to picture these men who were winning the war for you as im-maculate and shining young heroes agog with enthusiasm for the Cause. They had seen too much dirt and filth for that. They hated the war. They knew it. And they were very realistic indeed about it. Instead of sitting on an exposed hill-top in the imminent danger of death they would have much preferred to have been on a drunk, or in bed with a girl, or eating a steak, or going to the movies. They fought because they were part of a system, part of a team. It was something they were obliged to do, and now that they were in it they had a technical interest and a pride in it. They wanted to win and get out of it—the sooner the better. They had no high notions of glory. A great number of people at home who referred emotionally to

*Each night the patrols
went out seeking information.*

'Our Boys' would have been shocked and horrified if they had known just how the boys were thinking and behaving. They would have regarded them as young hooligans. And this was because the real degrading nature of war was not understood by the public at home, and it never can be understood by anyone who has not spent months in the trenches or in the air or at sea. More than half the Army did not know what it was because they had not been in the trenches. Only a tiny proportion, one-fifth of the race perhaps, know what it is, and it is an experience that sets them apart from other people.

We went higher onto Longstop to join the Argylls, and as we moved off, the men shouted at us to keep down so that we would not draw the fire on to their position.

The Argylls, too, were resting after the bad night, and their eyes were red-rimmed with fatigue. The commanding officer had been killed. His deputy, a tall major who was a Highland farmer, had been drinking wine with us at Thibar only a few days before, but now a great gulf of experience separated us. He was still as hospitable and level-headed and kind, but there was something he could not communicate. We were very near the top of Longstop here. From the surrounding caves Germans were still being routed out. We overlooked a German gun-pit, empty now of men, but the black snouts of the guns still pointed toward us. In every direction the rocks were chipped with shell-blast and the camel thorn was rooted from the ground. A light heat haze hung over the far end of the hill, where the Germans were still hiding and shooting.

When the third day came it was evident that the enemy defences were pierced, and as we stood near the summit that afternoon new units were going in to mop up the rest. Longstop was taken in the only possible way, by men going in yelling with the bayonet and meeting the enemy face to face.

22

GENERAL ALEXANDER ordered a wholesale regrouping of the armies and at urgent speed. All the Americans, three divisions, were swung into the northern sector around Sedjenane. The French, with their new Valentine tanks and American vehicles, were wedged into the Pont du Fahs gap. On the coast Montgomery's forces were ordered merely to maintain a series of holding attacks. This left only the Medjerda Valley, and upon the Medjerda the General concentrated all

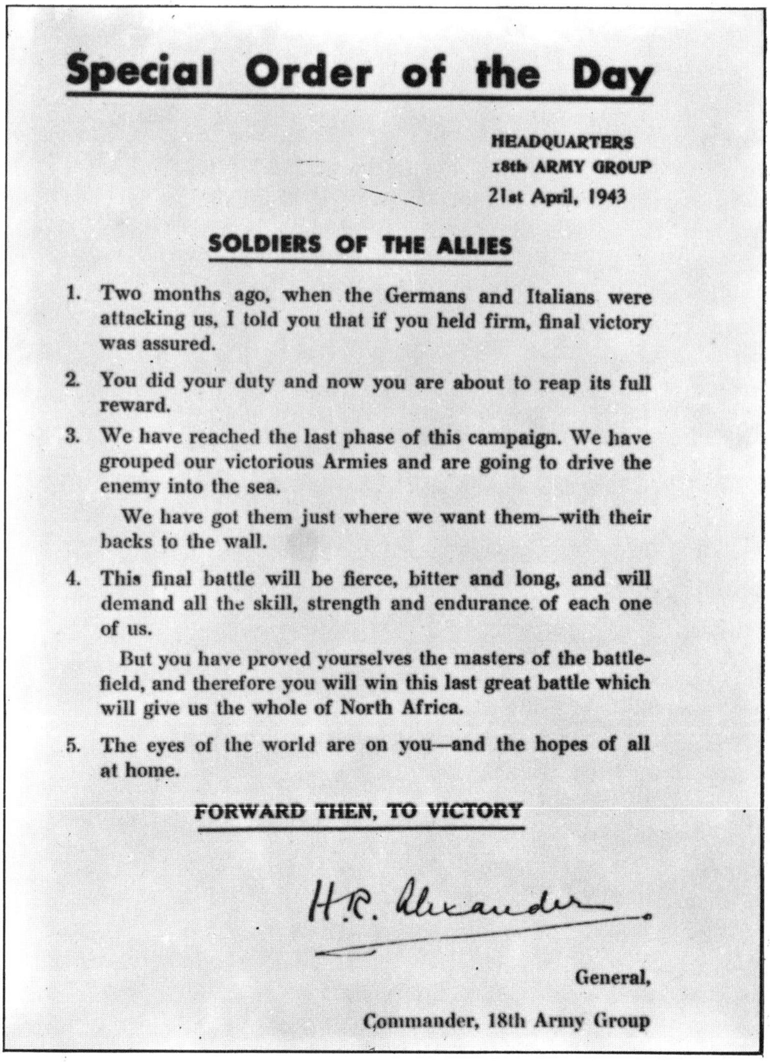

General Alexander's battle cry.

Special Order of the Day

HEADQUARTERS
18th ARMY GROUP
21st April, 1943

SOLDIERS OF THE ALLIES

1. Two months ago, when the Germans and Italians were attacking us, I told you that if you held firm, final victory was assured.

2. You did your duty and now you are about to reap its full reward.

3. We have reached the last phase of this campaign. We have grouped our victorious Armies and are going to drive the enemy into the sea.

   We have got them just where we want them—with their backs to the wall.

4. This final battle will be fierce, bitter and long, and will demand all the skill, strength and endurance of each one of us.

   But you have proved yourselves the masters of the battlefield, and therefore you will win this last great battle which will give us the whole of North Africa.

5. The eyes of the world are on you—and the hopes of all at home.

FORWARD THEN, TO VICTORY

H. R. Alexander

General,
Commander, 18th Army Group

Looking down on Mateur and the rolling hills still to be conquered.

his great hopes for a knock-out blow. He wanted only the best of his British forces here. Already the 78th Division, the 4th and the 1st Infantry Divisions were in position. To these were added the 6th Armoured Division from the First Army and the 7th Armoured Division and the Indian Division from the Eighth Army.

These last two desert divisions were obliged to make a spectacular forced march from the coast in order to reach the Medjerda Valley in time. They were unable to pause even long enough to camouflage their vehicles from the desert yellow to the mountain blacks and browns.

The scene on the roads during these days was bewildering. Tens of thousands of vehicles crammed the passes day and night, and when, after darkness fell, we were sometimes caught in the mountains away from our base at Thibar, it was an unnerving thing to drive past the immense convoys of blacked-out trucks and tanks. Not infrequently vehicles tumbled headlong into the valleys and ditches below, and the strain upon the drivers was intense.

The battle plan was quite simple. Now that the line was barely a hundred and thirty miles long, we were going to apply severe and continuous pressure along its whole length—the Americans striking toward Mateur, the British along the Medjerda Valley, the French at Pont du Fahs and the British again at Enfidaville. As soon as the pressure was applied in force then the blitz would go in up the Medjerda Valley, a needle-thrust aimed straight at Tunis. Two infantry divisions, the Indians and the 4th, were to break the crust of the German line. Then the two crack armoured divisions, the 7th and the 6th, would pour through and continue until they reached the sea.

A sector only three thousand yards wide was chosen for this thrust, and it was to go directly up the road from Medjez-el-Bab through Massicault and St. Cyprien to Tunis.

That was the broad plan. Although surprising and unpredictable things occurred and the plan had to be altered and extended, its essential structure remained the same to the end: by the night of May 5th the enemy's last battle line round Tunis lay exposed to immediate assault. At dawn on the following day the British blitz went in.

As I say, we had taken a sector of only three thousand yards for this last assault. This cauldron seemed to us at that time the whole battle and the whole world, but in reality it was a tiny piece of the line, not two per cent. of its entire length. Like the arc of a bubble now, the German line stretched round Tunis, and Alexander proposed to prick it in this one place.

Von Arnim was issuing printed orders of the day to his men: 'Behind you lies the sea; before you lies the enemy. You must go forward. You must fight to the last round and the last man'—the sort of pamphlet they issued at Stalingrad.

Alexander made his last reshuffles behind the lines. One-half of the force was from the Eighth Army and one-half from the First. That was right. Both armies should share in this honour. Lieutenant-General Horrocks was made the Corps Commander. He had been borrowed from the Eighth Army because he was a veteran, an aggressive man, a successful commander with three or four recent victories to his credit.

In the same way Air Marshal Coningham bound his two air forces together, the one from the desert and the one from the mountains, and it was an instrument of air war such as Africa had never seen before—thousands of aircraft. They had three jobs: to smash the enemy in Tunisia, to prevent what was left taking to the boats, to knock out the enemy ports and airfields in Sicily and southern Italy.

The tanks are gone, the bedouin and the goats remain.

Top-level discussions: ABOVE: *General Anderson and General Bradley meet in the mountains.*
LEFT: *General Eisenhower and General Montgomery talk in a cornfield.*

From the opening of the battle to the end I saw something I had never seen in a campaign before—shoals of Allied fighters patrolling back and forth, protecting the ground troops every hour of the day.

The guns had begun bellowing soon after midnight on May 6th, one shell landing every five yards every few seconds. It is simply not possible to explain the effect of that. Even if one is there, the full enormity of the noise and the brilliance of the light does not persist in the memory; and the Germans receiving the barrage do not speak clearly of it because each shell that fell near them was every shell; they could see nothing beyond their immediate trench and hear nothing except the monstrous noise of the explosions near at hand.

Under this roof of shells the sappers went forward at 4 a.m. In the flickering light of the explosions they cut the barbed wire and felt on the ground for the mines. Then the Indians and the British Infantry charged through. In the midst of the web of mines and mortars and bullets, the battle was on.

In that triangle of villages around Sidi Salem, Sidi Abdallah and Peter's Corner the Germans were manning their positions in the usual way when the British fell on them. While it was still dark the Indians and the Tommies came creeping through the wheat. Over the last few hundred yards they rose to their feet and rushed the enemy positions. They swarmed into the enemy dugouts. They yelled their war-cries, each man taking courage from the excitement of his neighbour, and they poured a hail of bullets across that three-thousand-yard front that was more terrible than the earlier barrage.

The German line was perhaps a mile or two miles thick—that is to say, there

Medjez el bab; they put a Bailey on the broken span of the beautiful old bridge.

was a loosely connected series of trenches and defended positions of that depth. At daylight the British were right in the midst of this line and our penetration was being measured in thousands of yards. It was scarcely noon when the leaders of the forward companies were reporting over their portable radios that they were meeting reduced opposition. They had burst clean through the German line and come out into the vacant space behind.

It was only a narrow breach, but that was all that Horrocks wanted: he had pricked the bubble; he was behind the German line; he was through the minefields. For seven or eight hours the tank crews of the 6th and 7th Armoured Divisions had been waiting. A few tanks had gone in with the infantry, but the bulk of them were waiting in the rear under the cover of the trees. He now turned to these vital reserves and said 'Go'.

The tanks charged ahead. They went straight at the gap the infantry had made for them, and they passed through practically unscathed. It was like releasing the flood-gates of a dam. In scores, in hundreds, this vast procession of steel lizards went grumbling and lurching and swaying up the Tunis road. Tunis itself lay barely thirty miles away, the line was pierced. Visors down, dust streaming out behind them, they shot ahead straight for Tunis. They took no account of the Germans on either side of them, no account of the fact that the road behind them might be closed. The line was pierced, and that was enough. They roared on. With them flowed the artillery and the anti-tank guns, the fuel and the ammunition wagons, the workshops and the recovery vehicles, the jeeps and the command cars. Out in front and on either flank rode the armoured cars on reconnaissance. When night came they were all on the road to Tunis.

On the morning of the 7th the Medjerda Valley had become a hateful place: it had turned from green to dirty yellows and greys; the fields of wild flowers had withered entirely; the ripening wheat was flattened; the dust was appalling.

234

Nearing Medjez-el-Bab visibility was barely two hundred yards, and on the dozens of newly made sidetracks it was much worse than that. Huge trucks lurched suddenly out of the gloom and we turned aside fifty times at the last moment to avoid a collision. General Alexander, driving a jeep, shot past us over a culvert. He was travelling at almost reckless speed, both his hands tight on the wheel and his face was whitened like a baker-boy's with white dust. For the first time we thought, 'Can Tunis fall to-day?' No one said this. No one liked to say it. But we all thought it as we raced down the side-tracks toward the main road.

Inside half an hour we were on yesterday's battlefield and no enemy anywhere, just empty trenches and gun-pits. Past the villages which the Germans had held for months, past Sidi Salem and Sidi Abdallah, were there had been nothing but death and killing the week before. Over a ruined bridge and round by Peter's Corner that was once an enemy stronghold. Nothing there now. Nothing but the rusting broken tanks around which the wheat and flowers had grown tall, as if the earth itself wanted to hide those hideous machines.

And then, on the main road, there it was again, for the third time in one month—the army careering forward in pursuit of the enemy. But this made the other cavalcades look puny and of no account. Miles before Furna the vehicles were touching almost bonnet to tailboard. They stacked themselves two and three deep along the road. The infantry lay sprawling on their kits on top of the lorries and their rifles

An American patrol infiltrating into Bizerta.

lay stacked together as though the war was over. At Furna still the procession went on; it was not so thick now, but still it stretched away in the distance. Only twenty miles to go. It was there on the white stone: 'Tunis 33 kilometres.'

Presently a mosque and another group of white farm-houses showed up across the plain—St. Cyprien. We ran into the village and stopped at the first farm-house. That was a pleasant moment. We had found the front—if you could call it a front. Standing there were the men and the guns of the Royal Horse Artillery—the Desert Rats, the original Desert Rats. The men I had seen in Syria and Abyssinia and the Desert. The guns that had fired from the very beginning of the African war for Wavell and Straffer Gott, for Jock Campbell and Alec Gatehouse. The twenty-five-pounders that used to accept and turn back the German tank-rushes in the desert though they were never meant to fire at tanks. They had come all the way from Alamein and they had been through everything: young Cockneys and Lancaster boys in shorts and shirts and burnt by the sun, men of the 7th Armoured Division who had fired the first shots in the African war, some of the finest gunners in the world.

Presently we fell in with a group of armoured cars reconnoitring the road. That was good; our own cars could not even stop a rifle bullet. They were travelling fast and we went with them, each vehicle spaced about fifty yards away from its neighbours. I counted the kilometre stones. Only eight miles now. It was gentle country, almost market-gardening country. The Arabs stared out of their huts without comprehending. The smoke ahead got heavier and heavier.

At Kilometre 9 all Tunis broke into view—the wide bay, flanked by mountains, the spreading town, one of the largest in Africa, not much harmed by bombs, but smoking now with a score of large fires. We stood poised on the summit for a moment before we dipped down in to the suburbs. Looking around, I saw I was again among the Desert Rats. The Red Jerboa in the red circle was painted on the battered mudguards, the most famous symbol in the whole Desert War. And the men in the vehicles were the Eleventh Hussars, the reconnaissance unit that had led the Eighth Army across the desert since Wavell's time. With them were the Derbyshire Yeomanry, the men who had led the First Army through all the hard fighting in Tunisia, and they carried the symbol of the mailed fist.

It is useless and stupid to argue which of these units was the best or debate who got into Tunis first. They arrived together. They were the representatives of the two most famous British divisions, the 6th and the 7th Armoured. They were both magnificent reconnoitring units. It was almost poetic that the Hussars and the Yeomanry should have come up to Tunis together. For those who had been in Africa from the beginning, there was something else, an incommunicable thing. It was beyond excitement of the immediate sense of triumph. Some of the men there were only by chance alive. They had fought so often, taken so many risks, seen so many of their friends die in the desert. They knew almost too well what it was to have hope and lose it, to hang on blindly and then to recover hope again. And so this was a moment of extraordinary emotional fullness and it was a thing of deep pride to see the men from the hills and the men from the desert come into Tunis together.

Crowds of French people rushed into the street and they were beside themselves in hysterical delight. Some rushed directly at us, flinging themselves on the running-boards. A girl threw her arms round my driver's neck. An old man took a packet of

236

The welcome in Tunis was hysterical.

cigarettes from his pocket and flung them up at us. Someone else brandished a bottle of wine. All the women had flowers that they had hastily plucked up from their gardens. A clump of roses hit me full on the mouth and there were flowers all over the bonnet of the car. Everyone was screaming and shouting and getting in the way of the vehicles, not caring whether they were run over or not.

The double doors of a big red building on the right-hand side of the street burst open and at first I could not understand—the men who ran out, scores, hundreds of them, were British, in flat steel helmets and British battle-dress. Then it came to me—they were prisoners whom we had rescued. They stood in an undecided group for a moment on the side-walk in the rain, filling their eyes with the sight of us. Then they cheered. Some of them had no heart to speak and simply looked. One man, bearded up to his eyes, cried quietly. The others yelled hoarsely. Suddenly the whole mass of men were swept with a torrent of emotional relief and wild joy. They yelled and yelled.

Meanwhile another patrol of armoured cars had taken the right fork, the Rue de Londres, down to the centre of the town. They took the city entirely unawares. Hundreds of Germans were walking in the streets, some with their girl friends. Hundreds more were sitting drinking apéritifs in a big pavement café. No one had warned them the British were near. The attack had gone so quickly that here in the town there had been no indication that the Axis line was broken. Now, suddenly, like a vision from the sky, appeared these three British armoured cars. The Germans rose from their seats and stared. The Tommies stared back. There was not much they could do. Three armoured cars could not handle all these prisoners. In the hairdressing saloon next door more Germans struggled out of

237

the chairs and, with white sheets round their necks and lather on their faces, stood gaping.

The three armoured cars turned back for reinforcements.

In this mad way Tunis fell that night. Here and there a German with desperate courage emptied his gun down on the streets and hurled a grenade or two. But for the most part these base troops in Tunis were taken entirely off their guard and there were thousands of them. All night there was hopeless confusion in the dark, Germans and British wandering about together, Italians scrambling into civilian clothes and taking refuge in the cellars, saboteurs starting new fires and igniting more dumps, men putting out to sea in rowing-boats, others grabbing bicycles and carts and making up the roads to Cape Bon, and others again, bewildered and afraid, simply marching along until they could find someone to whom they could surrender. All night the fires burned, and they were still going in the morning when the British infantry began to flood into the town in force.

We had entered the city at fifteen minutes to three on May 7th. It was just six months since the landing in North Africa, just on three years since the African war had begun.

*

While all this sorting-out was going on in Tunis tremendous events were happening outside the town. The Americans had broken clean through the mountains to the west and north of Medjerda Valley, and were mopping up prisoners in uncounted thousands. The 7th Armoured Division wheeled northward from Tunis and pur-

The road to death: German graves between Gafsa and Gabes.

The road to captivity: an entire German army laid down its arms

sued its old enemy, the 15th Panzer Division, up the coast road as far as Porto Farina, outside Bizerta. The Germans made one abortive attempt to escape by sea—bodies were being washed ashore for days afterwards—and then surrendered. Those two divisions had been fighting one another across the desert for years.

The Fighting French had come through Pont du Fahs in one epic rush and were counting their prisoners by the truck-load. On the coast the skeleton Eighth Army was again locked in a most bloody battle around Enfidaville.

But all this did not account for the main bulk of von Arnim's forces. They were in a state of disorder, but they were still intact. In a vast disorganized mob the majority of them had made for the Cape Bon Peninsula, where arrangements for evacuation ought to have been made. Cape Bon was defensible. A stiff double line of hills ran across its base, and von Arnim's last coherent plan was to get as many of his men and weapons as possible behind those hills before the British arrived.

It was not until a few days later that I realized what a masterpiece of design our break-through had been, and what enormous risks had been taken. In our headlong thrust to Tunis we had left huge numbers of the enemy in pockets on either side of us. It was an extremely narrow thrust, and the major risk was that the enemy might close in behind us and entirely surround the head of the British army. Fifty things might have gone wrong. As it turned out, the sheer depth and swiftness of the thrust entirely disorganized von Arnim's command. Von Arnim himself was put to flight. So were his corps and divisional headquarters. The result was that the big pockets of fresh fighting troops on either side of the British break-through were without orders. They saw a great column of enemy vehicles and tanks rushing past them, and they simply deduced that the game was up. They headed at full steam for Cape Bon.

Now, having taken this first major risk and got away with it, Alexander and Anderson decided to go one further.

They decided to split the German army in two halves by occupying the Hamman Lif–Hammamet line across the base of Cape Bon Peninsula before von Arnim could. In that way one-half of the Germans would be bottled up in the Peninsula, the other half would be isolated outside, and neither would even get a chance of getting to the boats. There was, of course, not an instant to lose, and already, before Tunis fell, the orders went out to the 6th Armoured Division: 'You will break through the enemy position at Hamman Lif and then, wheeling south between the hills, proceed to Hammamet.' Even on paper it seemed to be a fantastic thing to ask of any division. For one thing it meant their tackling an enemy at least ten times numerically stronger. But Alexander had the Germans on the run and he meant to keep them running even if it cost him an entire division or more. Some of our finest infantry—the Guards—without waiting for daylight, set off into the unknown. The subsequent march of the 6th Division must place it and its general in the very highest place in the military history of the war.

They broke clean through to Hammamet inside the next ten hours. They roared past German airfields, workshops, petrol and ammunition dumps and gun positions. They did not stop to take prisoners—things had gone far beyond that. If a comet had rushed down that road, it could hardly have made a greater impression. The Germans now were entirely dazed. Under the German military training you had to have a plan. But there was no plan. Only the boats remained—the evacuation boats which had been promised them. In a contagion of doubt and fear the German army turned tail and made up the Cape Bon roads looking for the boats. When on the beaches it became apparent to them at last that there were no boats—nor any aircraft either—the army became a rabble. The Italian Navy had not dared to put to sea to save its men. The Luftwaffe had been blown out of the sky. In other words, the Axis had cut its losses and the Afrika Korps was abandoned to its fate.

On May 10th I set off up the Peninsula through Hamman Lif to see one of the most grotesque and awesome spectacles that can have occurred in this war—an entire German army laying down its arms.

23

TEN kilometres outside Tunis we began to meet Germans and Italians coming toward us on the road; at Hamman Lif their vehicles had thickened to one every hundred yards; outside Soliman it was one solid mass and there was hardly a British soldier to be seen anywhere.

The German officers piled into their little
staff cars and drove themselves to prison.

All the Axis soldiers were driving. They drove in ten-ton Diesel lorries, and by standing upright and close together, they had managed to jam about forty or fifty men into each vehicle. Many of the lorries towed a trailer of the same size and an equal number of men were crowded into the trailer.

For eighty miles this procession was crawling slowly along the roads of Cape Bon Peninsula toward the British lines. Most of the German officers were travelling in blunt-nosed little staff cars adapted from the Volkswagen. Others had ordinary touring cars and saloons and there was a good sprinkling of command vehicles. The Italian officers were in Toppolino Fiats and Lancias. Some of the trucks were very old and much battered by desert wear. They staggered along under their unusual burdens, emitting great jets of acrid brown smoke. In the smaller cars the officers had piled up their bedding and any chance thing they had laid their hands on at the last moment—extra gallons of petrol, packets of cigarettes, a favourite folding-chair, a violin, a basket of oranges, a suitcase full of civilian clothing. There were many motor-cycles and side-cars.

When a vehicle broke down, its passengers went along the line begging lifts, and when they were all absorbed in the overcrowded lorries the procession went on again. The soldiers still wore their insignia, showing that they were sailors or soldies or airmen, but they had thrown away their weapons and their steel helmets.

No one was in charge of this horde, not even the Axis officers. No one had accepted its surrender. It was a spontaneous and natural sequence of the Allied victory, a result no one could have foreseen, but still a natural result. The Axis mob had retreated to the tip of the Peninsula and found itself unable to get away. They were trapped. They had no orders. The finely balanced Wehrmacht system, the careful stepping down of responsibility from corps to division and from colonel to regiment, from N.C.O. to soldier, had disintegrated into a thousand pieces.

By a natural instinct the men sought the preservation of the last thing left to them —their own lives. The prisoners I saw—and I suppose I passed thirty thousand on this first day, mostly Germans—were not exhausted; they were not hungry or shell-shocked or wounded; they were not frightened. I saw their dumps under the trees from Soliman to Grombalia and away up the Peninsula, and the weapons they had thrown away; they had ammunition and food and water, they had enough weapons and supplies to make a series of isolated stands in the mountains for weeks had they chosen to do so.

But they did not choose because they had lost the power of making military decisions. From the moment of our break-through on May 6th orders had stopped flowing through the German machine.

It appeared to me as I travelled among the prisoners, especially the Germans, that they lacked the power of individual thought and action. They had been trained as a team, for years the best fighting team in the world. They had never been trained to fight in small groups or by themselves. They were seldom forced to make adaptations and makeshifts on the spur of the moment, because they were usually on the winning side and their almost perfect supply machine had placed the finest weapons in their hands. The German Army organization had been a miracle of precision in every phase of the African war. The fighting men always got their ammunition and their food. It used to come by air while we were still using carts. They even got their mail twice a week from home. And so they leaned heavily on the machine and trusted it. They never tried out the odd exciting things that we did—things like the Long Range Desert Group. They were never much good at guerrilla fighting or patrolling at night. From May 6th onwards the Germans were for ever in doubt, and doubt created despair.

I stress the Germans in all this. The Italians at the end showed much more initiative. Indeed, the young Fascists were indignant at several places when their German companions gave up. A few of the Italians at least wanted to fight it out, guerrilla fashion, to the death.

However, the Germans prevailed because of their greater numbers, and so for the next two or three days we came on an endless succession of these amazing scenes along the road. The extraordinary thing was that once the enemy troops had decided to surrender they had no thought whatever of taking up arms again. Two days before they were concentrating all their minds and bodies on killing Englishmen and Americans. At this moment they were entirely free to pick up their rifles and shoot us. But they did not seem to be even morose or resentful.

They had lived such a practical and physical life in the field that they had had no time to develop any grandoise theories about the war and the honour of Germany. They did not worry about the future. Since whole armies were surrendering, it did not seem to any one man that he was doing anything extraordinary by giving up. Indeed, the whole astonishing spectacle was more and more like another army manœuvre.

We rode back at last to Tunis, past the prisoners, who now stretched in a procession reaching from the tip of Cape Bon far into Tunisia. Weeks were going to elapse before a final count revealed the total at over a quarter of a million prisoners, the biggest single haul made by the Allies since the war had begun. In all, the Axis had lost close on a million men in Africa. Now they had nothing, absolutely nothing, to show for it.

I personally had expected the African war to finish in havoc, a cataclysm of destruction and death and frightfulness. These friendly, peaceful scenes at the end were almost an anti-climax. In the British army alone the doctors had budgeted for six thousand casualties in the final break-through. Actually they got the astonishingly low number of two thousand.

There remained still, on May 11th, a large knot of resistance in the mountains between Zaghouan and Enfidaville, where the Eighth Army was still fighting. But in the afternoon came the momentous news that von Arnim had been captured near the aerodrome of St. Marie du Zit and had asked for terms.

In the southern sector the New Zealanders and the German 90th Light Division broke off their fighting at last. These two divisions were the élite of the British and German armies. For two years they had mauled one another across the desert. We had killed two of the 90th Light's commanders. The 90th Light had almost killed Freyberg. They had charged up to the gates of Egypt in the previous summer, and it was the New Zealanders who broke the German division's heart outside Mersa Matruh. There is hardly a major battlefield in the desert where you will not find the intermingled graves of the New Zealanders and the men of the 90th Light. And now at last it was all over.

Eight minutes to eight o'clock on May 12th is the official time given for the cessation of all organized enemy resistance in Africa.

No special incident marked that moment. This tragedy of three years and three acts simply ended with all the actors crowding on to the stage too exhausted to be exultant or defiant or humiliated or resentful. At the end the battlefield fell to pieces and lost all pattern and design, and those who had fought hardest on both sides found they had nothing to say, nothing to feel beyond an enveloping sense of gratitude and rest. The anger had subsided at the surrender, and for the first time the German and Allied soldiers stood together looking at one another with listless and passionless curiosity.

The last of the German generals came down to the landing field and was flown off to captivity. The last of many thousand enemy soldiers trudged into the internment camps.

And in our ranks the soldiers stripped off their uniforms, washed, and fell asleep in the sunshine.

All Africa was ours.

But there was no escape. Cape Bon, May 1943.

ACKNOWLEDGEMENTS

I wish to thank the Imperial War Museum for permission to publish most of the illustrations in this book. Others I wish to thank are Mr. Geoffrey Keating, Mr. Edward Ardizzone, the Commonwealth War Graves Commission and Radio Times Hulton Picture Library.

Whatever merits this new edition may have are due to my wife who has edited the text and selected the photographs. Indeed it is as much her book as mine.

A.M.

INDEX